W9-AFN-361

Statutes of Liberty

The New York School of Poets

Geoff Ward
Senior Lecturer in English
University of Liverpool

MACMILLAN

First published 1993 by
THE MACMILLAN PRESS LTD
Houndmills, Basingstoke, Hampshire RG21 2XS
and London
Companies and representatives
throughout the world

ISBN 0-333-47389-2

A catalogue record for this book is available
from the British Library.

Printed in Great Britain by
Antony Rowe Ltd
Chippenham, Wiltshire

Contents

Copyright
Acknowledgements

I should like to thank the following individuals and publishers for permission to quote from material for which they hold the copyright: John Ashbery and the Ecco Press for permission to quote 'Two Scenes' and 'The Thinnest Shadow' from *Some Trees*, copyright © by John Ashbery 1956, published in 1978 by the Ecco Press; John Ashbery for permission to quote lines 1–8 from '"They Dream Only of America"' and lines 1–24 from 'Wet Casements', from *Houseboat Days* (New York: Viking/Penguin, 1977); Alice Notley for permission to quote 'Angst' by Ted Berrigan; Alfred A. Knopf, Inc., for permission to quote from *The Collected Poems of Frank O'Hara* by Frank O'Hara, copyright © 1971 by Alfred A. Knopf, Inc.; Farrar, Straus and Giroux, Inc. for permission to quote excerpts from 'Growing Dark', 'The Snow', 'Song' from *The Morning of the Poem* by James Schuyler, © 1976, 1978, 1980 by James Schuyler; Darragh Park, literary executor of James Schuyler, for permission to quote the last seven lines from 'Flashes', pp. 51–2, *Freely Espousing* (Sun Books, 1979) and lines 13 to 21 of 'Blue' from *The Crystal Lithium* (Random House, 1972). Every effort has been made to locate copyright holders and obtain their permission for material to be used in this book: if I have inadvertently failed to do so, I can only apologize, and assure any such copyright holder that I will be happy to put matters right in any subsequent edition of this book.

List of Abbreviations

James Schuyler:

FE	*Freely Espousing*
CL	*The Crystal Lithium*
MP	*The Morning of the Poem*
FD	*A Few Days*

Frank O'Hara:

CP	*The Collected Poems of Frank O'Hara*
AC	*Art Chronicles*
SP	*Selected Plays*
SSWNY	*Standing Still and Walking in New York*

John Ashbery:

ST	*Some Trees*
TCO	*The Tennis Court Oath*
RM	*Rivers and Mountains*
TP	*Three Poems*
VN	*The Vermont Notebook*
SPCM	*Self-Portrait in a Convex Mirror*
HD	*Houseboat Days*
W	*A Wave*

Ashbery/Schuyler:

NN	*A Nest of Ninnies*

Preface

My personal debts are many and varied. I am grateful to the University of Liverpool for granting a period of leave, during which a good portion of this book was written, and to my colleagues in the Department of English Language and Literature and elsewhere, particularly Tony Barley, Simon Dentith, David Seed, and John Thompson. The British Academy, and the University of Liverpool Research and Development Fund, provided grants on separate occasions for research visits to New York which were of incalculable help in enabling me to write with confidence about what I have now seen, as well as read about. I am grateful to the staff of the Museum of Modern Art, particularly Janis Ekdahl (Assistant Director of the Library), while Waldo Rasmussen (Executive Director, International Circulating Exhibitions) who worked closely with Frank O'Hara, helped me get a clear and detailed sense of his work and life outside the poems. For hospitality in New York and Boston, I thank Jean Blondel and Bill Corbett, Steve Finbow and Clare Lees. Tony Tanner in Cambridge and Barry Wallenstein at the City University of New York kindly invited me to give papers to their colleagues and graduate students that helped sharpen my thinking, particularly in relation to the politics of New York poetry, debated in Chapter Four. Neil Reeve's decision to publish an early version of Chapter One as an article in *The Swansea Review* came as a real encouragement. I am grateful to the editors of *The Cambridge Quarterly* for commissioning reviews of contemporary poetry, portions of which have been reworked in what follows. As Series Editor, Denise Riley encouraged this book from the start, and in the closing stages gave it all the benefits of a rigorously close reading, and a deep knowledge of the poetry.

It is customary in the preface to an academic book to thank the staff of university libraries, where research is supposed to be done, and I am grateful to the Inter-Library Loan Service in the Sydney Jones Library at Liverpool. Unfortunately I have never been able to work in libraries, and so wrote this book at home using, for the most part, my own copies of texts. I have been collecting poetry by O'Hara and the New York School since the mid-1970s, an enjoyable but not always straightforward pursuit, given transatlantic distance and the

ix

fugitive nature of 'small press' poetry publishing. In consequence I owe a major and continuing debt to the independent British book-sellers who specialize in this area, and without whose knowledge, and sometimes complex efforts, this book could most definitely not have been written: I thank Paul Green, Alan Halsey, Peter Riley, Iain Sinclair and, above all, Nick Kimberley from his time at Compendium.

John Ashbery answered all my (frequently banal) questions with unfailing patience, good humour, and readiness to get dates and details right. I expected erudition and intellectual hospitality be-cause the poems have those qualities, but the poems are in a sense common property; I had no right to the kindliness, and the wish to be straightforwardly understood, that I was shown. James Schuyler died while I was preparing my typescript for the press. Schuyler wrote poems of great rhetorical subtlety, their seemingly casual and improvisatory air suddenly revealing emotional depths and com-plexity. Apparently insecure and reclusive until very late in his life, he had started to give successful public readings at the time of his death. I saw him read with John Ashbery at the 92nd Street Y in the winter of 1989, a bear-like man with Dennis Healey eyebrows and a surprisingly confident manner, reading superb, mostly unpublished work, that will add to his growing reputation.

To Marion Wynne-Davies I owe much more than I can say here. Among her invaluable gifts to me has been the understanding that a book finally gets done when serious play is put to work. This book says that a poem is the play of words, against time: Clifford Ward, my father, is the only voice I hear that could persuade me that, in the end, there is a broader perspective in which even time will be folded up, and put away. *Statutes of Liberty* is dedicated to the memory of my mother, Marjorie, who would have heartily disliked the subject, and been delighted to see the book.

Introduction:
The New York School
of Poets

I too walk'd the streets of Manhattan island, and bathed in
the waters around it,
I too felt the curious abrupt questionings stir within me . . .

(Walt Whitman, 'Crossing Brooklyn Ferry')

If Whitman were alive today and chose to go bathing in the waters
off Manhattan, 'abrupt questionings' would not be the only thing to
stir inside him. But New York is as infamous on account of the
chemicals its denizens ingest, as for those its industry expels into the
water. As the emblem of a contemporary condition of toxicity, New
York is an infernal *primus inter pares*; the most concentrated dose so
far of what is present in more diluted form elsewhere, be it vagrancy
or insider trading, crime or vanguard art. It is the city to which other
cities look for a sign, most often a warning, of the episodes to come
in their own unfolding narrative. In one sense a triumph over Nature, its skyscrapers and subway system *are* the new Nature, as fields
of concrete and forests of scaffolding dwarf the species that created
them, 'while nature itself, in the form of parks, a snowfall, cats and
dogs, is a detail in the stone and steel of his habitat'.[1] To take your
hungry, your tired, your poor and stratify them, is the real promise
of the Statue of Liberty; but if a race and class-based pecking order
divides New York as never before, this city is, in a phrase from John
Ashbery's most famous poem, 'alive with filiations, shuttlings'.
(*SPCM* 75) The homeless prowl the West Eighties in hopes of better
pickings, while in the galleries urban refuse turns into art: self-
divided, New York is also uniquely self-reflexive. To walk around
Midtown in the lunch hour, and (doing exactly what the locals warn
you never to do), pause to take it all in rather than looking where
you're going, is to witness something wonderfully appalling. Human dots and dashes mimic and dodge each other in a giant mural
by Keith Haring, one ongoing wave of self-reinvention. Seen by itself
as jaded and cynical, New York is the only modern city that can still
inspire an unironic awe.

1

When France fell to the Nazis, Paris ceased to be the world's art capital. Around 1943, the foreign policy of the United States made a decisive shift from isolationism to internationalism. In the unprecedented economic boom of those years, and as America looked to express its new cultural supremacy in a time of Cold War, immigrant Surrealists found conditions propitious to the relaunch of the avant-garde, for a public newly instructed in the principles of modern art. From the meeting-point of European influence and the shared tendency towards abstraction among those New York painters who had worked on the Federal Art Project, Abstract Expressionism was to emerge.[2] This movement signified, to resurrect the sub-title of an important survey of its works by Irving Sandler, the triumph of American painting; the successes of Abstract Expressionism were commercial and national, yet managed to retain (at least until recent times) an untarnished image of artistic vanguardism, of the painter as an intrepid visionary, working on the margins of what is privately bearable and publicly tolerable. The more ferocious antics of a figure such as Jackson Pollock show the intense psychic pressures experienced in trying to live up to, while working around, such an image of the avant-garde artist. And so it might be said that the New York School, a term coined by Robert Motherwell, was in many cultural respects a kind of phenomenon new to America but familiar in Europe. To art historian Dore Ashton, 'the myth of the romantic New York School was essentially construed from the old *art pour l'art* sources'.[3] Behind Ashbery's New York, alive with filiations and shuttlings, may lie Baudelaire's Paris, *'Fourmillante cité, cité pleine de rêves'*.[4]

The poets with whom this study will largely deal have all had connexions with the New York School, and with painting in general, which colour their work in varying ways. John Ashbery (1927–) has earned his living as an art critic for most of his working life, first for the Paris *Herald Tribune*, later as Executive Editor of *Art News* from 1965 until 1972, and more recently as critic for *New York* and *Newsweek*. A selection of Ashbery's art criticism, *Reported Sightings*, was published in 1989. James Schuyler (1923–1991) had much less of a direct involvement with the art world, and was indeed something of a recluse until his mid-sixties, at which point he began to give extremely assured and successful public readings. Schuyler's poetry, with which Chapter 1 is concerned, is in itself extremely painterly. The artist Fairfield Porter is said to have joked that Schuyler's poems were more visual than his own work. At the time of his early death,

Frank O'Hara (1926–66) was an Associate Curator at New York's Museum of Modern Art. Having joined MOMA in 1955 as a special assistant on the International Program, he contributed to the organization of many important travelling exhibitions, including the first selection of Abstract Expressionist works to circulate in Europe. O'Hara's association with the painters was, famously, personal as well as professional. In addition to writing critical essays and monographs such as *Jackson Pollock* (1959), O'Hara incorporated among the many projects of his poetry a soap opera-cum-art history Lives of the Painters (and other Poets). Read as they can be as a growing and single work, *The Collected Poems of Frank O'Hara* do not merely issue from but document with unparalleled colour and detail the artistic milieu of postwar New York.

This study touches on painting only incidentally, and no informed or ingenious parallels will be claimed between the techniques of brushwork (or drip-painting) and the inscription of poetic hieroglyphs. It is important nevertheless to note that, insofar as the poets named here may be read as a group, that group did emerge in a historical relationship to the painters of the Abstract Expressionist movement. That relationship was defined by antithesis as much as continuation. Where Abstract Expressionism denotes an art often of monumental severity, such as the dark and portentous canvasses painted by Mark Rothko for the Seagram Building, the poets are witty, sociable, and bored with alienation and top-heavy symbols. (In fact the Seagram Building is mentioned in a late poem by O'Hara chiefly as a place where he dropped his hot-dog in one of the fountains, while trying to get a speck out of his eye.) There are further differences. Where the bar-room and other behaviour of Pollock's circle frequently took machismo to the point of parody, the presiding though not universal temper of the poets is homosexual. Some consideration will be given here to the overlapping contexts in which an artistic côterie might be driven as well as led to self-support. Such contexts can be commercial, as well as sexual. As David Trotter remarks, O'Hara the poet 'knew just how invisible avant-gardes can be', when during the same period his salaried labours were adding to the painters' celebrity.[5]

There is a distrust of poetic levity in university departments of English, except in cases where historical distance has lent gravitas to the joke. The New York poets are all expertly addicted to witticisms and poetic comedy; if that much is not clear from what follows then I have failed, indeed. But comedy is anathema to many brands of

criticism, and not merely in Britain. By referring to Frank O'Hara
and Kenneth Koch as 'comedians of the spirit', Harold Bloom damns
them with praise so faint as to condemn.[6] To Bloom poetry must be
agonistic, conflictual, illusionistic *en route*, and of necessity self-de-
ceiving, but of the highest and most legible seriousness if it is to be
counted part of the canon. The claims Bloom has made for the poetry
of John Ashbery over the years have been massive, and form an
argument, partly on his behalf, against the whole notion of a New
York school of poets.[7] Bloom's liking for Ashbery's work preceded
and looks like outliving the vogue for deconstruction with which
this book also deals, and to which it is not unfriendly. (Call me old-
fashioned.) The suggestion in Chapter 3 is, broadly, that Bloom has
had to deafen and blind himself to Ashbery's wit, and to his significant debts to Auden and to Surrealism, in order to make the poet fit
the particular laurels and toga that the critic has in mind, and which
were designed only for tragic statuary. That said, my own chalky
habits of evaluation will become apparent, quickly enough. To read
O'Hara, Ashbery and Schuyler as they deserve, is to open their work
to, and see refracted in it, the full retrospect of the American Renaissance, and of the changing structures of European poetry from Romanticism to the present. To lower one's sights, and in particular to
pander to the notion that poetry should be modest and casual, is to
block out knowledge of the challenges to which these three poets
have at least risen. O'Hara's work takes on more than either the
ephemeral 60s 'happenings' or the boxed-in ironies of the Movement
with which it is contemporary.

Of course O'Hara's poetry looks casual. It often was, in as much as
it was knocked out at speed, like Byron's. But as in the case of Byron,
the surface lightness is intimately related to its opposite; if O'Hara
laughs, it is so that he also may not weep. As with *Don Juan*, where
enjoyment of the picaresque bounce and chatter begins to cede to a
more sombre tone which, once heard, resounds everywhere, so the
poetry of Frank O'Hara is often to do with the varieties of death; the
necessary murder of influence or inhibition, poetry as an *acte gratuite*
against silence and darkness, ambiguities of desire and love, the loss
of friends and heroes. An underlying seriousness is there in the
beautifully warm and comic Lunch Poem about a movie-star's collapse ('oh Lana Turner we love you get up'), and the cooler, mysterious 'Getting Up Ahead of Someone (Sun)' with the premonition of
its closing line: 'each day's light has more significance these days'.
(*CP* 449, 341)

This book is not sufficiently wedded to deconstruction to adhere completely to Bloom's agenda. Neither however does it run to the opposite extreme, by displaying that allergy to the canon which is one of the characteristics of Postmodernism, as defined by Jean-Francois Lyotard; 'an incredulity towards metanarratives'.[8] But no hierarchy of the canonical is so fixed in its meta-nature that it cannot be revised in the light of contemporary developments. It might be prudent to enquire by whom, historically, and on what grounds canonical works are determined as being, to adopt one of the OED's meanings for 'canon', 'genuine and inspired'. If I want to read O'Hara's poetry, I am free to go on doing that without writing about him. I wrote this book in order to express, however inadequately, my sense that the poetry of Frank O'Hara is demonstrably great poetry.

And that meant that there was less space in which to write about other poets who might be thought integral to an account of New York poetry. The city's poetic culture is of course as various and indeed as self-divided as any other aspect of its expressive life. Those seeking an account of the work of Victor Hernandez Cruz and his catalysis of the Spanish-infused Nuyorican scene will have to look elsewhere, as for wholly different reasons will admirers of Charles Reznikoff, Paul Blackburn, Sam Abrams or Carol Bergé. It was easy, if regrettable, to omit performance poetry *à la* John Giorno, which has to be heard; the same applies to those poets such as Barry Wallenstein who work in a jazz context, and to the spasmodic brilliance of New York rock lyrics from Lou Reed to Patti Smith and Laurie Anderson. Much more debatable is my relative neglect or outright omission of such names as Anne Waldman, Edwin Denby, Bernadette Mayer, Lewis Warsh, Dick Gallup, Peter Schjeldahl, Tony Towle, Paul Violi, Frank Lima, Lorenzo Thomas, John Godfrey and others whose work crops up regularly in *The World*, Kenward Elmslie's Z magazine and their inheritors. For one thing, this book is intended partly for a British audience, who may well be puzzled by Ashbery and have barely heard of O'Hara. In the future one might hope for an updated and comprehensive selection of poems along the lines of Ron Padgett and David Shapiro's *An Anthology of New York Poets*, published in 1970, as a necessary introduction. But I make no apology for focussing discussion on the work of Ashbery, O'Hara and Schuyler. Many of the younger New Yorkers derive their habitual tones and images, at least to some extent, from a baptism by full immersion in the repertoire of their elders. For divergent reasons, there was long hesitation over certain missing names, chiefly those of Alice Notley, Ed Sanders, and above all Allen Ginsberg, who has lived in New York on and off for many years, and whose poetry no doubt contains more references to the city than does John Ashbery's. But Ginsberg is still associated with other literary constellations (as well as the open cosmos), and so shines only dimly, here.

Some words of explanation concerning the labelling of a New York school of poetry may be called for at this point. 'The Poets of the New York School' – note the different emphasis – was a phrase adopted by John Bernard Myers, to register his sense of an emergent generation of writers whose work he wished to represent in a series of pamphlets; the series would bear the name of his gallery, Tibor de Nagy editions. These publications began in 1952, ran sporadically for around fourteen years, and included such items as the four-page broadsheet *Semi-Colon*, Ashbery's *Turandot* and Frank O'Hara's *Love Poems (Tentative Title)*. 'It was particularly appropriate in the case of all these new poets that they should find their first publisher in an art gallery director because all of them, in one way or another, were intimately bound with the aesthetics, the people, the politics, the social life and the concerns of the New York art world.' Myers had fallen under the influence of André Breton, acting as managing editor of *View* magazine between 1944 and 1947, when Breton left New York to return to France. In Myers' eyes, the New York School of painting was the American offspring of Surrealism, and his new poets of the fifties were umbilically connected to both. Hence the emphasis on one continuing 'New York School' of arts. It is a partial picture, but valid as far as it goes. In the fifties the poetry pamphlets, unlike the paintings, tended to remain unsold. Consequently there was an element of ironic comedy from the beginning in the use of the portentous term 'school'. However, according to New York dance critic and poet Edwin Denby, in conversation with Anne Waldman, that element had been operative for the painters too, making the poets' adoption of the term a 'double-joke':

Met these four boys Frank O'Hara, John Ashbery, Kenneth Koch, and Jimmy Schuyler (who I had first met abroad) at the Cedar Bar in '52 or '53. Met them through Bill (de Kooning) who was a friend of theirs and they admired Kline and all those people. The painters who went to the Cedar had more or less coined the phrase 'New York School' in opposition to the School of Paris (which also originated as a joke in opposition to the School of Florence and the School of Venice) . . . So the poets adopted the expression 'New York School' out of homage to the people who had de-provincialized American painting. It's a complicated double-joke.[9]

In sum, the important factor is surely that the poets had before them the conspicuously successful example of the New York paint-ers, whose encouragement and interests may have been a stimulus, but whose success cast a shadow over the writers' efforts to 'de-provincialize' poetry and reach a wider public than their own côterie.

The poets who appealed most to Myers were, understandably, the painterly ones, including Kenneth Koch, for whom as he rightly remarks 'the surface of a work of art *is* the work of art'. By looking briefly at Koch's writing it may be possible to establish a sense of the New York poets' house style, in so far as such a thing exists.

Kenneth Koch (1925–) had his first collection *Poems*, with prints by Nell Blaine, published by Myers in 1953. Aside from his many books of poetry he has written a novel (*The Red Robins*), a guide to the teaching of creative writing, and been an editor of *Locus Solus*, whose special issue on collaboration is cited in Chapter 3. It is when the work of each approaches its greatest intensity that the poetry of Ashbery, Schuyler and O'Hara begins to diverge, not only from the work of the other two, but from its own usual broad intentions. All three, but particularly O'Hara, seem led almost reluctantly into some of their most powerful writing. By contrast, Koch appears to want to retain the house style, but then blow the house apart in a spate of language, upbeat, comic and almost cartoon-like in its vibrancy. He is the most frantically and farcically humorous of all these poets, often drawing his best jokes from a self-reflexive attention to the poetry world, as here, in the Whitmanic 'Fresh Air':

Where are young poets in America, they are trembling in
   publishing houses and universities,
Above all they are trembling in universities, they are bathing the
   library steps with their spit,
They are gargling out innocuous (to whom?) poems about maple
   trees and their children,
Sometimes they brave a subject like the Villa d'Este or a
   lighthouse in Rhode Island,
Oh what worms they are! They wish to perfect their form . . .

Here on the railroad train, one more time, is the Strangler.
He is going to get that one there, who is on his way to a poetry
   reading.
Agh! Biff! The body falls to the moving floor.

It's good; the problem is that it will never be as good the second time.
As time has passed, Koch seems to have lit on that very perception
as a bottom-line fact in human affairs and human ageing, and its
double focus powers much of his more complex work. One relatively recent piece, 'The Circus', looks back to the time of writing a
very early poem of the same name, offering a wry and mournful
account of the changes of years in between. 'Fate', a curious long
poem from which it is hard to excerpt, one of Koch's best, deals with
a memory of meeting O'Hara, Ashbery, and the painters Larry Rivers and Jane Freilicher in a West Side apartment in 1951, the main
topic of conversation being the young Koch's recent, first trip around
Europe. The memory of telling friends who are at present absent,
one of them being, indeed, dead, of experiences and places which
they had not known, begins a curious unravelling and auto-
deconstruction in Koch's initial attempts to articulate memory through
a characteristically Romantic rhetoric of creative assertion. Where an
equally Romantic individualism usually qualifies any poet's decla-
ration of loyalty to a 'school', however avant-garde the curriculum,
here Koch seems to have needed a particular grouping of names to
signify as such in the public domain before he could then write it
back into his poem as a private, indeed an interior and finally a
vanishing subject. The cumulative effect of the diffident and tremu-
lously swerving line-endings, very different from Koch's usual breathless bravura, is engaging and disturbing in itself. Elsewhere, things
are generally more hectic, and it is the colour and the facetiousness
of poems by Koch like the one beginning 'You were wearing your
Edgar Allan Poe printed cotton blouse', that are characteristic of his
activities.[10]

With the exception of James Schuyler, the writers with whose
work this study deals have tended towards prolificity, in Ashbery's
case prodigiously so. Not only do the New Yorkers write with facility, they parade that quality openly in the often invertebrate forms of
their poems. So many of the long works, from Koch's 'Sleeping with
Women' to Ashbery's 'Litany' could easily have been shorter, or for
that matter thirty pages longer. (The former was, at one point.) The
structureless structures of the endless list, the pseudo-narrative, the

neo-Surrealist collage, can be read as offering procedural analogues for the faintly nauseating terms in which John Bernard Myers describes the New York art-world of the fifties; 'a situation which was open, yeasty, limitlessly permissive'.[11] The blame for some of this can be laid at the door of Walt Whitman, rather than the painters. Whitman's severance of American from English poetic tradition inaugurated an aesthetics of monstrous absorbency, total inclusion. Perhaps this has gone wider than even Whitman's bequest, and become a common factor in American aesthetics. Readers of this book are unlikely to need reminding that some of the poems are contemporary with a noted B-movie, *The Blob*, in which a pink jelly from Outer Space hoovers up most of the contents of an American small town, with undiscriminating appetite. The most effective poems of the New York group are frequently those whose capacity for tireless exploration and absorption comes up against, if not Steve McQueen's ice-wagon, then some equally cold shower that has consequences for the formless forms of the poetry. In this area it is above all James Schuyler's management of rhythm and the linebreak – sometimes the quiet pulse of sustained thought, sometimes the faint shudder or holding back recalling the acutely vulnerable or the infirm – that give the lie to a wholesale dismissal of all technical innovation in recent American poetry.

The first generation of New York poets – O'Hara, Schuyler, Ashbery, Koch – have in general been more attentive to this area than the 'second generation' figures such as Ted Berrigan and Ron Padgett, whose activities get properly under way in the mid-sixties. Here Bloom's theorization of the anxieties of influence is spot-on; so many of the younger poets seem as much confined as defined by their learning from Frank O'Hara. In the Postscript, I offer a sketch of what has become of the New York influence in recent years. This entails some consideration of the 'Language' group of poets, and of one or two British writers who have been able to utilize O'Hara's example in ways that open and are not enclosed by it. In one sense the New York school of poets was a loosely collective practice from O'Hara's and Ashbery's time at Harvard in the late 1940s, to 1976, the year when John Ashbery won all three major American literary awards for his *Self-Portrait in a Convex Mirror* and so was airlifted to the slippery slopes of the university syllabus. This book is an attempt to recover the years in between, and to examine some of the developments in literary theory that have accompanied Ashbery's rise to fame.

1

James Schuyler and the Rhetoric of Temporality

POETRY OF DEEP AND LAYERED SPACE

To adopt and amplify a term used in passing by Harold Rosenberg, modern artists have been driven to choose an art of deep, or of layered, space.[1] To an art of deep space, as the term immediately implies, would belong all questions and certainties of religion, metaphysics, or the extremes of subjectivism. Any hierarchical ordering of perceptual data will likewise tend towards an art of deep space. The tradition of Romantic landscape painting that depicts the inner as much as the outer world, epitomized by Friedrich or Turner, would clearly be a deep space genre by these lights, and one that has continued to evolve up to the present day. For example, jumping to the years following the Second World War, and the translation of Werner von Braun from Nazi armourer to architect of the NASA space program, the word 'rocket' would take on an understandable ambiguity, signifying both military conquest and America's Cold War colonization of outer space. The avant-garde painting of this period, exemplified by the work of Jackson Pollock or Mark Rothko, absorbs the bequest of Friedrich's European landscape tradition and pushes it to a new intensity of inwardness.[2] That body of work may be viewed as both an assertion of inner-space subjectivity over the claims of the social centre, and an unintentional homage to a New World empire pleased to fund massive abstracts on a par with the more literal explorations of deep space engineered by its technological élite. Being Abstract, this Expressionism would depict nothing so specific and so potentially dangerous as an issue. So it is that Jackson Pollock's art can be seen, with a deal of irony but no real contradiction, as both the heroic act of a marginal Romanticism and as the latest adornment of bourgeois culture (used, as it was, and with the artist's full consent, by County Homes Inc. of Tarrytown, New York, to help sell their executive villas.)[3] To get further into the politics of the New York art world at this point would be to digress. It's worth

10

noting, though, that the only professional ambit in which James Schuyler recorded himself as having been employed was the Department of Circulating Exhibitions at New York's Museum of Modern Art (making him, briefly, a colleague of Frank O'Hara). To reinsert Schuyler for a moment into a text of history: he was involved with modern art in its moment of greatest public ambiguity, when the triumph of the avant-garde was accomplished with the blessing of the US State Department through its funding of MOMA's International Program.

However, to return to the terms with which I began, the more crucial and pugilistic advances of painting this century tend to have been made in the service of an art of layered, rather than deep space. A layered space art would be typified by the innovations of Mondrian, Léger, or Picasso in his Cubist phase. Here the paint is variously organized into sequences of shapes and flats which, be they referential or non-representational, are freed from all metaphysical ambition and urge their claim on our attention by virtue of their *intensity*, rather than their place in some order. Such an opposition between the arts of deep and layered space can also be seen in the history of modern poetry. The work of William Carlos Williams presents a layered-space manifesto as influential in its sphere as Picasso's Cubism. Crucial early poems such as 'The Great Figure', which in time would clearly come to help determine the practice of Schuyler and O'Hara, press the case for a materialist poetic in which any metaphysical depth to the visible surface, or the experienced moment, is happily denied. So the line 'I saw the figure 5' is weighted equally at both ends, the first-person deserving no priority over the numeral in Williams' layered space world.[4] In this area it may well be Frank O'Hara who is Williams' closest descendant, rather than Ginsberg or Creeley or others who have wanted to state that connexion overtly. It is O'Hara who wants to reject any trace of metaphysics as a taint, and whose texts both celebrate the energy of a world (New York) composed of a series of discrete sense-events ('A Step Away From Them') and must also pay the price for the separateness and unrepeatability of each moment ('Joe's Jacket'). That loss may signify the reopening of deep space. It is still the case that O'Hara's avowed rejection of metaphysics – more extreme than Schuyler's and vastly more so than Ashbery's – makes of it a perimeter marker for an opposition between deep and layered-space aesthetics and for the argument that follows.

No doubt a division of all modern art using the model I propose may seem as reductive or susceptible to immediate exception as any other binary opposition applied to the structure of literary texts. And even if the terms were thought acceptable, it is true that most poets have shown the influence of both kinds of mind-set, rather than an extreme commitment one way. T. S. Eliot, for example, in one sense a high-priest of deep space, retains even in his late work an attachment to collage and the art of the fragment that qualify in interesting ways his commitment to a metaphysic of wholeness. Conversely, the ructions engineered in French poetry of the twenties and thirties by the Surrealists issue from an avowed attempt to colonize the deep spaces of prophecy, dream and reverie at the behest of a layered-space, Marxist humanism. But as his friend Trotsky complained to André Breton, the resultant art keeps a little window open onto the beyond, through which the supernatural can get in. To put it another way, the Surrealist poem would seem finally to be penned within a tradition of lyric brevity, its margin of white space actually a deep space for metaphysical speculation that locates it within the Symbolist tradition, rather than in relation to its nihilistic Dada-base. And then there are poets who retain a purchase on layered space while announcing a commitment to the deep. Here the English and American Audens are at one, for while conversion may have modified his ethical outlook, it brought no otherworldly spiritualization to Auden's worldly poems.

It may be that tensions between the arts of deep and layered space go back to the origins of European Romanticism, including its attempt to work out the implications of the French Revolution for artistic and political practice. Romantic texts that refer directly to the Revolution are well-known and surprisingly few in number. Instead, this historical crisis is very rapidly interiorized by Romantic art, and imaged in a symbolic, fantastic or oblique fashion. Regicide and insurrection had overturned the pyramidal order to produce, at least in prospect, a levelled or layered-space society. The objective gains, violence and contradictions of the Revolution, with the double-edged dangers and attractions that followed its displacement of a deep-space order by a layered-space egalitarianism, were still being worked out in our Cold, and other modern wars. In a sense we are still inside the questions posed by the first-generation Romantics, and no vanguard art-manifesto this century has driven such a wedge between its poetry and that of its forbears as did *Lyrical Ballads*. Poetic writing since that time can indeed be viewed as the driving of a wedge between itself and other kinds of language. It follows that such linguistic violence would have its analogues in the image of the poet: the terms that Paul de Man applies to Baudelaire, as 'not the father of modern poetry but an enigmatic stranger', are helpful and perhaps need to be felt in relation to any strong poet, setting aside for a moment the matter of debts and bequests.[5] Yet the violence in the act of self-severance must itself bear testimony to an underlying familial attachment to at least certain writings from which the poet claims separation. In this narrow sense there is substance to Harold Bloom's credal assertion that the meaning of a poem or poet can only be another poem or poet.

But if we are still in the Romantic period, it is a period whose underlying and defining tensions are still unresolved. Hierarchical, metaphysical, religious models still compete with a layered-space opposition. Curiously, it seems to have been easier for poets who were nearer to the French Revolution in time to come to some kind of accommodation between the contesting world-views which the revolution set going. For example Wordsworth managed a relatively easy negotiation between an art of fragmentation and the metaphysics of wholeness. Shelley in one sense turns Wordsworth's deep-space metaphysics into a layered-space revolt, preserving his sense of a phenomenological circularity, an 'unremitting interchange' ('Mont Blanc') between self and the world, but situating this dialectically, in time, and therefore with some radical possibilities for change and progress. By contrast Keats's perpetual drive towards intensification of sensation in the present moment, which seems at first to make him a layered-space writer, does not prevent him from locating sensation in metaphysical twilight zones that are very much the province of deep space. Victorian writers tend on the whole to make a clearer choice between a deep and a layered-space art than did the Romantics, but that choice seems typically to carry a trace of guilt, erupting in occasional but crucial texts such as Browning's 'Childe Roland' or Henry James' *The Turn of the Screw*, both of which might be said to incarnate the momentary subversion of a layered-space, humanist ethos by anxieties from the deep. Artists of the early twentieth century were driven less by guilt and more towards drastic sorts of position-taking: for Yeats, Eliot, Pound and Lewis the choice between a hierarchical and a levelled world was exceedingly clearcut.

The major poets of the New York School – John Ashbery, Frank

O'Hara, James Schuyler – were influenced by texts that issued from periods of political upheaval. Specifically, one would point to French Surrealist writing and to the more disturbed writings of 1930s England: Auden's *The Orators*, for example.[6] However, work by the first two was to find its first publication in the late 1940s and early 1950s, a period of growing affluence and relative political quietism in America. The kind of promptings towards change that had seemed urgent to Breton or Auden in the thirties were now, if they occurred at all, simultaneously assuaged by palliatives and rendered impotent by the massive entrenchment of Cold War attitudes. Understandably therefore it is the oneiric and stylistic elements in the European writers which touch the New Yorkers, rather than their referential and political sides. Coupled with this, we find in all three of the New York poets a sociable, conversational manner – anecdotal, self-consciously witty, and with a marked interest in the mingled pleasures and anxieties of company. This is sponsored in part by the later, American Auden, whom the younger writers knew personally as well as textually.[7] In sum, their work would seem at first to operate at a very distant remove from the convulsions and dilemmas that I have alleged to be governing agencies in a continuing historical narrative of Romanticism. The remainder of this chapter will be given over to the poetry of James Schuyler in an effort to show how the contesting world-views of deep and layered-space may be seen at work in his writing, and with what consequences, both for that writing and for the current debates in literary theory that one might want to bring to bear on it. I will argue that recent theory, exemplified for this occasion by the work of Paul de Man, seems to both illuminate the poetry and, in various unexpected and instructive ways, to be critiqued by it.

SCHUYLER'S MORTAL WORLD

Although James Schuyler (b. 1923 – d. 1991) was born before Ashbery and O'Hara, his first substantial collection *Freely Espousing* did not appear until 1969, three years after O'Hara's death. A tense and oblique elegy for O'Hara, 'Buried at Springs', appears towards the end of what is otherwise Schuyler's lightest and brightest book. Some of the poems were over a decade old at the time of collection: we might surmise that Schuyler's practice did not merely develop more slowly alongside O'Hara's, but that O'Hara's methods were in a sense absorbed and filtered by Schuyler, his more exploratory and

prolific output converted to a series of moves, a repertoire, that
Schuyler could then deploy at will:

> It's like what George and I were talking about, the East West
> Coast divide: Californians need to do a thing to enjoy it.
> A smile in the street may be loads! you don't have to undress
> everybody.

> ('December')

The wit, the chattiness, the meandering air that suddenly gusts
home with an acerbic one-liner; these are Schuyler's own, to be sure;
they are also in the New York atmosphere: but we can hear in
addition, and specifically, a deployment of O'Hara. Like his poems,
these lyrics must be, or at least seem, 'dashed off like the easiest
thing' ('May 24th or so'). Schuyler is a subtle as well as an overtly
comic writer, and his mimesis of New York life is a latter-day *commedia
dell' arte*, with O'Hara part and parcel of his *zibaldone*, the stock of
learned devices that a Masker might deploy at will across a range of
comedies, set off against purely improvised skills, and probably
leaving the audience pleasurably unsure as to what was rehearsed
and what plucked from the air. Theatrical metaphors were used by
Bill Berkson for a memoir of O'Hara that could aptly be read as a
way in to Schuyler: 'For him, composition was a matter of performance, of "staying on the boards', and Berkson continues, writing of
O'Hara's lightness and poise in 'A Step Away From Them':

> The technical quality in these lines once referred to as 'casual' is
> actually very intense. At each break, instead of a thump or heave
> or 'dying fall', you get a vibration or click . . . The next word is
> prepared for, the way a fine dancer prepares for the next attitude,
> carrying it in the momentum of an all-over movement.[7]

The agility in both poets does indeed have a technical aspect, but the
'click', the end-stopped quality of these poets' measure, is also the
articulation in verse of a layered-space world-view:

> not to be in love with you
> I can't remember what it was like
> it must've been lousy

> ('"The Elizabethans Called It Dying"')

            Everything chuckles and creaks
            sighs in satisfaction
            reddens and ripens in tough gusts of coolness
            and the sun smites

                                                           ('Today')

Many of these early poems by Schuyler have a similarly uplifting
ending. They are saying that the deep spaces of memory, of the
cosmic, flatten under inspection: what's gone is gone, and the sun is
just the sun, there's no time like the present, and this is acceptable
because the only time we have *is* the present. And so we can, to pick
up Auden's motto from 'Lullaby', 'Find our mortal world enough'.[8]
In fact *Freely Espousing* is quite insistently a poetry of observation,
watching the world go by, or grow, catching things on the turn. The
true precursor is therefore neither Auden nor O'Hara but William
Carlos Williams:

            a bird
                snapped by
                                it's raining
                just in one spot
                                flashes
                    in puddles
                            on a tar roof

                                                           ('Flashes')

Even the line breaks recall one of Williams' poems of urban observation. By this layered-space view, to capture such moments in poetry
is to record all there is, without any spurious metaphysical depth.
But although Schuyler is relentlessly attentive to street scenes, changes
in the weather, the movements of people or animals caught for an
instant in a new light, the poet does not try to set himself in abeyance
during the act of watching, or as Williams generally did, restrict
himself to a narrow and predictable tonal range. (I must tell you!
This young tree/cat/plum/mother of three . . .):

                an elm ascends
                    smoothly as an Otis Elevator.

                                                           ('May 24th or so')

It's funny early spring weather, mild and washy
the color of a head cold.

('3/23/66')

If these comparisons strike us as accurate, that is to say recognizable, they are also incongruous, new to cognition. Personality and subjectivity are by no means as subjugated to observation and description as the poems seem at first sight to imply. Many later poems by Schuyler are openly confessional. *Freely Espousing* doesn't ever go that far, but neither are its poems contained entirely by the influence of O'Hara's wit and Williams' watching.

In the 1960s, James Schuyler's was a poetry of quirks. In him, or outside: a quirk implies what was to be expected, but then diverges from it. ('Thank you for your letter/and its extenuations.') A quirk is an interesting tic, related to incongruity and ultimately to irony. ('A man passes/in calendula-coloured socks.') A doubleness is asserted, but a doubleness which draws attention to some crucial dislocation between its two parts: between what's said and what's meant, or between expectation and reality. To some extent this is merely to locate in rhetoric the implications of a layered-space world-view, for when metaphysics and origins and eschatology are put in question, existence would seem to be located only in the present moment. Though there has been a lyric tradition in praise of exactly that, the Romanticization of the Moment – in the 1890s, say, and the period of High Modernism – is fundamentally a reappropriation by deep space aesthetics of some unacknowledged anxieties. The cult of the Moment as it appears in Virginia Woolf or Ernest Dowson is able to sidestep difficulties of dealing with a temporal, layered-space world by putting art or experience into that timeless, deep space parenthesis to which religion used to speak. The Paterian aesthetic (which endures as late as Woolf and Joyce) is basically a Romantic prioritization of the subject, a posture of mastery in relation to time, the artist as highpriest of the art-cult enabled to arrest the flux of temporality so as to retrieve and preserve a given moment. Schuyler does of course do this himself: 'Silver day/how shall I polish you?' (*MP* 16); but the slightly camp tone of the apostrophe (most *embarrassing* of poetic rhetorics, as Schuyler well knows) is actually a sign of his attachment to a more rigorous modern tradition which, if it can be said with confidence to start anywhere, starts with Baudelaire. It is Baudelaire who proceeds into exactly those areas signposted as the province of deep space, in order to record mercilessly their flattening into our usual piecemeal habitat. Thus he refuses both illusion and the mirage of our ever emancipating ourselves from the need for illusion.

> Je ne vois qu'infini par toutes les fenêtres

('Le Gouffre')

> Grands bois, vous m'effrayez comme des cathédrales;

('Obsession')[9]

Words such as *'infini'*, *'rêve'*, *'inconnu'* recur endlessly in his work, but just where those signifiers seem to gesture most forcefully towards a metaphysical opening into deep space, Baudelaire denies the possibility of tenure on anything except yearning, and refuses palliatives to what is revealed unflinchingly as a temporal destiny. The *'Grands bois'* will be anthropomorphized only one line later, and the Infinity of 'Le Gouffre' is an enigmatic nothingness that returns us to our ineluctable, layered-space world: ' – *Ah! ne jamais sortir des Nombres et des Êtres!'* It is ironic that by his writings about drugs, and development of a Bohemian style, Baudelaire should have expanded the range of possibilities for a deep-space lyricism by which his own thought refuses at last to be seduced.

Baudelaire's death-mask is evoked by Schuyler at the opening of his longest piece, which gives its title to *The Morning of the Poem*. It may be helpful, though less agreeable, to look for a moment at what I would suggest is a momentary falling-off in one collection by Schuyler, interpreting it in exactly these terms: as a would-be escape into deep space where the poet's earlier work knew better. But first, consider the production of maple syrup:

> Maple syrup production is off, the *Times* says, due to the vogue for
> maple furniture.
> Willingly or not, you can't give your Cape Cod cobbler's table
> with a lamp attachment above a ship's-type wheel back to its grove.

(*FE* 54)

This indictment of the dining-room rapacities of 1960s proto-Yuppies has its serious ironies. Willingly or not, you can't give your modern, layered-space commodity, whose connotations are purely those of status and a bourgeois nostalgia (Cape Cod cobblers) back to the non-modern, mysterious dark woods of deep space. In the layered-space world there is no access to origin, and no final explanatory order: the signifier slips from the signified, the centre cannot hold. So when Schuyler concludes one of the weaker poems from *A Few Days*, 'This Notebook', as follows, he says something about the larger book of poems in which 'This Notebook' is contained:

> Little notebook, I
> love you, and the friend
> who gave me you.

> (*FD* 6)

This time the apostrophe is merely sentimental, embarrassing in a non-provocative way. Worse, the lines seek a mirror-reversal of their sentimentality in the relationship between reader and writer, a nostalgic falsehood that would fit back together the broken halves of the sign, representation and reality. Then 'I' would be whole again, and 'you' unchanging. That would undo irony, which is a slippage between saying and meaning, a Fall that we must live through for having abolished hierarchy and moved into a layered-space world. *A Few Days* yearns to return to deep space, to metaphysics:

> I'm so in love
> I want to die and take
> my happiness to heaven!

> ('Tom')

This tomfoolery is either excessive, or not excessive enough. Camp religiosity has not proved entirely without value to contemporary poetry: John Wieners, for example, has immersed himself gleefully in that interestingly swampy area where excess of meaning is allied to slippage in the sign. But the would-be conformation of signifier to signified is in the case of Schuyler's poem too nostalgically smooth, clichéd. Indeed the book insists throughout on smooth conformations: 'The Rose of Marion', pink and many-petalled, sits in a glass on a desk in a house in *'of course*, Marion, Cape Cod,/Massachusetts' (my italics). In the next poem Rachmaninoff is 'played by Richter/

(*who else*?)' (my italics). An awful poem about a dog, 'Oriane', does this ubiquitously. It is a nostalgia for a deep-space wholeness that never truly existed, of *complete* harmony between origin and ending, word and thing, utterance and meaning, the player and the played. Elsewhere in the book, such smoothness seems half to be aimed for, then, intriguingly, missed on purpose. After a sexual dream, awakening and regrets:

> That's all
> over now, though I still and
> always will like to dwell
> on your thighs.

('Sleep')

Like any pun, 'dwell' is an instance of both excess and slippage, its Surrealism driving out sentimentality. And there are some magical poems in *A Few Days*. 'At Darragh's I' tears strips off nostalgia, or more specifically, fireflies:

> in Maryland we used to catch
> them and put them in jars
> and watch their silent, sexy
> signal. We also used to tear
> their phosphor off: children
> can be real fun people!

And the conclusion of that poem is absolutely characteristic of Schuyler's expertise in its oscillation between Surreal enigma and social banality, dry East Coast wit and a kind of delighted playing with primary colours:

> Then we all pile into
> the Toyota and drive off
> into the
> World of Roses.

(FD 15)

Schuyler's effects are complex, but they are also delicate, exceedingly poised, and almost always throwaway. To supply any kind of commentary is to go on a fool's errand, in that any kind of language attached to the poems will seem not merely laboured but redundant, somehow previewed and returned by a poetry that remains conspicuously unimpressed. Schuyler's writing appears to be completely self-aware, but it is not hermetically sealed: after all, kindness and comedy are as much the product of self-awareness as is vanity.

If slippage is linked to the Fall from a religious to a layered-space world, the comedy of pratfall can wrest an ironic victory from disaster. As Baudelaire notes in his essay 'Of the Essence of Laughter', 'the phenomena produced by the Fall will become the means of redemption'. During the whole of *A Few Days* there is only one fall against the curb, necessitating stitches, and one close shave in the traffic. In his best book, *The Morning of the Poem* (1980) Schuyler falls over constantly, and in one of the strongest texts, 'Afterward', manages over the space of two pages to trip over, get pneumonia, diabetes, poisoning as a side-effect of medication, a pinched ulnar nerve, and then:

> . . . when I came out
> feeling great wham
> a nervous breakdown: four
> weeks in another hospital.

He also suffers the smoker's nemesis, fire in bed (*'extase, cauchemar,/ sommeil dans un nid de flammes'*) but begins the poem by dropping his tablets on the floor:

> I cannot
> open this container: and
> do and the pills all lie
> "star scattered on" the
> rug, which by mischance is
> the color of the pills. Do
> you ever swear out loud
> when you're alone? I do
> and did, like that painting,
> *The Gleaners.*

(*MP* 22)

The container that is Schuyler's poem spills the beans, but such confessional gestures are far from resembling a complaint by Lowell or Sexton. A painting, or a poem, can never 'swear out loud', but only inscribe, unspontaneously. That doubleness, self-awareness, is not the same as the attempts in *A Few Days* to fake a match between representation and reality; nor does it resemble Lowell's attempts to get the reader enviously embroiled in his sense of his own complexity. The duality in Schuyler's self-figuration and its pratfalls are a psychological dramatization of the convulsion within the sign. 'Joy is a unity. Laughter is the expression of a double or contradictory feeling; and it is for this reason that a convulsion occurs.' Thus Baudelaire, in his essay on the essence of laughter, which asks:

> . . . what is there so particularly diverting in the sight of a man falling on the ice or on the road, or tripping on the edge of a pavement, that his brother in Christ should promptly double up uncontrollably, that the muscles of his face should suddenly begin to function like a clock at midday or a mechanical toy?[10]

This reads like a premonition of the kind of 'convulsion' Wyndham Lewis would exploit throughout *Snooty Baronet* or *Self Condemned*. For the comic to exist there must be 'two beings in the presence of each other' a duality which Schuyler both internalizes and dramatizes as the self who falls, and the self who recreates that fall within the poem's theatre of irony. Apparently it takes two to fall, in love or in a poem. It is curious however that although Baudelaire is keenest to stress the discrepancy between the experience of he who trips and he who watches, the 'contradictory feeling' that produces laughter, the material of the fall does become grist to a kind of redemption as complicity between the two is reasserted just at the moment of their greatest separation. The watcher is condemned by his own doubling-up and rictus grin to replicate the spasms of the twitcher in the road. In this chain-reaction of contradiction and broken signs may be read an ironic restitution of compassion, a paradoxical empathy-through-ridicule. For Baudelaire, this remains a matter for relatively bleak and dispassionate observation; it is central to Schuyler's 'Afterward'.

Abstract art can never be cruel. Consider the paintings by Willem de Kooning that captured most attention in the 1950s and 60s. In works such as *Parc Rosenberg* and *Ruth's Zowie* (both of 1957) pigment is flung, slashed and splattered on the canvas with extraordinary vehemence, a phase of exploration that would culminate in the less impulsive but equally powerful *Door to the River* of 1960. In terms of the physicality of painterly method emerging as the subject of the work, I have never seen a more violent painting than de Kooning's *A Tree in Naples*, done at the end of this phase and now hanging in the Museum of Modern Art. These canvasses are abrasive, abandoned, filled with ire and wildness – but never cruel, because their basically non-narrative character makes that impossible. Other works such as *Woman and Bicycle* (1952/3, from de Kooning's famous 'Women' series) are extremely cruel, but have to return to recognizable depiction of the human frame – in, of course, a stylized and distorted form – in order to achieve their satirical cruelty.

A number of hypotheses might be drawn from a comparison between Schuyler's poetry and the painting of de Kooning, so central to New York's sense of its own best art at the time of the poetry's emergence. The New York poets were adept in techniques of defamiliarization, and techniques that stress the materiality or potential opacity of language: examples that come readily to mind include Ashbery's *The Tennis Court Oath* (1962) and O'Hara's *Second Avenue* (1953) through to Kenward Elmslie's *Circus Nerves* (1971). Analogies between these techniques, and methods deployed or discovered by the Abstract Expressionist painters, can readily be found. They would however be less significant than the sharp differences of emphasis and method between the poets and the painters, which are not solely a consequence of working in different media. The poets were actively writing against as well as with the grain of Abstraction in order to define their own art. Like the painting of Larry Rivers, but with more serious intent, the work of Schuyler and O'Hara in particular returns to figurative, representational poetry in narrative and anecdotal form alongside or *from the far side* of abstraction. Once the human figure has re-entered writing, it can be made to fall, and the comedy of cruelty as well as pathos is possible once more. But laughing-at can be subtly related to laughing-with, as empathy and a necessary sense of isolation move carefully around each other in these lines by Schuyler from a poem called 'Growing Dark':

> When
> I was young I
> hurt others. Now,
> others have hurt
> me. In the night
> I thought I heard
> a dog bark.

Racking sobs.
Poor guy. Yet,
I got my sleep.

(*MP* 12)

This is as simple and as difficult as one of Auden's love poems from
the Thirties. It is not solely a mordant acknowledgment of the cal-
lousness that is a gift of middle age, glossed by the middle-aged as
energy-conservation. The hurt that was caused and that is now
returned, the wracked sounds of a dark night of the soul and the
need for a healing oblivion, all co-exist in a tremulous poetic frame
that turns towards the reader for completion. The deliberate, trembly
awkwardness of Schuyler's linebreaks, utterly distinctive and unlike
anything in the other New Yorkers, is a form of turning to the reader.
There is an unsentimental but moving *plea* in Schuyler's poetry,
which can be comic or as cool as Baudelaire in its diagnosis of the
fall, but is as attentive as Baudelaire to redemption.

THE RHETORIC OF TEMPORALITY

Other pericopes from Baudelaire's dissertation on laughter are quoted
by Paul de Man in a now celebrated essay of 1969, 'The Rhetoric of
Temporality', to which I would briefly like to turn. De Man's analysis of the structure of Romantic writing is based on an opposition
between symbol and allegory. The symbol, it is argued, assumes
increasing importance towards the end of the eighteenth century,
within an aesthetic aiming to bridge the gap between experience and
its representation. It is part of the totalizing ambitions of Romanticism that when the symbol should have closed the gap between
subjectivity and its expression, a configuration of symbols should
close the gaps between themselves, leading not simply to a general
truth as that might have been understood earlier in the eighteenth
century, but to universal meaning. The importance of such a conceptual idealism to the organicist view of the universe propounded by
Coleridge in particular would be generally agreed. De Man's use
of the term 'allegory', which he opposes to the symbol, is rather
more provocative and personal, despite its having originated in
Hans-Georg Gadamer's *Wahrheit und Methode*. Where the symbol is
potentially infinite in its ramifications and always productive of a

multiplicity of meaning, allegorical meaning is discrete and suppressive of analogy. De Man begins to build an implied world-view on his chosen rhetorical term: the prevalence of allegory 'always corresponds to the unveiling of an authentically temporal destiny. This unveiling takes place in a subject that has sought refuge against the impact of time in a natural world to which, in truth, it bears no resemblance.' Allegory becomes as it were the secret meaning of Romanticism, always accompanying in order to undo its ambitions, and disclosed in the ironies of a text such as Wordsworth's 'A slumber did my spirit seal', where the speaker's attempts to arrest the hand of time are savagely corrected by the death of the loved one – the irreversible disclosure of our temporal plight, and the pains and evasions it catalyses. Allegory can therefore be used deconstructively in order to illuminate, in however harsh a light, what de Man feels to be crucial problems in Romantic practice, such as the apparent contradiction between an organicist philosophy of integration into the world of Nature, and 'the assertion of a radical priority of the subject'.[11] The latter can be made by the identification of allegorical figuration to disclose a selfhood severed from all that is not it, cut off from origin and explanation alike, and seeking to cover its nakedness by various defensive strategies. The consequent proximity of allegory to irony will be clear, and is the cue for de Man's attention to Baudelaire in the final section of his essay.

The relevance of such an argument to Schuyler's poetry will also I hope be clear, for despite the historical gap that separates his work from the early Romantic period, there are vital continuities which de Man's propositions help set in relief. The obsession with the recorded observation and the exaltation of New York that we see in Schuylers' and for that matter O'Hara's work make of that city a totality very close to the Romantic picturing of Nature, one massively networked Symbol. A marvellous long poem by Schuyler, 'Dining Out with Doug and Frank' (*MP* 31–40) builds, in an apparently casual and sidelong way, into a massive and threatened hymning of New York as a honeycombed text of anecdote, remembrance and common knowledge under sentence of death from Time disguised as the construction industry:

> To be on
> the water in the dark and
> the wonder of electricity –
> the real beauty of Manhattan.

> Oh well. When they tore down
> the Singer Building,
> and when I saw the Bogardus building
> rusty and coming unstitched in
> a battlefield of rubble I deliberately
> withdrew my emotional investments
> in loving old New York. Except
> you can't. I really like
> dining out and last night was
> especially fine. A full moon
> when we parted hung over
> Frank and me. Why is this poem
> so long? And full of death?

By de Man's reading, this would undeniably be an evasion of the temporal, and not simply in its overt dislike of changes in the Manhattan skyline. The deliberate use of cliché is an insistence on *common* knowledge, denial of the subject's plight – to de Man, essentially a randomness. Even a strain of *timor mortis* can be construed as temporizing in the face of time by its identification of personal fear within a genre. Elsewhere, it is true that many of the poems that seem dedicated to scrupulous observation do in fact privilege the ego over the perceived, as I tried to show in relation to *Freely Espousing*. Take these lines from a poem in *The Crystal Lithium* (1972) describing clouds in a 'beautiful New/York sky':

> tin ceiling sky
> up into and on
> which a white cup
> (more of a mug)
> falls, falls up-
> ward and crack
> splits into
> two glazed
> clay clouds

> (CL 9)

Again the fall is redeemed, reversed into a comic rise, but aren't the clouds so *excessively* observed as to be in fact not observed at all? Ingenious projections from a human scene, they are an act of colonization by a radically prioritized subject who sees his own mug in the sky. But then viewed from the perspective of 'An East Window on Elizabeth Street', even the birds seem to be up to the same thing:

> a bird is building a nest out of torn up letters
> and the red cellophane off cigarette and gum packs.

> (CL 15)

Refusing to acknowledge a conformation between signifier and signified, the unlettered bird builds a house from what is read or discarded prior to smoking, making as Schuyler did its environment an extension of itself. This can happen in relation to other people, as well as the non-human surround. The poem 'June 30, 1974' is dedicated to the poet's hosts, Jane and Joe Hazan, and to a life of 'tranquil joy' in the country, a pastoral retreat from New York to a more classicist, Horatian or at least late-Auden perspective on urban folly and the superior pleasures of company: 'Home! How lucky to/have one, how arduous/to make this scene/of beauty for/your family and/friends. Friends!' etc. What's noticeable however, and anticipated once more by the poet's expert deployment of embarrassment and archness, is that he is actually alone here. The poem concludes (with a typically upbeat ending):

> Enough to
> sit here drinking coffee,
> writing, watching the clear
> day ripen (such
> a rainy June we had)
> while Jane and Joe
> sleep in their room
> and John in his. I
> think I'll make more toast.

> (MP 7–8)

The individual life, the lives of others in the vicinity, and the non-human surroundings with the possibilities they afford for pleasure and contemplation, are celebrated for that precious but provisional balance in which they can be held for the moment the poem records. But it could equally be argued that in these lines we see how the

author-parasite has both battened on his hosts' larder and got a
poem out of them, the four Js, one of whom is a non-human month,
flattening and textualizing the symbols of Home! and Friends! into
allegorical supports for a coffee-gorged subject whose temporal en-
trapment seems far from painful. If we were to insist ruthlessly on
the necessity for poems to conform to the categories urged by Paul
de Man, we would presumably have to interrogate the relative satisfaction with temporality that these poems seem to exhibit, until
they were prepared to yield some residual attachment to a covert
ideology governed by the symbols that they had seemed only to
touch lightly. And, following a violent excision of one's sense of
humour, this can be done: the speaker's parasitism is simply the
normal, agreeable relationship of guest to host; his good fortune, to
be in such company and surroundings will not persist; but to use de
Man's terminology, he is undone by this, attempting to cushion his
separateness from a world he does not resemble by a strategy of
Romantic reinsertion. The world and its weather are falsely por-
trayed as a larger home into which everyone will fit harmoniously:
aptly, given this resurrection of the poetic Logos as conveyer of
harmonies, everyone's name begins with J, including the author's
Christian name.

In truth, none of these readings will really do. De Man's pairing of
symbol and allegory comes very close to presenting the second as
the unconscious of the first. It therefore resembles many strategies of
contemporary literary theory, whose practical application turn out
for the most part to be confined to a rejigging of the canon. The old
novels are made to yield new interpretations which the texts do
logically support, but which their authors and an older generation of
critics would have regarded as scandalous. But such instruments
rapidly become blunt when applied to contemporary poems such as
Schuyler's, which are clearly involved in the generation of multiple
and contradictory meanings from the outset. There is no 'hidden
reading' of 'June 30, 1974' whose deconstructive disclosures could
entirely erase its referential aspect, that of a text celebrating certain
sorts of human situation and company. Equally, there is no blandly
referential reading to be had, whereby the kinds of solitude and mild
egotism, carapace for our temporal plight, could also be omitted
from the poem's meanings, which are in any case generated by an
insistently poetic language which constantly draws attention to its
own artifice. Deconstruction may shed a certain light on the poetry,
but it does not in the end disclose anything that the poetry did not

know about itself. The remainder of this essay will trace the implications of this relationship for poetry and for a mode of criticism that has put on the mantle of art by pluming itself on the issue of cultural vangardism.

SHADOWS AND MARGINS

In an essay published in homage to Paul de Man, the critic Barbara Johnson had this to say about the attention paid by deconstructive reading to the 'shadows and margins', rather than the representational or intentional aspects of texts:

> Deconstruction thus confers a new kind of readability on those elements in a text that readers have traditionally been trained to disregard, overcome, explain away, or edit out – contradictions, obscurities, ambiguities, incoherences, discontinuities, ellipses, interruptions, repetitions, and plays of the signifier.[12]

It is the case that the kind of nineteenth-century text to which critics like Johnson and J. Hillis Miller have paid attention will, being in one sense long dead, submit to all kinds of scandalous repositioning of its limbs without demur. The passage of time will in any case have betrayed the presence of all sorts of shadowy contents which authorial intentionality would have wished to keep hidden from inspection. And the institutional usefulness of Professor Johnson's methods to jaded teachers and ambitious students is also clear, though not at all invited. But the applicability of such deconstructive methods to contemporary poems such as Schuyler's is questionable. A poem by O'Hara beginning

> The root   an acceptable connection
> ochre   except meaning-dream partly
> where the will falters   a screw polished
> a whole pair of shutters   you saw it
> I went in the door   the umbrella

> (CP 380)

seems similarly not to be in need of a Yale key to unlock its 'hidden' tendency to generate 'ambiguities, incoherences, discontinuities, ellipses'. If anything, I suspect a new reader would be more likely to reverse Barbara Johnson's methods entirely and begin an encounter with the New York poets by searching for a few pre-Postmodernist continuities as handholds during reading. When Christopher Norris, a lucid explicator of Deconstruction, says the following about de Man and Jacques Derrida, he too seems to herald novelties that contemporary poetry already knew from the inside:

> Allegory in de Man exerts something like the power of deconstructive leverage that Derrida brings to bear through his key-term *différance*. That is to say, it introduces the idea of a differential play within language that everywhere prevents (or constantly *defers*) the imaginary coincidence of meaning and intent.[13]

Far from wishing to suspend a recognition of that slippage, which would leave the poem in the thrall of a transcendental aesthetics wilfully blind to the rhetoric of temporality, O'Hara insists on 'differential play' and, by the arrangement of words on the page, a fundamental deferral/differentiation of any settlement of the wayward energies straining around the bar of the sign. However, it might in turn be a simplification to argue that a poem such as 'What Appears To Be Yours' marks the furthest outpost of poetic vanguardism with which theory might now, please, have the decency to race to catch up. There exist other poems by O'Hara and by Schuyler that know about that kind of groundbreaking detonation of signifiers, but which deploy it as one device in the armoury, while the most exploratory aspects of the writing move on into a territory which is as hard to characterize as it is vital to their practice. Schuyer's best work – the whole of *The Morning of the Poem*, most of *The Crystal Lithium* and *Freely Espousing* – requires that vanguardism as an ironizing presence in its attention to social realities, within which it ministers against anything so nostalgic and insufficient as the notion of literary realism. Poetry and deconstruction may meet again, in passing, at a shared perception that social reality is itself textual in a broad sense: to engage with slippage of meaning is to be involved with the real world, as has been clear at least since Freud's theorizing of *lapsus linguae*. Freudian method can readily be brought to bear on literary texts so as to disclose, say, unconscious erotic puns in early James, but again, how could one diagnose *lapsus linguae* in a poem like Schuyler's 'The Dog Wants His Dinner', which so clearly knows that trick backwards?

> The sky is pitiless. I beg
> your pardon? OK then
> the sky is pitted.

(*CL 61*)

Later: 'Yesterday the/air was squeaky clean today/it's dull and lifeless as an/addict's armpit. Surely you/mean leafless.' And so on. Yet the poet's boxing clever about the traditional kind of unconscious revelation can hardly lift him free of other kinds of involvement with semantic slippage. Perhaps to be unfaithful to a lover is to discover in the bedroom that rift between saying and meaning that spells irony in a rhetorical context. (Perhaps there is no escape from rhetorical context.)

> How I wish you would come
> back! I could tell
> you how, when I lived
> on East 49th, first
> with Frank and then with John,
> we had a lovely view of
> the UN building and the
> Beekman Towers. They were
> not my lovers, though.
> You were. You said so.

('This Dark Apartment' *MP* 4)

Words in a sense are always late for the event, and explication late for the words. But if saying always swerves away from meaning, language generates new life in the mouth or the mind, begetting and issuing from a world no less real for its omission of the original, intended meaning. 'I/think of you and then/my thought slides/on, like slipping/on a lightly iced/walk. I have no more/poems for you, chum,/only for the ice and snow.' (*MP* 27)

I would suggest tentatively that a return to the key terms proposed originally in this essay might preserve something of what is valuable in de Man's opposing concepts of symbol and allegory, while respecting those elements in Schuyler's poetry that seem to take it beyond what 'The Rhetoric of Temporality' can account for. While allegory is in de Manian rhetoric the rival of symbol, and may work to undermine it, the arts of deep and layered space need not be seen as existing in such a strictly contentious relationship. They *may* do so of course, for example wherever a humanist position battles against the claims of deep-space religion, or where a traditional humanism, itself now ossified into falsely transcendental categories, finds itself under attack from a layered-space perception less willing to see a fixed concept of 'man' as the 'centre' of what may not after all be 'his' world. But there may well in the work of any artist be a shifting coexistence of deep and layered-space forms, metaphysical and anti-metaphysical energies, whose mutual interrogation could compose the work or take it further on. In that light I close with a poem by Schuyler, 'Song' from *The Morning of the Poem*, in which opposed concepts of wholeness and fragmentation, the temporal and the symbolic, deep and layered-space, are turned over by a writing that recognizes their opposed qualities but records the potential of either to support, flow through or undo the other. In any case, Schuyler's poems suffer, if that is possible, even more than most good poems from not being quoted entire. Part of the pleasure of reading him is a pleasure in watching something held and carried to its own conclusion with poise and without being allowed to fall.

> The light lies layered in the leaves.
> Trees, and trees, more trees.
> A cloud boy brings the evening paper:
> *The Evening Sun*. It sets.
> Not sharply or at once
> a stately progress down the sky
> (it's gilt and pink and faintly green)
> above, beyond, behind the evening leaves
> of trees. Traffic sounds and
> bells resound in silver clangs
> the hour, a tune, my friend
> Pierrot. The violet hour:
> the grass is violent green.
> A weeping beech is gray,
> a copper beech is copper red.
> Tennis nets hang
> unused in unused stillness.
> A car starts up and
> whispers into what will soon be night.
> A tennis ball is served.

A horsefly vanishes.
A smoking cigarette.
A day (so many and so few)
dies down a hardened sky
and leaves are lap-held notebook leaves
discriminated barely
in light no longer layered.

(*MP* 17)

'Song' is, as its title announces, a progression from music to silence through one continuous poetic action. At the same time, this poem would seem to be very much a collage of layered-space bits and pieces, carried as it is to one side of the traditional, Romantic Ode to Evening as something quirkier and more fragmentary. The poem seems made up of part-objects: although a horsefly is a discrete, organic whole, and its behaviour recorded very accurately, the fact of its being there only to be denied – 'A horsefly vanishes' – puts a question mark against it. The cigarette lacking its smoker and the ball served out of nowhere are, again, well-observed but a touch Surreal. Up to a point this can all be ascribed to mimesis. One can see what is inside one's field of vision, and only that; some things do move too rapidly to be seen to go; the grass at sunset can turn a rather Pre-Raphaelite, 'violent' green. But if therefore the poem can be seen to depend from a tradition of observational poetry sponsored by William Carlos Williams it seems, like the elm that rose with the smoothness of an elevator some pages back, to express a surplus of meaning which is yet broken into pieces. Some shadow of irony, of a rift between saying and meaning, is cast even over the most sharply-observed data. In a way, 'Song' is a fragment made of smaller fragments, which would situate it in relation to a taste that began at the end of the eighteenth century, with the connected enthusiasm for ruins and republicanism. The collage is the modern art of fragments. It is an art appropriate to a layered-space sense of history, that has sought to level hierarchy and place an emphasis on change which necessarily recall us to our temporal and piecemeal existence. To an extent therefore, layered-space can be seen in close proximity to de Man's concept of allegory vis-à-vis symbol. The whole symbols of a grand ode are denied; reminders of the passing of time, of 'what will soon be night', of days that are 'so few', of the loss of light to see by that forces a closure on the poem – all these can be read as exposing the temporal plight of a subject who has looked for refuge in an environment from which he is truly separate.

And yet there is another, more marbled Romantic tradition, exemplified by Tennyson, which speaks exactly to our loss of light and life in an ambivalence of mourning, pathos and celebration. In the punning transition from arboreal to notebook 'leaves' Schuyler treads a time-honoured path, as his words both lament and arrest the passing of time. In consequence we might want to give some especially rigorous attention to any deep-space yearnings in the poem, to see if they mark the restitution of transcendental categories, the de Manian symbol, in which the timebound subject might seek to hide his vulnerability. And the word 'layered' does seem ambiguous in this context, meaning both something like what I have meant by it – nonmetaphysical flats and shapes of painterly colour or texture– and something offering the promise of more, mysterious light, 'above, beyond, behind' and thus by implication in the deeper spaces of metaphysics. And 'a cloud boy' does after all bring 'The Evening Sun': but this seems playfully apollonian or hermetic, an imaging of and not a subscription to deep-space mythology.

A de Manian reading would not appear quite to work, chiefly because the symbols here are more played than needed, and the allegory refuses to work as a canker inside them. As Schuyler himself writes in *The Crystal Lithium*: 'All things are real/no one a symbol.' (80) An opposition, which can also be an association, between deep and layered-space aesthetics seems more adequately to trace the contours of the poems' thinking in relation to literary history. 'Song' has a layered-space bias; there may be mimetic and even Horatian strains in Schuyler's work, but there is also, beneath the deceptive jokiness, a fierce separation of poetic from other kinds of language, and an equally assertive separation of this from various other sorts of poem. It may well be that the poetry of James Schuyler is brought most to its own poised and subtle life by an act of silent listening that would make the kind of superstructure I have provided not merely cumbersome but irrelevant. However, the number of people listening to Schuyler silently or otherwise is far from ideal. None of the New York poets has ever tried to solicit a university-based readership, and yet it is evident from the public career of John Ashbery that, however irrelevant the monopoly undoubtedly is to his sense of his own work, there is no significant readership for poetry now outside of syllabus-sponsorship. Yet even the advance guard of university criticism (*soi-disant*) either get it all wrong, or more usually ignore, contemporary poetry in favour of the distant past. Readers do, of course, frequently make their first encounter with avant-garde poetry at college, but this is much more likely to take place through readings organized by the university's Poetry Society than through the official syllabus as determined by the English Faculty. In a more lively time and place, wouldn't students be most intensely involved with the reading and writing of their own time, reaching from their own moment to locate the past, and not the other way about?

For the time being there is no way to praise and promote the poetry publicly except through the Institution's channels and debates. Meanwhile James Schuyler's poetry is more than equal to the attention that will be paid to it in time, and has its own resistant integrity:

The nimbus is back at four in the afternoon: no moon tonight. Before
    dawn I woke and made my oatmeal, orange juice and
Coffee and thought how this poem seems mostly about what I've lost:
    the one who mattered most, my best friend, Paul
(Who mattered least), the Island, the California wild-flower paper,
    the this, the that, Whippoorwill, buried friends,
And the things I only write between the lines. What can one write
    between the lines? Not one damn thing.

                                   ('The Morning of the Poem' *MP* 108)

2

Frank O'Hara: Accident and Design

GRACE AND THE IMPORTANT UTTERANCE

Frank O'Hara was dead at forty. Called on to speak by the graveside, the New York painter Larry Rivers began, 'Frank was my best friend', but later in his speech had ruefully to admit that there were 'at least sixty people in New York who thought Frank O'Hara was their best friend'.[1] Poet, critic, Assistant Curator at the Museum of Modern Art and associated with many of the painters called Abstract Expressionist, O'Hara led by any standards a packed and hectic life in which the threads of work, play, friendship and competition were deliberately allowed to intertwine at speed. His career, evidently successful in one way, also had something of the balancing-act about it. According to one close friend and colleague at MOMA, O'Hara had been 'under suspicion as a gifted amateur' during his early years at the Museum: a Harvard English major who switched from Music, graduating in 1950, O'Hara was first employed on the front desk, the sum of his relevant work-experience at that time having been dogsbodying in the theatre and a brief stint as private secretary to photographer Cecil Beaton. Consequently O'Hara did not have 'the credentials of art history training or a long museum apprenticeship to support his claim to direct exhibitions', and his closeness to the artists was thought a mixed blessing.[2] He did nevertheless go on to assist in the organization of many important circulating exhibitions, including *The New American Painting*, (1958–9), the first group showing of American Abstract Expressionism to tour Europe. Between 1961 and his death in 1966, he would supervise the definitive retrospectives of Kline, Motherwell, Nakian and David Smith, and at the time of his death O'Hara had begun to plan a Jackson Pollock retrospective.

Despite this professional success during a crucial period of consolidation for the new American art, it is important to retain a sense of the maverick and the transgressive as being both instinctive and

36

productive at all levels of O'Hara's (hyper) activity. Alongside the actual mixed-media collaborations in lithograph or film with Larry Rivers and others, his constant practice was to bring one form of expression to life by forcing it to abrade or include another from which it is conventionally distinct. So, many of the poems concern painting or music; the most personal of his critical essays, the 'art chronicles', attain a kind of prose poetry; the painters he helped canonize professionally would also be friends; his worksheets for their exhibitions resemble his poems in visual layout.[3] This multifaceted diligence was powered by interruption, on the page and elsewhere. He was very far from the Eliotean model of the academic: yet it is still Frank O'Hara who, of all the poets of his generation, insists most firmly and frequently that criticism, analysis and evaluation are integral to civilized life. One poem laconically observes of a friend, 'I suspect he is making a distinction/well, who isn't'. (*CP* 328) O'Hara is an acutely self-conscious writer who makes distinctions partly as a pre-emptive strike against their being made by others, against him. Warm about friends and besotted with New York, his poetry also gives off a coolly professional sense of life in that place as a game in which one had better stay ahead – which is achieved by never staying still. Like great chunks of the city, the poems are 'built yesterday as everything should be' (*CP* 358), nerves and restlessness hardening into something created and concrete. Incessantly opinionated, they refuse to be trapped inside any single attitude, their catch-me-if-you-can capacity to dazzle and magnetize an attempt to elevate the mercurial into work of stature. Like the more successful of the Mid-town skyscrapers, they are both fabulously ambitious and surprisingly delicate. These 'big, airy structures', as John Ashbery calls them in his introduction to O'Hara's *Collected Poems* (*CP* ix) are built both to compete against the weather, Ahab-style, and passively reflect its changing colours. Ashbery is repeatedly driven to paradox in describing his friend's work; the poetry is 'modest and monumental', and, in an absolute identification of art and the city, 'a scent of garbage, patchouli and carbon monoxide drifts across it, making it the lovely, corrupt, wholesome place New York is'. (*CP* x)

To both these poets, the City is a poem, a gesture against mortality that its constructions strive to block out, yet reinscribe through their own shadows. The depths of paradox in O'Hara are already there on the surface of his poetry, its vivid fragmentation. This chapter will largely be occupied in locating the sources and effects of fragmentation recorded in O'Hara's work, where avant-garde spikiness may mask the pathos of the broken; where a creative messiness of layered-space bric-à-brac, sponsored by Carlos Williams and the City of New York, may be layered in such thick impasto that it turns deep – the City as Nature, our new Sublime. Although I offer a vain attempt to sketch the range of O'Hara's writing, much can be gained from a reading of his early masterpiece 'In Memory of My Feelings', where a range of crucial influences are seen to be both gathered and discharged.

Inevitably, the mixing of media, the sharpening and the blurring of vision, went on far into the deep space of night:

> Two weeks before his death, during a weekend at Larry Rivers' place in Southampton, a particularly exhausting all-night session of drinking, talking and listening to music prompted J. J. Mitchell to ask Frank, as dawn was breaking, 'Don't you ever get tired and want to sleep?' Frank said, 'If I had my way I'd go on and on and on and never go to sleep.'[4]

This living for the moment, a kind of Romanticism common in artistic rhetorics of the last two centuries, appears to have been deeply ingrained in O'Hara's personality and its representation by himself and others. Sudden death, that cut off and stamped his existence with a generic *carpe diem*, was shockingly unexpected and yet in line with the darker intuitions of his poetry. A subtle poem of self-criticism, 'Getting Up Ahead of Someone (Sun)', ends with the softly ominous line 'each day's light has more significance these days' (CP 341), one given a tragic cast by our knowledge of the accident on Fire Island that was to terminate his life within a few years.[5] Although the strain of dark Romanticism is important, O'Hara was not his own sole subject for poetry. He mistrusted the 'confessional' manner popular in his lifetime and epitomized by the work of Robert Lowell, for its attempts to place if not enthrone the personality of the poet between the reader and the poem. O'Hara told one interviewer 'I think Lowell has . . . a confessional manner which (lets him) get away with things that are just plain bad but you're supposed to be interested because he's so upset.' Equally, however, he had doubts about the more experimental Black Mountain school of writing, detecting in Charles Olson's work a straining after 'the important utterance, which . . . is not particularly desirable most of the time', a congested, neo-Poundian gravitas that in a different sense from Lowell still gets in the reader's way.[6] Speed was of the essence. As O'Hara's oft-quoted mock-manifesto 'Personism' has it:

> I don't even like rhythm, assonance, all that stuff. You just go on your nerve. If someone's chasing you down the street with a knife you just run, you don't turn around and shout, 'Give it up! I was a track star for Mineola Prep.' (CP 498)

As so often in O'Hara the aim of the joking is to deflate pretentiousness, but even 'Personism' shows an exceedingly *driven* commitment to art. To equate the experiences of composing a poem and being chased down the street by someone wielding a knife is no truism. As so often in O'Hara, a self-protective wit that seems at first to mask a fear of the serious idea (and which lies at the root of the refusal by most American critics to take O'Hara seriously) reveals darkness, obsession and insecurity just where it seemed to be signing off with a throwaway punchline.

To read *The Collected Poems of Frank O'Hara* is therefore to call into question an antagonism, familiar in literary criticism, between an idea of poetry as the condensed expression of an extra-linguistic life to which it is umbilically attached – the view still dominant in Britain – and a more formalist sense of the poetic text as a free-standing construct. While a poem such as 'What Appears to Be Yours' (sampled in the previous chapter) does indeed mount a frontal assault on any conception of poetry or language as straightforwardly referential, the poems as a whole are shamelessly autobiographical, and certainly unwilling to be held captive by any neo-Mallarméan aspirations to a *poésie pure*. Notoriously diffident over the publication of his poems in book form, O'Hara may have sensed that they would best be viewed either as one-off improvisations, or in the huge, cross-referencing construction, *The Collected Poems*.

Although the positions occupied by O'Hara's poetics are at variance with the dicta of both the avant-garde and the East Coast establishment of his time, this did not isolate him. Somewhat as Auden characterized Yeats' perpetuation after death, O'Hara was to become his admirers: no other poet in recent times can have elicited such a flood of poetic tributes that don't merely show the poet's influence, as in so many verses by Ron Padgett or Jim Brodey or

Peter Schjeldahl or Michael Brownstein, but mention him by name
and with affection. John Wieners, whose early work O'Hara had
championed, Allen Ginsberg and James Schuyler are among the
elegists, but the process of lionization had already begun during
O'Hara's lifetime: Ted Berrigan, most tenacious of the poet-acolytes,
would hang around Avenue A waiting for a glimpse of his idol, a
Pepsi-generation De Quincey on the path to Wordsworth's cottage.
O'Hara's poems are themselves often affable and warm in tone.
They are also, often, cool, and to pursue that complementary opposition would be to dive deep towards the mainsprings of O'Hara's
writing. But it is the conspicuously emotional pull the poems choose
to exert at times that may continue to draw a corresponding warmth
from poet-readers. 'you can't plan on the heart, but/the better part
of it, my poetry, is open.' (*CP* 231) O'Hara both liked and exhibited
emotional expansiveness in his day-to-day life, the 'better part' of
which was the composition of poetry. Allied to that warmth is the
magnetic but cooler energy of wit, which he again exuded on the
page and *in propria persona*.

Likewise, the younger poets such as Berrigan who imitated O'Hara
most closely have attempted to develop a sharp sense of comedy as
well as tonal warmth. The question then arises of the degree to
which O'Hara originated this configuration of styles, and the degree
to which both the poet and his followers may have been carrying on
some other tradition. It may help in uncovering the operations of
O'Hara's skills in these areas to mount a brief comparison with the
methods of Lord Byron, a figure mentioned regularly and significantly in O'Hara's work. There is clearly no need to list those areas
in which their oeuvres have nothing whatsoever in common, but in
touching on such matters as the relationship between scepticism and
the comic, or between a high emotional charge and an art of improvisation, some affinities may appear that would contextualize
O'Hara in ways that cross time, as well as the avenues of Manhattan.
They are both great debunkers, for a start.

> why are you reading this poem anyway?

> ('Petit Poème en Prose', *CP* 427)

> Hail, Muse! *et cætera*.

> (*Don Juan*, III, 1)[7]

In both these cases, verse-convention is semi-seriously interrogated and takes a bruising. Both Byron and O'Hara understood but were fearful of a Romantic obsession with poetry, and in both a compulsive, at times manic urge towards Orphic utterance sits at odds with the cooler inclination to get writing in perspective as just one activity in a varied life. The line from 'In Memory of My Feelings' that was to be chiselled on O'Hara's gravestone, 'Grace to be born and live as variously as possible', has generally been read as a Whitmanian motto appropriate to a trailblazing American artist. But it could be taken as warning gently that poetry should be kept in perspective; and in fact 'Grace' in the poem refers to O'Hara's friend, the painter Grace Hartigan. Perhaps the conflict between the two views of poetry can only be resolved via the temporary truce of such a serious joke.

Of course to mock one's self is among other things to insist on the self's self-consistency, and so in an oblique way to assert it:

> . . . I think of myself
> as a cheerful type who pretends to
> be hurt to get a little depth into
>   things that interest me

('Post the Lake Poets Ballad', *CP* 336)

> I pass my evenings in long galleries solely,
> And that's the reason I'm so melancholy.

(*Don Juan*, Canto V, lviii)

It should be only initially surprising that Byron's habitual manipulation of rhyme, and O'Hara's ritual avoidance of it, should engender some broadly analogous tonal effects. In both cases – in the case perhaps of any strong poem – our sense of the poet's self hovering somewhere slightly behind the form of a given text is an achieved illusion. Indeed, by the lights of some recent philosophical enquiries presence itself is never anything but an illusion, which we may now be able to deconstruct, but beyond which we may not historically be able as yet to pass. There is an early essay by Jacques Derrida that seeks to unpick the metaphysics of presence underpinning Husserlian phenomenology, an enquiry on which it would at this point be digressive to report at length, but which reminds us that presence is

bound up with form, can only be detected in a form. 'Only a form is
evident, only a form has or is an essence, only a form *presents itself* as
such.'[8] One might argue that all that presents itself, all that is evident
of a poem, is verbal form. Form, however, has designs on the reader
who by reading brings it to life, and by co-operative linguistic sleight
of hand inscribes a depth of selfhood onto the flat page. So the
seeming autosubversion in the above quotations is not quite what it
seems. Perhaps debunking in O'Hara's and Byron's writing is never
straightforwardly all it seems. The two poets may have more than a
sceptical comedy in common. One of O'Hara's 'warmest' poems,
'Having a Coke with You', begins as follows:

is even more fun than going to San Sebastian, Irún, Hendaye,
    Biarritz, Bayonne
or being sick to my stomach on the Traversera de Gracia in
    Barcelona
partly because in your orange shirt you look like a better happier
    St. Sebastian
partly because of my love for you, partly because of your love for
    yoghurt

                                                              (CP 360)

The glamorous travelogue of the poem's first line is brought down to
earth by a case of Spanish tummy, somewhat as Don Juan's rhapso-
dizing on board ship is overturned by seasickness. It is partly in both
cases a revenge of physicality on the mind. Comic upsets restore
balance in the end. Looser in one sense at a formal level, O'Hara's
recourse to this kind of life-giving bathos once again resembles the
salutary bump so often found in the closing couplet of Byron's *ottava
rima*. Here the best part of two stanzas is taken to set up what will
then be knocked down in two lines:

    He thought about himself, and the whole earth,
        Of man the wonderful, and of the stars,
    And how the deuce they ever could have birth;
        And then he thought of earthquakes, and of wars,
    How many miles the moon might have in girth,
        Of air-balloons, and of the many bars
    To perfect knowledge of the boundless skies; –
    And then he thought of Donna Julia's eyes.

> In thoughts like these true wisdom may discern
>   Longings sublime, and aspirations high,
> Which some are born with, but the most part learn
>   To plague themselves withal, they know not why:
> 'Twas strange that one so young should thus concern
>   His brain about the action of the sky;
> If *you* think 'twas philosophy that this did,
> I can't help thinking puberty assisted.

(*Don Juan*, Canto I, xcii–iii)

This looks at first sight like a straightforward debunking of 'Longings sublime, and aspirations high' as gland-based hallucination. To revive the categories introduced previously, a layered-space view here punctures aspirations to deep space, the sublime. However, to inscribe within a text the demotion of speculative thought by the workings of biology is itself to offer the beginnings of a philosophical position. It would be easy to accumulate a hundred instances in *Don Juan* where metaphysical or other highfalutin aspiration is grounded with a comic jolt, but *Don Juan* would be a very different poem if its aim were simply to pull down idealism in a purely cynical or merely worldly way:

> Perfect she was, but as perfection is
>   Insipid in this naughty world of ours,
> Where our first parents never learn'd to kiss
>   Till they were exiled from their earlier bowers,
> Where all was peace, and innocence, and bliss
>   (I wonder how they got through the twelve hours) . . .

(*Don Juan*, Canto I, xviii)

This is no simple deflation of Christian mythology, any more than O'Hara's sour joke about a stomach upset makes his lyric less of a love poem. Byron actually comes down harder on the complacencies of secular humanism than he ever does on religious, deep-space aspiration, despite the many blasphemous jokes. If Byron had felt a complete want of interest in such figures as Adam and Eve, he need not have breathed textual life into them; at the least, objects of satire must be thought worth attacking to be brought in at all. And in fact Byron prefers a suggestion of mystery, a hint of deeper space, to

sheathe the tip of even his sharpest foil. Something similar may be at
work in the margins of O'Hara's poem. It is certainly not of prime
significance, but it can be no simple accident either, that 'San Sebastian' is mentioned in line one and 'St. Sebastian' in line three. Later
in the poem

                                                              I look
at you and I would rather look at you than all the portraits in the
   world
except possibly for the *Polish Rider* occasionally and anyway it's in
   the Frick
which thank heavens you haven't gone to yet so we can go
   together the first time

                                                          (CP 360)

Barbara Johnson has defined cliché as 'an authorless quotation', and
that second line is an authorless quotation of the kind Frank Sinatra
would croon through a million New York wireless sets in the year
this poem was written. Deep-space by virtue of its extreme and
lyrical subjectivism, it is set up to be knocked down by the jokey
genuflection at Rembrandt in the line that follows. Or so it seems at
first: the preference for the *Polish Rider* is such an *authored* quotation,
so ridiculously definite a Critic's Choice, that it ends by undermin-
ing the whole idea of rational preference and restores feasibility to
the unimpeded emotionalism of the previous line. The 'cliché' now
sounds like a convincing statement of feeling, while the judgment
about painting seems absurd. In keeping with this, the slipped-in
'heavens' that will follow is apparently insouciant, but its deep-
space associations are unavoidable. In consequence the lines are
undecidedly both a layered-space debunking of any lover's romanticism – O'Hara's debunking, in a sense, of his own Byronic postur-
ing – together with the metaphysically-minded opposite of that
attitude, a feeling however hedged by ironies that there is in love
something divine, and that 'the world' can seem a smaller thing than
love's energies. This conjuration of a deeper space is in truth equally
Byronic, but as distant from Byron's usual modes of self-representation as an unabashed love poem is distant from O'Hara's usual
scepticism. The final indeterminacy of tone in both the nineteenth-
and twentieth-century texts is not what one might be led to antici-

pate from the definition and extraversion of each author's customary self-representation.

It would be accounted less surprising to uncover semantic or tonal indeterminacy in any post-*Waste Land*, post-Surrealist writing than to find it in Byron, for of all the Romantic poets, Byron lays most stress on the determinate nature of the self, its integrity, difference, and distance from the world that is not it. We feel only rarely in Byron that pulsing, the call-and-response of a phenomenological interchange between self and the world, that mutual formation of landscape and mind, intrinsic to the Wordsworthian credo. Byron will try occasionally to beat time with it, as in some of the more meditative episodes in *Childe Harold's Pilgrimage* (for example, III, 13), only to reject it for the fierce arrythmy of a separate selfhood, that *figure* which his writing always yearns to create, then present as its own source. For all his diffuseness, what Ashbery labels a trifle disingenuously 'the inspired ramblings of a mind open to the point of distraction', O'Hara too relished the poem's emergence as a vortex of energies at whose still centre was the *figure* of Frank O'Hara, imaging in words something like the classic photo of the poet by Fred McDarrah, reproduced at the front of *Art Chronicles*. Yet such an image, sign of that integrity of a governing personality of which the poem needs desperately to believe it is the offspring, is indeed marked in Byron's writing, but only as a reiterated absence. That sense of the self as multiple or kaleidoscopic, which is part of any modern American poet's inheritance from Whitman and Dickinson, is acknowledged only with reluctance and a sense of vertigo in Byron. In a powerful irony to which Byron's writing is hostage but from which it can negotiate no terms of release, that singularity of personality on which the poetry is built, and which distinguishes it from the work of the other Romantic poets, is in truth a phantom possibility retreating before the advance of any given poem. A second irony ensues. Wordsworth's sense of self is phenomenological, Merleau-Pontyan *avant la lettre*, the world generating human observers whose acts of perception supply its significance. In Byron the self is manifestly separate from the world, and yet turns out to have no separate reality beyond that of a mirage, always advancing, like the possibility of an afterlife, beyond reach of the questions that are the writing's only 'heart': 'The goal is gain'd, we die, you know – and then –/What then? – I do not know, no more do you – ' (*Don Juan*, 1, cxxxiii–iv); 'What are we? and whence came we? what shall be/Our *ultimate* existence?' (VI, lxiii); 'Here we are,/And there we go: – but *where*?' (V, xxxix). The urgency of the questions deflects attention only initially from an uncertainty in the 'I' as radical as that attaching to the mystery of our 'ultimate' existence. To put it another way, there is no escape in Byron from the mutual interrogation of deep and layered-space positions, because each seems mysteriously seeded in the other.

At crucial points in the text, language unpicks its own verbal weaving, its *textus*, in search of an answer to these torments, but finds none.

> Could I embody and unbosom now
> That which is most within me, – could I wreak
> My thoughts upon expression, and thus throw
> Soul, heart, mind, passions, feelings, strong or weak,
> All that I would have sought, and all I seek,
> Bear, know, feel, and yet breathe – into *one* word,
> And that one word were Lightning, I would speak;
> But as it is, I live and die unheard,
> With a most voiceless thought, sheathing it as a sword.

> (Canto III, xcvii)

This is the most Shelleyan moment in Byron's poetry, the usual gravity and sonorousness dislodged by a pell-mell spray of verbs recalling *Epipsychidion*, a moment where Byron strains for the one magical word that would end words and their unending separation from the reality they are doomed to shadow and never embody. But the word 'word' can only be sheathed once more within 'sword', as metaphors again start up their proliferation, leading expression away from its object. The alleged reality to which signifiers point is finally as conjectural as the 'I' that claims to supervise them. But as any close reader of Byron or O'Hara will testify, this recognition of fictiveness by no means spells release into a painless universe. The word 'sword' may drip real blood; to weigh 'heart' down with a question mark may be to break it. To see through illusions of the nominative is not necessarily to feel neutral, let alone happy, in one's emancipation; indeed, to see *through* is not necessarily to be emancipated at all. This is one of the themes of a great poem by O'Hara, 'In Memory of My Feelings'. Likewise, one might argue that to read Byron carefully is to retain an involvement with the comedy and pain and redemption which the writing articulates, while acknowledging the phantom or provisional nature of those supposedly firm subject-positions from which the text argues such categories can only issue.

I have lingered with Lord Byron, and there will be readers of O'Hara to whom this may still seem puzzling or inappropriate. Byron, however, was one of O'Hara's touchstones; along with the figures of Rachmaninoff and Pasternak, his associations are not merely those of cultural bric-à-brac, but become part of the poet's personal mythology. Direct use is made of Byron in a number of poems, pre-eminently 'In Memory of My Feelings', 'Those Who Are Dreaming, A Play About St. Paul', and 'Ballade Number 4'. However I would like to at least hold open for consideration in this chapter the possibility that other poems by O'Hara are less explicitly but at a deeper level Byronic. This would not simply be a question of temperament or method, though there are obvious affinities between the author of *Don Juan*, whose 'conversational facility' could rattle off stanzas 'Just as I feel the "Improvvisatore"', and Frank O'Hara, who left poems in letters or his laundry, and knocked out two of his finest poems – 'Sleeping on the Wing' and 'Adieu to Norman, Bon Jour to Joan and Jean-Paul' – in response to a direct challenge to his facility as an improviser. Both poets are wits, jester-philosophers who puncture pretension to deep-space. Yet in both cases, not only does a window giving onto deep-space, a refusal to relinquish metaphysics, shimmer in the margins, but a perpetual reverse reading becomes necessary whereby margin becomes mirage, where deep becomes layered becoming deep again, where metaphysics and nihilism seem not so much opposed as latent in each other.

Of course the possibility would then arise that all such binarily 'opposed' categories – belief and scepticism, for example – are ultimately rooted in each other. The distinctly bleak conclusions of Paul de Man's thinking become visible at this point. By the lights of his deconstructive analysis, and according to the most mournful passages in the later Cantos of *Childe Harold* or a poem of the order of 'For the Chinese New Year & for Bill Berkson', these categories by which we set such store are fig-leaves to cover our existential nakedness. It is easier to contemplate intellectually than to live inside such a version of events, whereby we are as cut off from our phantom, incomplete subjectivity as we are from each other. This is given ample acknowledgment by de Man's emphasis on madness towards the end of 'The Rhetoric of Temporality', by the sheer quantity of thrashing pain in the third Canto of *Childe Harold* and by the snarled and snarling termination of O'Hara's 'For the Chinese New Year . . .':

no there is no precedent of history no history nobody came before nobody will ever come before and nobody ever was that man

you will not die not knowing this is true this year

(CP 393)

That last line carries a number of meanings, to put it mildly. The little word 'this' includes everything of living for the instant that Romantic poetry from Byron's time to ours has wanted to celebrate, but turned around to show its darker side. When 'there is no precedent of history', when the instant of experience is all we have, then there is no we or you or I: 'nobody ever was', for to be somebody would have required a continuity of identity beyond the single instant. Ritual, society, measure – the fireworks of the Chinese New Year – exist to assert such continuities in principle but deny them by exploding into nothing in the darkness. To know that 'this is true' would be appalling, perhaps unliveable. But it's OK: the legend in the poem's fortune cookie predicts that you will not die not knowing this is true this year. You may well die, though, and knowing that it is true, sooner or later. And then no-one can really help, or be changelessly himself for long enough to be saluted, 'nobody ever was that man'.

'Who was that Masked Man?', people would ask as the Lone Ranger, a Corsair or Lara for the television age, swept by in a cloud of dust. Byron himself was a masked man: Venetian roué, freedom fighter, fat, thin, as pale as Géricault's 'Portrait of a Young Man' or got up to fight in Albanian costume. His life and writing are a firework disintegration of glittering selves that in any given passage emphatically assert the opposite; the heroic single self, not yet dying, knowing what's true, defiantly cheating death. And, as O'Hara's motto looks back to Lord Byron, it looks forward to de Man. The conclusion of 'For the Chinese New Year . . .' is not widely at

variance with the much-quoted remarks that come towards the end
of de Man's late essay on Shelley:

> *The Triumph of Time* warns us that nothing, whether deed, word,
> thought or text, ever happens in relation, positive or negative, to
> anything that precedes, follows or exists elsewhere, but only as a
> random event whose power, like the power of death, is due to the
> randomness of its occurrence.[9]

I am not trying to force an implausible, transhistorical convergence
of three figures – Byron, de Man and O'Hara – who are so clearly
unconnected in so many areas. Nor is it the ultimate drift of the
present argument to propose that any writing can be forced by
deconstructive pressure to concede its reliance on fictive handholds
that guard the writer and reader from a bleak (but accurate) view of
our miserable condition. It simply wouldn't work – to take only a
few examples of writers from O'Hara's intellectual background – on
Emerson, for whom belief and scepticism lived in rude health, open
cohabitation and mutual support: on the Surrealists, whose beliefs
were powered by political scepticism: or for Auden, whose lucid
humanism consistently calls on belief and scepticism to make room
for each other, but never in a ratio that critical reading can view
either as a merger, or dissolution. Instead, I am suggesting that
Byron and O'Hara share certain characteristics that set each apart
from his contemporaries. O'Hara was not influenced by Byron: rather
they are both poets for whom the comedy and wit they exhibit so
habitually is powered by pressures of mortality. They are writers for
whom the construction in writing of a plausible simulacrum of their
non-writing selves – not quite the same thing as autobiography – is
vital. Yet in both cases this simulacrum is known to be a cover,
holding at arm's length and yet in a painfully tight grip a knowledge
of mutability alternately dark and explosive. Deconstruction can
help to bare what Barbara Johnson calls the 'rigorous, contradictory
logic' texts exhibit in their self-difference, at least in the case of
Byron, as we have seen.[10] As with the imperviousness of Schuyler's
poetry to Freudian analyses, so O'Hara's poetry is braced pre-
emptively to meet any determination to spot contradiction. Although
de Manian method may have little to contribute to a reading of 'For
the Chinese New Year & Bill Berkson', the philosophical *tone* of that
poem is close to the atmosphere of de Man's fierce disillusionment.

There is a lingering trace of post-war existentialism in the work of both writers.

By alleging similarities, or for that matter differences, between Byron and O'Hara (or between prose and poetry, man and woman, Venice and Manhattan, literature and theory) one immediately represses differences internal to each entity, ways in which a phenomenon such as a poem or a writer differs from itself. To speak of that solid mass of wood-pulp *The Collected Poems of Frank O'Hara* and compare it to *Don Juan*, or to set 'Byron' and 'O'Hara' in juxtaposition, may be to imply a unity of writing or personality, where it might be more fruitful as well as accurate to work with internal contradictions and differences. In thus gesturing towards *différance* (difference/deferment) I defer to Derrida, as any juxtaposition of the categories of metaphysics and nihilism must recall an influential essay by J. Hillis Miller, 'The Critic as Host'.[11] Hillis Miller's use of a metaphor drawn from the relationship between parasite and host deliberately allows associations to cling to his argument that are faintly sinister. De Man's investigations of *différance* carry associations of danger, slippage, vertigo. Such negative connotations are generally absent from Derrida's writing, which is libertarian in tendency: the crucial paper on *différance*, lest we forget, was contemporary with *les évènements de Mai 1968*. That said, the most culturally influential manifestations of poststructuralism have been more unguardedly anarchic, drawing from *différance* the notion of a wild pluralism, represented to the reader with varying degrees of sophistication. Recently this tendency has been developed in tandem with feminism and postmodernism, as in Julia Kristeva's redefinition of the semiotic, and the 'poetic' gyno-criticism of Hélène Cixous. In large measure, it was the later writings of Roland Barthes which catalysed this reorientation of *différance*, away from its more vertiginous implications and towards a celebration of multiplicity. The overall drift of texts such as *A Lover's Discourse* (1979) and *Roland Barthes* (1975) is paraphrased as follows by Barbara Johnson:

> The writerly is infinitely plural and open to the free play of signifiers and of difference, unconstrained by representative considerations, and transgressive of any desire for decidable, unified, totalized meaning.[12]

This affinity between textual polysemy and transgressive desire is one that Barthes had related explicitly to his own sexuality, or rather, to a triumph of 'plural' sensuality over the demarcations of gender and conventional sexuality:

> . . . *difference*, that much-vaunted and insistent word, prevails because it dispenses with or triumphs over conflict. Conflict is sexual, semantic; difference is plural, sensual, and textual; meaning and sex are principles of construction, of constitution; difference is the very moment of dispersion, of friability, a shimmer; what matters is not the discovery, in a reading of the world and of the self, of certain oppositions but of encroachments, over-flows, leaks, skids, shifts, slips. . . .[13]

Barthes is both more genial and more polemical than de Man or Derrida in his valorization of transgression and his linkage of 'difference' with pleasure and desire. Does his version of *différance* shed more light on the work of such a knowing and comic writer as O'Hara? An early poem begins, 'Oh! kangaroos, sequins, chocolate sodas!/You really are beautiful!' (*CP* 15) and it may well be that this kind of breathless juxtaposition, so wilfully facetious and provoking to the poetic consensus of its time, may be better understood by the light of Barthes' emphasis on dispersion, friability, shimmer. Undoubtedly with both writers there is an obvious association to be made between textual deviation and sexual divergence from the sanctioned norm. However, to differ from the crowd, socially, psychically, in one's body, must surely be to encounter pain and exclusion sooner or later:

"who did you have lunch with?" "you" "oops!" how ARE you

 then too, the other day I was walking through a train
 with my suitcase and I overheard someone say "speaking of
  faggots"
 now isn't life difficult enough without that
 and why am I always carrying something
 well it was a shitty looking person anyway
 better a faggot than a farthead
 or as fathers have often said to friends of mine
 "better dead than a dope" "if I thought you were queer I'd kill
  you"

you'd be right to, DAD, daddio, addled annie pad-lark (Brit,
   19th C.)
well everything can't be perfect
you said it

('Biotherm', *CP* 441–2)

To be gay is immediately to spit in the face of the patriarch ('DAD'),
to enclose the word 'father' in 'farthead'. To maintain thereafter a
transgressive joyance in dispersion and shimmer may be hard in an
America where car bumper stickers read 'Kill A Queer For Christ'.
Barthes' most libertarian writing as a theorist of literature was done
in the 1970s, a post-Stonewall and pre-Aids hiatus of Gay Liberation.
O'Hara didn't live to see that time: his poems issue from the grey
fifties and the early sixties, when alleged sexual permissiveness
extended only to heterosexual activity: '"if I thought you were queer
I'd kill you"'. In consequence, Barthes is able to speak of a 'difference' that 'dispenses with or triumphs over conflict', a smooth eli-
sion that disguises more straightforward differences between an
active triumph over, and a mere avoidance of, conflict. A poem such
as 'Biotherm' does indeed transgress many received ideas of literature, exhibiting and transmitting a pleasure in disfigurement,
polysemy and 'dispersion': but it retains some tenure on pathos,
conflict and pain.
   One important influence here, as for so many poets of O'Hara's
generation, lay very much in the American grain.

O'HARA IN THE AMERICAN GRAIN

Most older readers of O'Hara made their first acquaintance with his
work through the selection offered by Donald Allen in his influential
anthology *The New American Poetry*.[14] In that company, three things
stand out: unlike the majority of his contemporaries apart from John
Ashbery, O'Hara had been finding uses for European ways of composing, chiefly Surrealism; that levity, asking in complex ways to be
taken and not to be taken at face value, was to be an issue; and that,
for all these differences from his colleagues in the anthology, O'Hara
shares their indebtedness to the poetry of William Carlos Williams.
Although the Donald Allen anthology has had to be updated in the
light of subsequent developments (as *The Postmoderns*), O'Hara's

place in the American literary canon is still pretty much prescribed by the wish to locate him as a junior partner in Dr Williams' practice.[15] By my lights Williams – as we have already seen, in relation to Schuyler – is very definitely an artist in layered-space, polemical in this direction to the point of aggression. And on the face of it, O'Hara is thereby his closest descendant; as Richard Gooder observes, 'no poet has ever been freer of metaphysical pretensions than O'Hara'.[16] The following brief examination of Williams' poetry is offered in order to determine the true extent and nature of his influence on O'Hara.

To read Williams deconstructively might be to interpret the bulk of his work as a revenge on his own early attachment to a Romanticism as florid in style as it was metaphysical in implication:

> For I must read a lady poesy
> The while we glide by many a leafy bay[17]

This represents the kind of improbable and egregiously sub-Keatsian claim Williams was still making in his twenties. It is only with the first, 1914 version of 'Pastoral', beginning 'The old man who goes about/Gathering dog lime', that we begin to see the poised but broken lines and the culturally antipathetic snapshots that form the basis of Williams' aesthetic.[18] To notice the fouled pavement underneath the leaves, decrepitude as well as the lady, gives Williams the energy of heresy which is an important component in his bequests to New York, Black Mountain and the Beats. In the poem could be found a social and materialist equality which the public world would either ignore or actively suppress. 'No one/will believe this/of vast import to the nation' is therefore Williams' simultaneous comment on the poor man's shack and on his own, militantly threadbare poem.[19] At its best, this egalitarianism can still startle by its rigour, and is not reducible to a disguised moralizing aimed only at glaring social problems; the poetry does imply the desirability of a potentially equal attention to all things. When Kenneth Koch praises O'Hara for offering a poetry that could contain 'aspirin tablets, Good Teeth buttons, and water pistols', he bestows approbation on what is basically a continuation by O'Hara of Williams' aesthetic of inclusion.[20] This permissiveness, when it is simply vented and not tested for its moral or political or psychological implications has had effects on American poetry about which it would be hard not to feel ambivalent. It is a very simple aesthetic. Significantly, Williams cannot

always quite adhere to his own prescriptions, and both the poems
and manifestos adopt contradictory positions vis-à-vis thought and
its objects. 'No ideas but in things' runs the famous motto, yet that
objectivism (which would undergo more productive modification in
the hands of George Oppen) is contradicted in documents of the
same period which do still echo Keats. 'To refine, to clarify, to
intensify that eternal moment in which we alone live there is but a
single force – the imagination.'[21] That 'eternal' sounds odd, coming
from the poet who, to return to the firetruck poem cited in Chapter
1, put the first-person singular at the beginning and the figure 5 at
the other end of his line, to show that their claims were not unequal
in this post-metaphysical world. It may be that Williams' earliest
poetic models made such a deep impression as to be able to reassert
their claims in his later work. Or it could be that there is no final
escape from deep-space, because it is seeded in the aesthetics of
layered-space as part of an ineluctable doubleness. Consider the
poem called 'Nantucket':

> Flowers through the window
> lavender and yellow
>
> changed by white curtains –
> Smell of cleanliness –
>
> Sunshine of late afternoon –
> On the glass tray
>
> a glass pitcher, the tumbler
> turned down, by which
>
> a key is lying – And the
> immaculate white bed[22]

The materials of the poem are mundane, but out of them Williams is
able to weave something enigmatic and haunting. There is mystery
here, not simply the materialist tease of anthology pieces like the
infamous 'Red Wheelbarrow' or 'The Great Figure', where to the
reader's inevitable question, Is that all? the poem replies, That's the
whole point. In those poems – in much of his poetry – Williams'
polemical insistence on the absence of meaning in the world, beyond
what humans impose on its glowing things and surfaces, its merely

layered space, leads him to throw away half his technique in order
to highlight the other half. Pun, metaphor, and anything suggestive
of *depth* has to go; we begin then to hear what Donald Davie once
called 'the excruciating tone of the faux-naif', all the more damaging
for being no mannerism but the rhetorical expression of the world
view on which these poems rest. To Williams, the task of the poet
was to demystify, to purge writing of metaphysics, and to celebrate
what actually impinges on the senses as the sum total of what is. To
enable the reader to see as if for the first time becomes the aim, but
Williams failed to see (or did see, and didn't care) that such a recourse to origin, to a primary moment of authentic perception, is
nothing if not metaphysical. Derrida's ironic adoption of key terms
from Husserl for the purposes of critique is once more germane:
'Phenomenology has criticized metaphysics as it is in fact only in
order to restore it. It has informed metaphysics about its actual state
of affairs in order to reawaken it to the essence of its task, to its
original and authentic purpose'.[23] Williams' Modernism aims to lib-
erate perception from metaphysics, but in a deeply American (because prelapsarian) gesture, stops short of the realization that the
very privileging of perception is itself metaphysical; the poet remains, in Emerson's notorious formula, a floating eyeball; an Adamic
condition sheltered from the storm of poetry's own deconstructive
rigour. I return to Derrida's 'Differance':

> What then is consciousness? What does 'consciousness' mean?
> Most often in the very form of 'meaning' (*vouloir-dire*), conscious-
> ness in all its modifications is conceivable only as self-presence, a
> self-perception of presence . . . The privilege accorded to con-
> sciousness thus means a privilege accorded to the present; and
> even if the transcendental temporality of consciousness is de-
> scribed in depth, as Husserl described it, the power of synthesis
> and the incessant gathering-up of traces is always accorded to the
> 'living present'.[24]

Thus it is that Williams' preference for an exclamatory present tense
is wedded to his ascription of 'the power of synthesis' to a privileged
consciousness. The mystery of his lapses into a Keatsian Romanticism antithetical to his own tenets may now be solved. The poetry
insists that there are 'no ideas but in things', but to look into the
margins of the writing, to begin to deconstruct it, is to see the
survival of deep-space metaphysics in the privileging not of things,

but of subjectivity. The poetry supposes that prior to or outside the
signs and *differance* into which subjects are born, consciousness is
somehow possible, gathered up somehow into its own, original
presence. Ironically, this idealist residue might be said to leave
Williams' practice in a position historically prior to that of Byron, in
whose texts a much-vaunted integrity of self-presence is broken
down in the incertitudes of its own *vouloir-dire*.

This is why 'Nantucket', which we may now be able to read,
works so well. Like 'The Great Figure' this is a poem of depicted
things, thereby engaging with but attempting to supersede the procedures of Pound's Imagist phase. But it is not possible to ask 'is that
all?' as might be done vis-à-vis the poem of the firetruck. Although
this is ostensibly a celebration of things-in-themselves, those things
refuse to retreat modestly into their positions as items in layered-
space. That is partly because the poem refuses a spatial hierarchy, or
depth; the key, the bed and the tumbler appear to be the same size,
as they might in a painting by René Magritte. Therefore the methods
of layered-space polemic are ironically responsible for ushering in
metaphysical depth. It is the very refusal to hierarchize entities that
gives them their strangeness here, their near-Surrealism. A preg-
nancy which might only be the imminence of human use, or might
be a metaphysical aura, hangs over the still scene; to argue, as
Williams is not able to do, that those two possibilities are one and the
same is to read the poem's own difference from itself, its contradictory but logical restitution of deep space. The poem works smoothly
because its insouciant refusal to account for its own voice (where is
the speaking subject located? how is that subject placed in relation to
the concept of an author?) need not be a problem in a lyric of such
brevity.

So far, it would seem that the categories of deep and layered-space
retain their usefulness, as the confirmation gained from Williams'
poetry that the first may be seeded in the second still preserves and
does not collapse the difference between the two categories. We
have also seen that certain emphases within deconstruction do seem
able to provide a critique of subjectivism and its attachment to ideas
of origin that can help to expose both the limitations and the secret
logic of some modern poetry. I want to look now at a 1956 poem by
Frank O'Hara, 'A Step Away from Them', in order to establish more
clearly the nature of O'Hara's relationship to Williams' practice, and
to test his poem within a deconstructive frame of reference. The

poem was collected first in *Lunch Poems*, and is a paradigm or stand-
ard-bearer for that collection:

> It's my lunch hour, so I go
> for a walk among the hum-colored
> cabs. First, down the sidewalk
> where laborers feed their dirty
> glistening torsos sandwiches
> and Coca-Cola, with yellow helmets
> on. They protect them from falling
> bricks, I guess. Then onto the
> avenue where skirts are flipping
> above heels and blow up over
> grates. The sun is hot, but the
> cabs stir up the air. I look
> at bargains in wristwatches. There
> are cats playing in sawdust.

> > (CP 256)

As with Williams, the poem is clearly based in recorded acts of
perception, and whatever 'power of synthesis' it may wish to display is located in a recreation of the Husserlian-Williamsian 'living
present': I go, I look, there are. (The poem may also be a reaction,
conscious or otherwise, to Williams' poem 'New England', a highly
sexualized evocation of 'masculine risk' as displayed by hard-hatted
construction workers 'walking on the air'.)[25] Later in the poem O'Hara
will pass the soon to be torn down Manhattan Storage Warehouse:
'I/used to think they had the Armory/Show there.' The Armory
Show of 1913 was the first exhibition of post-Cézanne, Impressionist
and early Cubist painting on American shores. It caused a storm.
Clearly, the building (even if this was the wrong one!) would be of
significance to the modernist curator Frank O'Hara, but Williams
saw the actual exhibition many times and its effect on him was both
intense and well-documented.[26] So, 'A Step Away from Them' is
influenced by Williams at the levels of style, literary allusion and
cultural matrix.

Superficially, and in keeping with this, the poem's 'I' would seem
at first to be another floating eyeball. The poem is full of flipping,
playing, blowing, agitating, clicking and honking but the first per-

son seems almost equally cheered by any or all of New York's lunchtime noises. Is that 'I', then, gathered up into its own illusion of wholeness, hoping by locating ideas in things to distract attention from the subliminal shifts of its own ineluctable self-difference? The poem does end with an emphatic statement of self-presence:

> My heart is in my
> pocket, it is Poems by Pierre Reverdy.

Elsewhere there is plenty of textual evidence to verify O'Hara's attachment to the poetry of Reverdy. Nevertheless, the more I read these lines the more camp they seem. The 'heart' here is knowingly a figure of speech, very different from the suffering 'heart/that bubbles with red ghosts' from 'In Memory of My Feelings', composed only six weeks before 'A Step Away from Them'. Here, the heart immediately becomes another poet's text; the 'I' is self-displaced. And at no point does the O'Hara 'I' lay claims to a unity preexisting the *'fôrets de symboles/Qui l'observent avec des regards familiers'*, that our cities have inherited and are.[27] For this poem's things are almost all signs, in a physical as well as a Saussurean sense: 'JULIET'S/CORNER', 'the posters for BULLFIGHT', 'Neon', and a Times Square tobacco ad whose 'sign/blows smoke over my head'. But unlike the *confuses paroles* in the sonnet by Baudelaire from which I quote and which inaugurated the whole era of Symbolist poems of the sign, New York's noises will never cohere metaphysically. When 'Everything/suddenly honks', that is a simultaneity and not an orchestration. 'it is 12:40 of/a Thursday': as in de Man's application of 'allegory' in his essay of 1969, temporality undercuts symbol.
    In fact it undercuts everything.

> First
> Bunny died, then John Latouche,
> then Jackson Pollock. But is the
> earth as full as life was full, of them?

Violet ('Bunny') Lang, a close friend (and so close textually that one of the *Collected Poems* attributed to O'Hara was actually written by her), and painters great and small, all turn to earth. What gives the opening sentences of 'A Step Away from Them' their poise and pertness is their discrete nature as perceptual incidents, a singularity that may be celebrated but which also sets limits on a life. However undemonstratively, that melancholy seeps out into the edges of the poem, somewhat as the glimpse of Billie Holiday's face on the cover of the New York Post lets death seep into every detail of 'The Day Lady Died'. This is a quieter poem. Like many poems by James Schuyler, it repels boarders gently but firmly; any critical reading, most certainly including this effort, will seem to make heavy weather of it. The sadness in its margins may or may not be taken as a sign to deeper spaces; that is, to draw a phrase from Henry James, fully half the reader's labour. I would suggest that the collection *Lunch Poems* is in subtle and perhaps deliberate ways not at one with itself; certain poems, for example 'A Step Away from Them', are set out like a brightly-lit shop window, to lure and catch the eye. The force of other, darker poems in the volume – 'How to Get There' or 'For the Chinese New Year & for Bill Berkson', say – will then be that much greater and more unexpected. And then, of course, the poems work in a dialectical relationship to each other, so that the final emotional affirmations of 'Steps' or 'St. Paul and All That' bring light to the other poems' darkness. This side of the reading process is interminable, fortunately. Poems are never the same twice, as 'A Step Away from Them', is not the same read in *Evergreen Review*, where it first appeared, in *Lunch Poems*, or in the Collected O'Hara.

In the fifties and sixties the more established poetry journals like *Poetry* or the *Kenyon Review* seem to have regarded O'Hara as a New York dandy who tossed off poems to amuse his côterie. This verdict from the *New York Review of Books* on the 1965 collection *Love Poems* would be typical: 'amiable and gay, like streamers of crêpe paper, fluttering before an electric fan.'[28] I hope to have shown that O'Hara at least deserves more than that damnation with faint praise. On the other hand, the comment is true to one aspect of his poetry, and it is characteristic of a poem such as the one I have discussed to leave its tones hovering between the grave and gay. Reading Frank O'Hara should be fun, both in the crêpe-paper sense, and in the more extended sense of 'fun' proposed by the Preface to *The Golden Bowl*.[29]

It would seem then, that O'Hara draws on and perpetuates a modern American poetry of observation developed by William Carlos Williams. Williams' pugnacious determination to rid poetry of the taint of metaphysics fails to conceal his own underlying metaphysics of selfhood. In a poem such as 'A Step Away from Them', O'Hara offers a poetic that stems from an engagement with Williams' layered-space project, but which (ironically) signals the possibility of

metaphysical extensions in quizzical and shifting ways. O'Hara's
extreme and haunted self-awareness puts the singularity of selfhood
into question. This interpenetration of deep and layered-space procedure recalls similar alternations between warmth and cool wit,
idealism and levity, egotism and loss-of-self in the poetry of Byron.
These, however, are affinities which ultimately have tentacular roots
in the most painful areas of experience articulated by both poets. I
want now to test the hypothesis that what characterizes these affinities with Byron, the supersedence of Williams, and the challenges
that O'Hara's poetry offers to deconstruction may all be located
along a spectrum of engagements between poetry and time.

'IT IS POSSIBLE ISN'T IT?' O'HARA'S TIMEKEEPING

'Are we just muddy instants?' asks an early ode. (*CP* 196) O'Hara's
poetry, so often written against the clock, strives to beat time at its
own game. The poems and the poet's life are promiscuously hungry
narratives of 'excitability and spleen to be recent and strong' ('Joe's
Jacket' *CP* 329), their commitment to the avant-garde a way to cheat
time by seeming to advance progressively, to change faster and
more purposefully than others. And there are attitudes and kinds of
textual practice in O'Hara which show him to be, as the phrase is,
ahead of his time. In another sense to think to get time on one's side
in this way is always an illusion. In de Manian terms, (or at least the
de Man of 'The Rhetoric of Temporality', for his ideas changed with
time), I would suggest that the idea of a literary côterie, so important
to O'Hara, might be read as a group symbol. The symbol, it will be
recalled, is in de Manian terms a Romantic concept tied into an
organicist picturing of the universe. It comes under attack from
allegory, which 'always corresponds to the unveiling of an authentically temporal destiny. This unveiling takes place in a subject that
has sought refuge against the impact of time in a natural world to
which, in truth, it bears no resemblance'.[30] The côterie might be read
as a symbol that attempts to cheat temporality by ingesting and
acknowledging certain of its powers. The artists' circle, be it in
Second Empire Paris or New York in the 1960s is therefore, leaving
aside its vanguardist claims, a microcosm of urban life which has
itself replaced Nature by the City. ('New York/greater than the
Rocky Mountains', *CP* 477) The lack of resemblance between the
subject and Nature is conceded by the twentieth-century city-dweller

who in places like New York has made a cult of living against the
'natural' grain, *à rebours*. But the côterie is still a humanist refuge
against temporality, seeking by the mutual support of its members
to stave off the negative impact of time on each individual subject.
This is of course to read the term 'côterie' textually, but we have to
a degree been invited by Romanticism to do just that, ever since
Friedrich Schlegel and the Jena Circle published their debates about
art in the form of staged conversations.

If one were to take a different tack, and look at O'Hara's citations
of côterie practices in his poems – namedropping, backbiting, off-
the-cuff criticisms and commendation – one could argue without
exaggeration that *The Collected Poems* gives us a more completely
rounded evocation of an artist's milieu than any body of verse since
Alexander Pope. The poems are themselves, to use the title of O'Hara's
selected criticism, Art Chronicles.

O'Hara had wanted such an artistic context from the start. A fine
early poem, 'Memorial Day 1950', (which only survives because
Ashbery once copied it out in a letter to Kenneth Koch, and Koch
kept the letter), is a fan's poem: its opening word is 'Picasso', and
O'Hara proceeds to fire off mentions of Gertrude Stein, Max Ernst,
Paul Klee, Rimbaud, Auden, Pasternak, Apollinaire and Dada as
charms against boredom and mortality. (*CP* 17) To write that one's
heart is in one's pocket and that it is the poems of Reverdy is to
continue in this vein with a little more tonal sophistication. And
much the same thing would appear to be happening at the close of
another Lunch Poem, 'Adieu to Norman, Bon Jour to Joan and Jean-
Paul' (*CP* 328–9), where Reverdy is mentioned once again:

and surely we shall not continue to be unhappy
we shall be happy
but we shall continue to be ourselves everything continues to be
    possible
René Char, Pierre Reverdy, Samuel Beckett it is possible isn't it
I love Reverdy for saying yes, though I don't believe it

Each proper name is chanted like a talisman against restriction and
in favour of possibility, against temporality: but he doesn't quite
believe it. Like Byron's 'one word', the magical lightning-word that
would rejoin what was broken, the chambers of the heart, the halves
of the sign, experience and its representation, one person and another, the will to believe falters and is sheathed in ironic comedy.

The reference to Reverdy is more melancholy this time. The earlier
references in the poem to 'Allen' (Ginsberg), 'Peter' (Orlovsky), 'Norman' (Bluhm), 'Jean-Paul' (Riopelle), not forgetting 'excitement-prone
Kenneth Koch', are an attempt to lift the contemporary côterie up to
the status of the gallery of heroes. And yet in another sense this is not
true and the names need no gloss. The tone, methods and final
effects of this kind of writing are very different from those present in
some of O'Hara's plays, many of which were strictly côterie productions, being written basically for those who performed in them. A
line like 'It's another case of nature imitating Alfred Leslie!' ('Awake
In Spain', *SP* 110) is simply an in-joke, conforming to the more
incestuous associations of 'côterie'. (Of course there are some flashes
of brilliance in the plays: 'Art's long, and conquered people are
short.' (*SP* 195) But the proper names in 'Adieu to Norman . . .' are
neither incestuous nor exclusive. Any of us middle-class speaking
subjects has a friend like Kenneth and a lunch appointment next
week with our own Joan or Jean-Paul. But it is part of this poem's
vitality and warmth as well as its anxiety to persist in the will-to-
believe, in friendship, in art. There is no escape from temporality,
but no escaping the attempt to escape it either.

The most celebratory expression of what remains possible, given
these pressures, may be found in O'Hara's occasional poems, of
which the most prominent are 'John Button Birthday' and 'Poem
Read at Joan Mitchell's', written within a fortnight of each other. The
occasion of the first is self-explanatory; the second was read at a
party for Joe Hazan and the painter Jane Freilicher (younger versions of two of the Js in Schuyler's 'June 30, 1974') on the eve of their
marriage. The poem for John Button derives ultimately from the
Coleridgean conversation poem, articulating as it does configura-
tions of selfhood on an apparently dialogic model; Ashbery enters
and speaks at one point, Button at another. That extraversion of
rhetoric to seemingly include other presences than the poet's in the
poem is once more to build in the theme of côterie as a buffer against
the onslaughts of time. Then again, to celebrate someone's birthday
has always meant to create a buffer against time by turning the
temporal into a positive:

>   And in 1984 I trust we'll still
> be high together. I'll say "Let's go to a bar"
> and you'll say "Let's go to a movie" and we'll go to both;

like two old Chinese drunkards arguing about their
favorite mountain and the million reasons for them both.

(CP 268)

Even Nature is invoked, Basho-style, with art and alcohol to help
stave off the temporal. The friendly argument stresses both the unity
of the couple and, more covertly, the unity of the single self, under
the sheltering symbol of the Birthday. But these sentiments are led,
inevitably, to express their own difference from themselves, and the
flow of the poem ceases here and there to disguise its fragmentation
as a collage:

> And then the way you straighten
> people out. How ambitious you are! And that you're
> a painter is a great satisfaction, too. You know how
> I feel about painters. I sometimes think poetry
> only describes.
>   Now I have taken down the underwear
> I washed last night from the various light fixtures
> and can proceed.

It might be noted that O'Hara's deprecation of his own art form is
immediately followed by an example of a kind of effect it would be
virtually impossible to achieve in painting. The comic and bathetic
shift of register from high art to underwear could only be done
temporally, would be unavailable to the painter for whom, whatever
detail or depth he builds in, a simultaneity of effect is unavoidable.
A painting could (just about) include the imagery of my first quotation; but it couldn't *lead up to it*, using timing to strike blows against
temporality, as O'Hara does. In O'Hara's occasional pieces the poem
is, in a sense as urgent as it is subliminal, 'the cry of its occasion', to
draw on a quotation from Wallace Stevens popular with poets of
O'Hara's generation. The poem should enact and not merely depict
the real, be 'Part of the res itself and not about it'.[31] The celebration
of a birthday, the assertion of a group-spirit, the assertion of self-
presence under cover of that camaraderie, and the articulation of a
poem are all grist to a repudiation of time that tries heroically to steal
the enemy's weapons. These poems occupy a distinct station in
O'Hara's oeuvre and yet can be grouped with his love poems, juxta-

posing as they do direct statements of affection as a warrant against change, with surprisingly candid admissions of defeat. The 'Poem Read at Joan Mitchell's' is delighted to be able to compromise its own leanings towards textual avant-gardism with a charmingly stagey, literally Byronic, image:

> let's advance and change everything, but leave these little oases in
> case the heart gets thirsty en route

> (CP 266)

The epithalamion's final oasis may only be a mirage where we ingest signs and possibilities, but if the will-to-believe is strong enough our thirst may still be slaked:

> we peer into the future and see you happy and hope it is a sign
> that we
> will be happy too, something to cling to, happiness
> the least and best of human attainments

More gradations may be visible now along the spectrum of involvements with temporality in O'Hara's poetry. Alongside those poems which operate in basic continuity with the Western lyrical tradition, lamenting the passage of time and erecting metaphysical conceits to clog that passage, there exist poems that regard such a stance as indulgence, and strive with an undecidable degree of intentionality to fight time with its own weapons. A poem such as 'John Button Birthday' knows however that to try and outstare time will always be to lose, and so solicits the enemy's company, celebrating, in order to gain, time. In the slender space of such a lyric O'Hara still finds time to build in large statements of poetics and cultural politics that call into question the distinction between literature and criticism, even as the foregrounding of genre in the occasional pieces makes a 'John Button Birthday' so definitely an exercise in 'light verse'. The lightest and the darkest moments in O'Hara, the most fragile lyricism and the most compendious thought, begin now to seem bewilderingly close, and my metaphor of a band or spectrum may more dangerously have to come to resemble the fan of cards in 'Hôtel Transylvanie', whose adjacent reds and blacks may or may not signal love, or its loss, while echoes of *Manon Lescaut* (*'chevalier*, change your expression!') sound a tragic note in the

already serious game. In such an art of layered-space, still troubled
in its margins by the deeps, the ineluctable and the throwaway seem
very close together. While preparing the manuscript that was to win
him a Hopwood Award in 1951, O'Hara told Jane Freilicher that 'the
light poems are the most truthful, so there you are'.[32] Of course we
need not believe him, but 'A Step Away from Them' shows this poet
to be adept at lyrics whose light tread is only a step away from the
grave.

The struggle with time becomes more acute and more ironic where
it is realized that temporality and difference are no merely external
threat, but are always already at work within the subject. To call a
poem a 'lie against time' as Harold Bloom so often does, may be to
tell only half the story, for even 'lie' may imply more self-consistency
and unity of utterance, however fictive, than a poem can manage. To
assert a unity of selfhood is to utter a white lie, to let fall a protective
blanket like snow or thick fog to cover for a while the pains and
wants and discrepancies of difference. Something like this is the
intuition of 'How to Get There', a meditation on false directions half-
buried in the *Lunch Poems* volume as a trap for the unwary, who
might have preferred to read the book as a set of variations on 'A
Step Away from Them':

White the October air, no snow, easy to breathe
beneath the sky, lies, lies everywhere writhing and gasping
clutching and tangling, it is not easy to breathe
lies building their tendrils into dim figures
who disappear down corridors in west-side apartments
into childhood's proof of being wanted, not abandoned, kidnapped
betrayal staving off loneliness, I see the fog lunge in
and hide it
              where are you?
                                                              (*CP* 369)

The third line casts judgment on the first as a lie against temporality
and its deathly implications for the subject, imaged in its ultimate
defencelessness as a child, vulnerable to abandonment or coercion.
But our refusal to face the possibility that words like 'our' may be
white lies runs so deep, is so much in the blood, that we 'dim figures'
and our figures of speech are alike built out of lies, of slippage. As
locally obscure as a fogbound neighbourhood, the poem alternates
between a dearth of comforting signification and an excess of mean-

ing: 'kidnapped' might or might not attach to 'betrayal', the enjambement is so chilling. And in a surreal moment of ambiguity, it is
uncertain whether the fog, as a white lie, 'hides' loneliness from a
recognition of itself, whether the speaker has trapped the squirming
fog under his coat, or whether it is childhood or betrayal that is
obscured. Later the tendrils of fog become telephone wires, 'trailing
softly' around the throats of white liars whose apparent communications are 'only an echo' of their loneliness which bestows all the pain
of isolation, without the consolation of a self-consistent self. This is
the poem's closing and fundamental irony:

> . . . didn't I have you once for my self?
> West Side?
> for a couple of hours, but I am not that person

The blurring of dialogue and monologue is both purposeful and
hardly matters. It could be any self talking to its or another's changed
self. Friability, shimmer, the leaks and skids and polysemy that
Barthes associated with a libertarian assertion of *différance* are in this
context mere will-o'-the-wisps that will soon lead to slippage, to a
fall in the fog.

Where 'How to Get There' shows no-one how to get anywhere,
focussing as it does on the differentiation within *différance* that makes
change omnipresent and continuity illusory, other poems seem almost intentionally to play on the other meaning, that of deferment.
'Ballad', which begins as follows, was written in August 1960, two
months before 'How to Get There':

Yes it is sickening that we come
                                    that we go that we dissembling live
    that we leave that there is anywhere in the world someone like us
it is that we are always like a that never that

                                                                    (CP 367)

We are never self-consistently we, I am never a unified I, but we or
you or I are always *like* others. Understood only in relation to other
people or things, a thing or a human self never exists only in itself.
Once again the arguments of Derridean deconstruction seem close to
those positions, or suspicions about tenure of any position, espoused
by the poem. And, arguably, it is as a result of the operations of what

Derrida calls the 'trace' that the poem has only a phantom unity, a set of absent meanings whose variance from the present signification are all that invests it with the effect of identity. Then again, the philosophical implications of 'Ballad' are in other respects not very distant from the Buddhist critique of Western metaphysics followed by West Coast contemporaries like Allen Ginsberg, with whom O'Hara was in friendly contact. And the poem's implications as well as its form may owe something to texts by Gertrude Stein, with whose writing O'Hara was certainly familiar. O'Hara would not have understood what 'deconstruction' meant, any more than Keats would have understood the term 'Romantic poetry' as applied to his work. Deconstruction cannot account for his work, and would not claim to. The totalitarian ambitions of structuralism, with its para-scientific reliance on codes, both brought to a pitch and found wanting in Barthes' *S/Z* (1970), offered the last attempt in literary criticism to *cover* the work of art, to completely explain it. In practice, the most deconstruction would claim would be an ability to unpick and expose a text's difference from itself, to show from the close reading of a text its conflictual modes of signifying. It is to phenomena of textual change, differentiation and instability that deconstruction does address itself with the greatest authority and detail.

That said, we do once more appear to have reached a point parallel to the brief discussion of a poem by James Schuyler, 'The Dog Wants His Dinner', in the previous chapter. ('Yesterday the/air was squeaky clean today/it's dull and lifeless as an/addict's armpit. Surely you/mean leafless.') How could a critic influenced by the literature of psychoanalysis dare to diagnose *lapsus linguae* in such a poem? The text has shifted onto the level of what it signals as intentional meaning a whole stratum of signification that criticism would have located as the unconscious operations in, say, a Victorian novel. Similarly, deconstruction claims to search out 'contradictions, obscurities, ambiguities, incoherences, discontinuities, ellipses, interruptions, repetitions, and plays of the signifier' as otherwise inscrutable gremlins which the text has tried to 'edit out' or consign to its margins.[33] But in O'Hara's 'How to Get There' obscurity, ambiguity, discontinuity and the rest are not merely available to the post-Surrealist poet as part of the armoury of poetic devices; they are the thematic substances on which the work meditates explicitly. What then, as alert readers, should we look for in the margins of O'Hara's poetry? Is there a Victorian, social-realist novel waiting to get out? And where are the 'margins' of an O'Hara poem, anyway? The

differential play of language which literary theory strives to expose
in texts such as those treated by J. Hillis Miller in *Fiction and Repetition* or Paul de Man in *Allegories of Reading*, Conrad or Hardy, Proust
or Rousseau, is so much to the fore in an oeuvre such as O'Hara's
that it needs no special argument or exposure. We may agree, then,
with Paul de Man, when he says that 'Poetic writing is the most
advanced and refined mode of deconstruction' while still holding
open to question his subsequent assertion that 'it may differ from
critical or discursive writing in the economy of its articulation, but
not in kind'.[34]

Such a blurring of the distinctions between criticism and literature is
a common insistence – perhaps, in fact, the only ubiquitous insistence – among those critics whose names have been associated with
deconstruction. Their discoveries along parallel tracks concerning
the powers of rhetoric, the rhetoric of power and the illusory nature
of any claim to a disinterested position have led to a shared elevation
of 'style' beyond any merely decorative or emphatic function.
Derrida's wordplay, Hartman's puns on Wordsworth and the worth
of words, de Man's grammatical swerves and lacunae (analyzed by
Barbara Johnson as if they were prose poems), all seek to break the
chains of modesty that have traditionally linked criticism to commentary, claiming instead that multiplicity of expression that has
always been an identifying feature of art. Whether the attempts have
been successful is of course another matter. Derrida's cultivated
obliquity, his thick webbing of puns, his goosing and force-feeding
of the footnote produce a verbal *pâté de foie gras* traditionally associated with Gallic afflatus and can seem as ponderous as his underlying philosophical revisions are monumental. In turn, Barbara Johnson
may be right to call certain passages in Paul de Man 'magnificent' in
their 'rigorous unreliability': it is true and admirable that a much-
quoted sentence like the following (from *Allegories of Reading*) is one
'in which evaluative terms flicker in and out, up and down, without
reaching a stable resolution, but also without enabling one to envis-
age a stance beyond evaluation'[35]:

Literature as well as criticism – the difference between them being
delusive – is condemned (or privileged) to be forever the most

rigorous and, consequently, the most unreliable language in terms of which man names and transforms himself.[36]

Ironically, however, the workings of difference may need to be traced inside the dubious assertion that the 'difference' between literature and criticism is 'delusive'. That consummation was devoutly wished by de Man, but the dream of his rhetoric represses their separate development, rooted in the pedagogical associations of criticism as against the *marginal* positioning of Romantic and modern poetry in society, and (to say the same thing in a different way), the brazen self-distancing of poetry from normal linguistic usage. The most admirable essays produced under the aegis of American deconstruction – Hillis Miller's 'The Critic As Host', Hartman's 'The Voice of the Shuttle', de Man's 'Shelley Disfigured' – deploy particular kinds of exactitude in scholarship and tone which are recognizable in their commitment, however reformist, to an academic genre which has nothing fundamentally in common with the separate evolution of poetic language in Wordsworth or Shelley or Ashbery. Alongside the customary wordplay, Barbara Johnson can show a lucidity and terseness which, while attractive undeniably, are dry even by the standards of the academy, and of a radically different texture from the poems by Mallarmé or Baudelaire about which she writes so persuasively. Of course, although poetry and theory may never actually touch, intercourse between them is constantly pictured in books of criticism. Poem and prose are thrust into an embrace which it is a distinguishing mark of recent criticism to have begun to acknowledge as its own creation. The relationships between poet and critic, text and text, have therefore been likened to the ambiguous clinging of parasite and host. The critic who quotes from O'Hara rewrites his poetry by excerpting, a parasitical attachment; and dead poets depend on live readers for the survival of their work. But no matter how complex or shifting these relationships, poetic and critical language remain as different in kind as ivy and bark. The one may cling to the other for dear life, but the distinction between poetic and critical language is far from 'delusive'.

We have seen, then, how pervasive is the theme of temporality in O'Hara's poetry, and with what unflinching rigour he charts its workings inside and outside our cherished fiction of a whole subjectivity. We have seen also how sharply prescient of deconstruction that analysis can be – so much so that literary theory, at least in this form, has little to contribute to a reading of poetry that has reached that stage of prescience through developments in its own separate tradition. In particular, it is clear that O'Hara built on approaches inaugurated by Carlos Williams. Ironically, O'Hara pursues Williams' antagonism to metaphysics with a rigour from which his predecessor flinched, yet it is still the case that flashes of a deeper space can be caught in the margins of the poems, seemingly as powerless to illuminate as they are insistent to be seen, like 'the beyond', in one of the many poems called 'Poem', which remains by its nature 'beyond', and so 'doesn't seem to be coming any nearer'. (*CP* 244) There appears to be no escaping either time or art's claims to escape it: O'Hara has to admit 'I don't believe it' at the close of a poem ('Adieu to Norman . . .') that seemed most powerfully and personally concerned with belief in art, and one's self as an artist. Are we then at a dreadful Point Zero with O'Hara, where the workings of difference leave the poetry no stability, beyond the dignifying fiction of a will-to-believe, stymied by the consciousness of its own fictiveness? The next section will be devoted to a close reading of these questions as they are encountered in one of O'Hara's most powerful poems, 'In Memory of My Feelings'.

'IN MEMORY OF MY FEELINGS'

Most of 'In Memory of My Feelings' was written over a four-day period in July, 1956. By O'Hara's standards this was not an especially prolific year, and the work composed at that time – 'A Step Away from Them' is another example – appears to take stock, to summarize and *deploy* techniques of poetic observation and self-representation that had been reached by more heuristic means in earlier phases of the poet's development. 'In Memory of My Feelings' is O'Hara's first incontrovertibly major poem, and his most technically proficient up to that time. It expresses both a gathering up and a final discharge of some major literary debts, to European Surrealism, and the debt to Walt Whitman that most American poets seem to have to work through explicitly. This particular combination of influences belongs distinctively to New York. What Surrealism and Whitman hold in common is an emphasis on the openness of the self, its multiplicity. This is foregrounded by O'Hara as a theme from the outset:

My quietness has a man in it, he is transparent
and he carries me quietly, like a gondola, through the streets.
He has several likenesses, like stars and years, like numerals.

My quietness has a number of naked selves,
so many pistols I have borrowed to protect myselves
from creatures who too readily recognize my weapons
and have murder in their heart!
                                        though in winter
they are warm as roses, in the desert
taste of chilled anisette.

                                                            (CP 252)

The opening lines are cool, and a dream-like ease of movement may
hide at first glance their rapid switches of subject-position. A later
section of the poem will be concerned with parenthood and the past,
but O'Hara's present concern is with the trans-parent, the aspects of
our selves that beget or protect or make enemies of each other. My
quietness encircles a man, who 'carries me quietly'; where then am
I, in relation to my own quietness? Transparent, the man can be a
window to other selves, but never be pinned down. Syntax replicates his elusiveness, making it unclear whether his 'several likenesses' resemble 'stars and years', or whether he is 'like stars and
years' in having likenesses. Through the magic lantern of the poem,
O'Hara flashes at almost subliminal speed his transparencies, of
Arabia and its development of 'numerals', of a rather Byronic Venice, of New York. As he moves rapidly, we must proceed slowly.
Everything here is transparent except the sense.

'My quietness has a number of naked selves'; nakedness is a
promise that one is about to touch bottom, a hope that is rudely
shattered by the taking up of arms. Quietness armed with a pistol is
not really very quiet at all, and syntax once more fans the possible
interpretations of whether self here equals 'pistol', whether 'I' contain more naked selves needing protection, or whether the 'creatures' who recognize my weapons do so because they are my
familiars, inside me already. And who are 'they', who taste in the
desert of alcoholic aniseed, look (or taste?) in the winter like extras
strayed in from Louis MacNeice's poem 'Snow'; creatures, selves or
pistols? O'Hara's conception of the multiple nature of selfhood is not
merely described but enacted in the multiplicity of meanings. Start-

ling and original in many ways, his bodying forth of the variousness of the self is comparable to the work of his contemporaries, and not merely in New York. Edward Dorn, at this period beginning his association with Black Mountain College, once wrote, 'Faced with any reality, we are no longer of one piece', an intuition developed during the course of a novel-length poem, *Gunslinger*, whose narrative 'I' literally dies part way through Book II, to be supplanted by other aspects of 'the shared mind'.[37] The political and psychic Babel of John Wieners' writing in the 1970s, the warring systems of signification in Jack Spicer's smoky conjurations, Allen Ginsberg's identification of the divided self with the consciousness of a generation, all share a conception of experience and the personality as both broken and multiple. This polemical replacement of a conception of the self as an inviolable unit by something more like a spectrum is sponsored in American poetry, to a degree anyway, by Walt Whitman's *Song of Myself*. However, Whitman often complicates a portrayal of selfhood in detail only to revive a more simple and unified Being at the level of cosmology. In O'Hara's poem the spectrum becomes in a different sense spectral, and as firearms are drawn for protection we see the darker side of the American dream:

> Ourself behind ourself, concealed –
> Should startle most –
> Assassin hid in our Apartment
> Be Horror's least.
>
> The Body – borrows a Revolver –
> He bolts the Door –
> O'erlooking a superior spectre –
> Or More –[38]

One need not be a chamber to be haunted, and in this lyric, so sharply prescient of *film noir*, Emily Dickinson argues something like the Whitmanian perception of the mind's multiplicity, only to remind the reader of the internal perils that make consciousness so much more dangerous than any straightforwardly external threat. Uninfluenced by Dickinson in 'In Memory of My Feelings' O'Hara is now in a position parallel to hers vis-à-vis the lighter or more celebratory conclusions of his own earlier work. In memory of Whitman, this poem erases by incorporating only to critique his influence; the

crucial passage comes in part 4. In memory of Lord Byron, part 1
follows the lines I quoted with a pastiche of lofty individualism:

> At times, withdrawn,
> I rise into the cool skies
> and gaze on at the imponderable world with the simple identification
> of my colleagues, the mountains. Manfred climbs to my nape,
> speaks, but I do not hear him,
> I'm too blue.

Such a rejection of 'the simple identification' of problematic identity
does not prevent the poem from being at a deeper level Byronian in
its registration of pain and guilt and loss as retaining their hard
reality even as the self that contains them appears to dissolve. But
O'Hara is bidding farewell here to a more simply dramatic idea of
selfhood as cloaked and discrete, in a witty display that is immediately succeeded by a quasi-cinematic montage in memory of Surrealism:

> An elephant takes up his trumpet,
> money flutters from the windows of cries, silk stretching its mirror
> across shoulder blades. A gun is "fired."
> One of me rushes
> to window #13 and one of me raises his whip and one of me
> flutters up from the center of the track amidst the pink flamingoes,
> and underneath their hooves as they round the last turn my lips
> are scarred and brown, brushed by tails, masked in dirt's lust

Poetic Surrealism is based on an expanded conception of metaphor.
In what one might think of as a 'traditional' metaphor, two terms are
combined so as to give the first added emphasis, and to unify the
pairing as in some way appropriate in its context: time is a great
healer, while life is a bitch, a bowl of cherries, or a pilgrimage. There
is always an element of disjunction in a metaphor, an acknowledgment that the second term derives from a different source from the
first, but that hint of *différance* is always to be contained finally by the
overall aptness of the phrase. In Surrealist metaphor, two terms are
juxtaposed so as to create a third which is more strangely potent
than the sum of the parts. This happens because the different sources
of the terms are paraded as such flagrantly, rather than smoothed

over by context or familiar usage. It could be said that a Surrealist
metaphor is a collage in miniature. 'Windows' and 'cries' are two
common words which, when set by O'Hara in Surrealist juxtaposition create a third term, 'the windows of cries', stronger than the
sum of its parts. Strength comes from the shock-effect of encountering in poetic language something we could never meet elsewhere;
no-one will ever look through or listen to the windows of cries, only
read them. The other ingredient in the efficacy of the Surrealist
metaphor is, nevertheless, its militant literalism. It behaves as if its
attachments were not metaphorical, but metonymic; we cannot determine whether the windows of cries are basically strange-sound-
ing windows, or transparent cries. The third term forces an equality
of attention onto the two originating terms, as in David Gascoyne's
phrase 'white curtains of infinite fatigue', whereby a reader is pre-
vented from making the metaphor-collage into a conventional statement about either curtains or tiredness by the equal weighting of the
component nouns.[39] Images of curtains and windows are very common in Surrealist writing because, while signifying dumbly literal
objects to be encountered or placed metonymically, they also imply
a beyond. Poetically, they are everyday doors to deep space, to the
mysterious but ultimately organic and organized universe. Finally,
then, Surrealist figuration achieves its strange resonances by oscillat-
ing undecidably between metaphor and metonymy, between implications of deep and layered space. In this it reinscribes the cult of
the Romantic fragment, which Friedrich Schlegel had characterized
as being both 'separate from the rest of the universe' and implying a
unity larger than its own, a deep-space organicism.[40]

O'Hara's 'money flutters from the windows of cries' is therefore
an adaptation of Surrealist procedure itself evidencing a persistence
of Romanticism. It is also, however, knowingly clichéd. In fact, the
phrase 'windows of cries' is lifted directly from 'Noeud des Miroirs',
a poem by André Breton.[41] Consequently O'Hara's use of Surrealist
technique during 'In Memory of My Feelings' has a staged side to it,
a deal more knowing and valedictory than the thoroughly Surrealist
poems of the early 1950s. Writing of the New York poetry scene of
this period, Kenneth Koch had attested to the explosive effect with
which O'Hara's 'wonderful, energetic and rather obscene' poetry
'burst on us all like a bomb', a commendation that needs to be read
alongside John Ashbery's reservations about not only the 'provocative' but the 'provoking' aspects of early O'Hara.[42] 'One frequently
feels that the poet is trying on various pairs of brass knuckles until

he finds the one which fits comfortably.' (CP viii) Ironically, by the 1950s French Surrealism could be read both as brass-knuckle avant-gardeism and as, in its antinomian way, one more manifestation of high art. 'What was needed was a vernacular corresponding to the creatively messy New York environment to ventilate the concentrated Surrealist imagery of poems like "Hatred", "Easter" and "Second Avenue."' (CP x) And so, for better or worse, there were to be no more lines like 'You come to me smelling of the shit of Pyrrhian maidens!' (CP 145) With 'In Memory of My Feelings' O'Hara commits his art to a more mature articulation of pain and the dissembling necessary to emotional survival, which stands as a memorial to certain writings as much as the 'feelings' of the title. The poem's 'I' must become a real snake in the grass in order to survive:

and animal death whips out its flashlight,
                                             whistling
and slipping the glove off the trigger hand. The serpent's eyes
redden at sight of those thorny fingernails, he is so smooth!
                                 My transparent selves
flail about like vipers in a pail, writhing and hissing
without panic, with a certain justice of response
and presently the aquiline serpent comes to resemble the Medusa.

This serpent must take on some of the attributes of a chameleon, and so be metaphorical, standing by analogy for certain changing aspects of the self in relation to experience, and yet be as earthbound and self-serving and intent on survival as a real snake, connected only by contiguity to the rest of the garden of earthly delights that is not it. This poem, which I am reading chiefly as a meditation on its poetic begettors, mourns its own emancipation from the parent-texts it must now ritually slay with the killing touch of parody or irony.

        And now the coolness of a mind
        like a shuttered suite in the Grand Hotel
        where mail arrives for my incognito,
                                       whose façade
        has been slipping into the Grand Canal for centuries;

Byron's turn. The mind, however, is often far from cool, and temporality makes experience as fugitive as it is intense. We try to mark time with one kind of firework display or another:

> 　　　　　　　　　　　　　　and it is a celebration,
> 　　the trying desperately to count them as they die.
> 　　But who will stay to be these numbers
> 　　when all the lights are dead?

As with the 'celebration' of John Button's birthday, it is time that truly marks us, as we attempt to regulate it. There may be a mournful satisfaction to be gained from trying to count the rockets as they splay into nothingness, but as with words and the reality they are doomed to chase and never catch, 'these numbers' stand for, but are not, either the experiences we have but may not keep, or the hand of time that we shun but which is always already inside us. Who will stay? No-one.

　　Still, you have to be up and doing, and art by delving into these matters can pass, but only in the most figurative sense kill, time:

> 　　Beneath these lives
> 　　the ardent lover of history hides,
> 　　　　　　　　　　　　　　　　　　tongue out
> 　　leaving a globe of spit on a taut spear of grass
> 　　and leaves off rattling his tail a moment
> 　　to admire this flag.

The poem is full of flags, money, ensigns, algebra, 'a sentimental longing for number', systems of signification whose clear limitations put into question their capability in mapping reality. The Chinese invention of fireworks, Arabs worshipping at Ramadan, the 'mountainous-minded' Greeks, who 'could speak/of time as a river and step across it into Persia, leaving the pain/at home to be converted into statuary', the Roman copies of that pain, France at the moment of revolution ('"Destiny, Paris, destiny!"'), the arrival of Columbus at the New World, O'Hara's own experience serving in the navy in the Second World War, all pass rapidly by with a tremendous and questionable vividness. What remains, when all these lights are dead? In its reactions to a world composed of fitful light and crumbling statuary, the poem wants its own broken format to be read as an index of truthfulness, but personal horror and desire still call out from the margins with an intensity that is, ironically, only increased by the supposedly larger nature of the pressures of 'history'. And so, if the poem must critique Whitman and the too-blithe hymning of selfhood's multiplicity, its darker attempts to do the *polis* in different voices must also bring it up against *The Waste Land*.

All poets of O'Hara's generation – born in the decade of *The Waste Land*, coming to maturity as writers in the period of Eliot's absolute cultural investiture – had, as it were, to enter into a competition that could not be won. It is possible that their interest in Ezra Pound was in large measure a way of dealing with that situation. Incarcerated in a mental hospital for political reasons by the Americans, marginalized as a poet also (and therefore available as hero-figure to a young avant-garde in search of a mythology), perhaps more exploratory than Old Possum in the consequences for prosody of their joint aim 'to break the pentameter', Pound was an Eliot cut down to manageable size, an ageing father who could be repudiated for his politics, studied for his methods, and supported in his vulnerability.[43] This displacement of an engagement with Eliot onto the more assailable and accommodating figure of Pound did not prevent the engagement from taking place with, understandably, some curious results. Charles Olson, (in his turn a paterfamilias with whom contemporary poetic writing has to deal), set out the choice explicitly in his sequence of poems, the 'ABCs':

> The word
> is image, and the reverend reverse is
> Eliot
>
> Pound
> is verse

Those are the closing lines of the first poem. It is a confirmation of my own thesis and an unexpected denial of Olson's own declared preference that the next 'ABC' should echo Eliot, much more than Pound. Lines like 'coiled or unflown/in the marrow of the bone' could literally have come from a lost Eliot manuscript, circa 1920, and the mysterious Dantesque figures Olson evokes recall 'What the Thunder Said' in both cadence and atmosphere, at least as much as they do Pound.[44] I cite Olson, but an analogous diagnosis of an encounter with Eliot where the polemics of the time were all in Pound's favour could have been made using texts by Robert Duncan, or Jack Spicer, or a number of prominent names from Donald Allen's *New American Poetry* anthology. The case is altered with Frank O'Hara

and John Ashbery because the affinities of their work to the French
Symbolist tradition running from Baudelaire and Mallarmé through
to the early twentieth century, a tradition barely relevant to most of
their American contemporaries, puts them more on Eliot's side from
the outset. (Indeed, one could argue that in some respects their work
is more faithful to that tradition, and has done more to keep it alive
for the wider world, than most of the significant French poetry
written since 1945, an unexpected confirmation of the model proposed by Eliot's essay 'Tradition and the Individual Talent', whereby
the avant-garde artist both subscribes to and modifies retrospec-
tively the work of his predecessors. Those seem also to be pretty
much the tenets underpinning O'Hara's art criticism.) However, 'In
Memory of My Feelings' is not to be read as Williams read Eliot and
as some American citizens read the city of New York, as at once
mandarin, threatening and faintly traitorous in its Europeanization.
The venom of O'Hara's serpent inoculates his poetry against a fatal
capitulation to Eliot or any other 'compound ghost'.[45]

O'Hara's poem makes its reckoning with *The Waste Land* not by
echoing its cadences, but by parallel engagements at the conceptual
level. Like Eliot's poem, it looks to the past for answers to present
miseries, only to find an at best ironic and fitful glance of recognition
assuring the enquirer that things were no better then. Ships, carrying
Columbus, Lord Nelson, the US Navy, pass in the night of O'Hara's
meditation like quotations from Webster, Baudelaire or the music
hall in Eliot, apparently discursive references that seem in the end
more like a hall of mirrors for a consciousness at crisis point in its
relation to temporality. Just as the literary allusions in *The Waste
Land* are familial or mirroring, and not educative as they often are in
Pound, so the historical sweep of O'Hara's poem may finally be read
as a series of spatial images standing for a temporal plight. Where
the poem engages Eliot's in argument and even competition is in its
attitude to the right relations between poetic rhetoric and personal
anxiety. Eliot's is a ventriloquial pathology, an exorcism avowedly
impersonal from whose margins it is not hard to conjure the personal as a long shadow cast by Marie's or Tiresias' or Thomas Kyd's
words on the page. O'Hara's poem criticizes that occultation of the
personal, and reinscribes it – not confessionally, as Lowell or Plath
might have done, but metaphorically, in the serpent imagery that
stands for both the will to survive pain and the canny urge to feed on
it for poetic purposes (in memory of my feelings) and so wreak

revenge on temporality, through art. As readers we must feel some
discomfort at the use of snake imagery, which stands here for both
honesty and a predatory economy, with all its connotations of danger and guile in the garden intact:

> When you turn your head
> can you feel your heels, undulating? that's what it is
> to be a serpent.

The poem is, at one level, about the necessity for a certain remorse-
lessness on the part of the poet, a readiness to feed off even the most
heartfelt experience for material:

> And now it is the serpent's turn.
> I am not quite you, but almost, the opposite of visionary.
> You are coiled around the central figure,
>
> the heart
> that bubbles with red ghosts

The process is more vampiric than heroic. Indeed, 'the hero' has only
a bit-part in the poem, accidentally stumbling over the poet while
'trying to unhitch his parachute', which O'Hara calls with a melancholy humour 'our last embrace'. The poem resembles 'Hôtel
Transylvanie' in the bitter and mournful tone with which it treats the
poet's homosexuality. In fact, much of the final section of 'In Memory
of My Feelings' is a meditation on a phrase of Emerson's from 'The
American Scholar' that O'Hara's sexuality renders savage and packed
with irony: 'love of the hero corrupts into worship of his statue'.[46]
   The nature of love, the image of the hero, and the representation of
both through sculpture and statuary were to recur prominently in
the series of odes O'Hara was to write over the coming period 1957–
8, publishing them as a separate volume in 1960. Other important
images from 'In Memory of My Feelings' that resurface in the odes
are flags, stars, horses as standard-bearers for an unfettered sexuality, the savage-who-isn't, the ambiguous gifts of fire and, not least,
snakes:

> make my lines thin as ice, then swell like pythons

> ('Ode on Causality', *CP* 302)

What the 'Ode to Joy' calls 'the sculptural necessities of lust' get their
weirdest presentation in the Causality Ode, a sort of elegy for Jackson
Pollock which, like most elegies, has very little to do with its subject.
The notorious swelling and thinning of his myriad dripped lines is
used opportunistically by the serpent-poet in a vivid example of
what the earlier poem was talking about:

> There is the sense of neurotic coherence
> you think maybe poetry is too important and you like that
> suddenly everyone's supposed to be veined, like marble
> it isn't that simple but it's simple enough
> the rock is least living of the forms man has fucked

(CP 302)

There are anxieties at work here that recall Rilke's feeling that as
Rodin's secretary, and as a poet rather than a sculptor, labouring
physically, he was the lesser man. James Schuyler had been secretary
to a prolific poet with a world reputation, W. H. Auden. And as
museum curators, reviewers, young middle-men, it must have
seemed to the group of New York poets that they were a secretarial
generation, vis-à-vis the Action Painters, macho heroes, who had
struggled from largely immigrant or hick backgrounds (Pollock
hailed from Cody, Wyoming), through poverty and political struggle in the thirties to the triumphs of post-1945 New York. The rural
background O'Hara paints for himself in the 'Ode to Michael
Goldberg ('s Birth and Other Births)' seems more a semi-fantasy
based on O'Hara's idea of the background a Pollock must have had.
The sense of living-in-the-aftermath isn't unique to the poets of this
time. It reappears, indeed is even more forcibly documented, in
what is perhaps the novelist Fielding Dawson's best book, *An Emotional Memoir of Franz Kline* (1967). However, a sense that he might
have been riding professionally on the back of that generation is
there in O'Hara's *poetry* – unlike Ashbery's or Schuyler's. It combines with a sense of his sexuality as necessarily masked, snatched in
episodes, and predatory. When people leave the gay couple alone
briefly, 'he takes you in his arms/for a few minutes terminated
physically by footsteps'. (CP 374) Interestingly enough, in that poem
of 1960 O'Hara refers to himself throughout as 'he', and when pick-
ing up the phone says 'hello/this is George Gordon, Lord Byron'. As
for so many gay writers in the days before Stonewall, and since,

there is a touch of self-hatred in the allusions to sexual orientation. I suspect that this combines with the other historical factors that have been mentioned, and indeed with a more traditional sense of the glories of the lyric as snatched, furtive and Promethean, to condense in the image of the serpent. The odes may be read as fanning like peacock eyes from 'In Memory of My Feelings': or, that poem is the first and best of O'Hara's odes.

At the end of that poem, everything is lost or has to die except the snake. The poem is the 'ruse' of its 'occasion', not the 'cry' as Stevens had it, and the more unflinching poet O'Hara 'must now kill' his predecessors' poems of influence and terminate his own poem of experience if the serpent that makes the next work possible is to be saved from their midst. It is an extraordinarily dramatic ending, and yet for that very reason one stands back, aware not only of reading sympathetically but of watching a performance. The serpentine ruthlessness the poem claims to admit but regret is in some measure what it wants. After all, as the snake makes its progress along the ground, the flattened Leaves of Grass spring up again:

>   Grace
> to be born and live as variously as possible. The conception
> of the masque barely suggests the sordid identifications.
> I am a Hittite in love with a horse. I don't know what blood's
> in me I feel like an African prince I am a girl walking downstairs
> in a red pleated dress with heels I am a champion taking a fall
> I am a jockey with a sprained ass-hole I am the light mist
>   in which a face appears
> and it is another face of blonde I am a baboon eating a banana
> I am a dictator looking at his wife I am a doctor eating a child
> and the child's mother smiling I am a Chinaman climbing a mountain
> I am a child smelling his father's underwear I am an Indian
> sleeping on a scalp
>   and my pony is stamping in the birches,
> and I've just caught sight of the *Niña*, the *Pinta* and the *Santa Maria*.
>   What land is this, so free?

This is the most shockingly comic moment in O'Hara's poetry, the passage most illustrative of the painter Grace Hartigan's comment that the poem is about 'how to be open but not violated, how *not to panic*'.[47] Arguably, the poem is about how to be open and violated, *and* panic, and get through it somehow with nothing of the hero, that lemming to his own appalling stoicism, but with some more flowing quality like an idea of democracy or a line by Whitman, with whom O'Hara competes, and in whose company he finally stands.

3
Ashbery and Influence

The monkish and the frivolous alike were to be trapped
in death's capacious claw
But listen while I tell you about the wallpaper –

(John Ashbery, 'The Ecclesiast')

THE ENGLISH ASHBERY

British puzzlement over John Ashbery may have become more respectful since *Self-Portrait in a Convex Mirror* won its clutch of awards, but it remains essentially unchanged. Reviewing Ashbery's tenth collection, *A Wave*, Gavin Ewart had this to say in a poetry round-up that included approving notices of Charles Causley and Craig Raine:

> John Ashbery's verse is like a a Moebius strip; it goes on and on and you can't get into it. A 'dish of milk is set out at night' in the very first poem ('At North Farm'). Is this for a cat, a fox, a hedgehog, a wandering spirit? No answer.[1]

By contrast, Craig Raine's poetry provides answers. His allegedly daring and innovative use of metaphor disguises only superficially a process very like that of the crossword puzzle: a definite answer exists, and the game is to find it. To take an example from Raine's collection *Rich*, a railway station doesn't look, on the face of it, like a 'terminus of zips' until a moment's reflection lifts the reader towards an aerial perspective: problem solved.[2] The real, underlying problem for such a poetry must lie in finding ways to lure an audience back for later readings, after the finite mysteries have all been seen through. Little would be gained, after all, from doing the same crossword twice. Raine's poetry is lifted above the comunications-fodder we imbibe daily by virtue of its density, its turned wit and ingenious use of metaphor. Yet it may, perhaps unconsciously, have made a compact with the essentially soluble and disposable nature of media discourse in that very ingenuity.

In other respects, the Martians, as they used to be labelled ('Metropolitans' would have carried more geographical accuracy), are basically young (in the sense of middle-aged) Movement writers, whose work shows no fundamental difference in procedure from the new British writing of the 1950s. Even some of the names are the same, with acidly-sexist Martin rather than downright-misogynist Kingsley Amis as the prose counterweight to Raine. The *Sunday Times* carried a long interview with Martin Amis in the same week that Raine was lauded by the *Guardian*. (Even more than the Movement, this generation of ex-Oxford journalist-artists has the media sewn up.) Amis betrayed anxieties over the crafted subtleties of characterization and verbal mimesis in his new novel:

> 'Did you get the joke about Lorne Guyland? . . . It's a play on the way New Yorkers say Long Island. You know: Lorngiland.'

Humbled by Amis's wit, the interviewer retreated into a deeply British suspicion of the clever-clever, misapplied vis-à-vis Ashbery but well deserved in this case:

> . . . *nobody* could be expected to understand every one of these curiously inverted jokes . . . His (Amis's) answer came smoothly: 'The only one who gets them all is the author, of course.'[3]

As with Craig Raine, getting the answer right (for what it's worth) is (in two senses) the end of the reading process. So to return to Gavin Ewart's puzzlement, if John Ashbery hasn't been willing in his forty years as a published poet to provide this kind of smart answer, we should at least be grateful to him for that.

At one level all of this is only the current version of a debate between English and American poetics that has existed since Walt Whitman severed the second from the first. Even so prolix an Englishman as Swinburne felt bound to censure Whitman's rejection of the single 'answer' in poetry in favour of an explosive and self-invented rhetoric:

> . . . to sing the song of all countries is not simply to fling out on the page at random in one howling mass the titles of all divisions of

the earth, and so leave them. At this rate, to sing the song of the language it should suffice to bellow out backwards and forwards the twenty-four letters of the alphabet.[4]

There is prescience in Swinburne's anxieties, and attention will be paid later in this chapter to the Language poets (*soi-disant*), poetic descendants of Ashbery showing a very literal concern with 'the twenty-four letters of the alphabet'. Swinburne's allegation here was one of excess in the sheer quantity of data, not an excess of semantic ambiguity. Still, with the passage of time the transmutations of Whitman's bequest in the hands of a poet such as Ashbery mean that the first has become the second. In poems like 'Into the Dusk-Charged Air' (*RM*) and in his most underrated text *The Vermont Notebook* (1975), Ashbery draws on techniques – dangerous techniques, perhaps – made available by Whitman in his great lists. A distinctively American perception of life as intrinsically multiplex runs from Emerson's Transcendentalism, his radical adaptation of Coleridgean Romanticism, through Whitman's poetry to the work of Stevens and now Ashbery. It is this that allows the question of for whom or for what a dish of milk was set out at night to hang in the air. As Harold Bloom has said about 'The Skaters' (*RM*), Ashbery 'accepts a reduction of Whitmanian ecstasy, while reaffirming it nevertheless'.[5] Here is a page from *The Vermont Notebook*:

Beggar-my-neighbor, pounce, fish, old maid, progressive euchre, bezique, backgammon, mah jongg, dominoes, hearts, contract bridge, Michigan poker, rummy, solitaire, Monopoly, Sorry, Parcheesi, Scrabble, Authors, checkers, Chinese checkers, chess, go, fan tan, honeymoon bridge.

Murder, incest, arson, rape, grand larceny, extortion, forgery, impersonating an officer, resisting arrest, loitering, soliciting, possession of a controlled substance, drunken driving, reckless endangerment, slander, mental cruelty, non-assistance of a person in danger, perjury, embezzlement, sodomy, child abuse, cruelty to animals, bootlegging, adultery, bigamy, bearing false witness.

(*VN* 17)

This is not from the Ashbery book on which most abuse has been heaped; that honour belongs to the early *Tennis Court Oath*: critics have merely ignored *The Vermont Notebook* altogether. However, its militantly literal recourse to the list as a poetic unit doesn't disguise its characteristically Ashberyan features. There is that dogged mono-tone, half-patient, half-sardonic, learned perhaps from Gertrude Stein (also a favourite of O'Hara's). And with that comes its equally Ashberyan opposite, a fabulous and Surreal exoticism, that lets the non-referential or droll or oneiric associations of 'honeymoon bridge' and 'Michigan poker' run free just as it relishes their social banality. Ashbery ducks under Whitman's heroic oratory, but allows his drive towards poetic democratization free rein through the lexicons of suburbia and the shopping mall. In just this way a great Ashbery poem, 'Pyrography' (*HD*) can be simultaneously a whimsical cata-logue of dream bric-à-brac and a seriously patriotic poem. Whitman's thundering egotism alternates incessantly with a fabulously nega-tive capability, an opening of the self into transparent hospitality that every bit of America, down to its rejectamenta, might have its say. Ashbery's poetry may parody this demonically, but it perpetu-ates it too.

The British like to pretend that whatever is new is merely fashion-able disturbance, and that we did it all a hundred years ago anyway. Why pay any attention to Surrealism, comes the cry, when we had Edward Lear and Lewis Carroll? And weren't we among the first to appreciate Whitman? We were. The problem, as Ashbery has noted in interview, is that the British perception of Whitman as a kind of Hicksville stump-orator, all beard and sweat and Howdy Ma'am, may be affectionate, but it is also reductive and patronizing.

> . . . the British feel that Americans, if they're going to be accepted as writers, have to act 'like Americans'. They have to be loud-mouthed, oratorical. That might be why Whitman was very widely accepted, and they loved Bret Harte, whom nobody reads anymore, just because he came to England and walked around in boots and cowboy hat. *This* is an American, so we can, you know, we can understand this, because the Americans are a bunch of Yahoos. And if you're not a Yahoo, they don't quite know how to take it . . .[6]

Of course being a Houyhnhnm also has its drawbacks – but Ashbery's observation still rings true. The British hope sincerely that, when it comes to his language, the writer will always be in possession of a controlled substance, if not quite in the sense used by Ashbery in the page quoted from his *Vermont Notebook*. If he is going to lose control, then he must not do so semantically, like the foreigners Stevens, Ashbery, the Surrealists: it would be better if he drank, like Dylan Thomas, and lost control that way, while remaining a controllable presence poetically. Drinking is OK for the British poet. So is swearing.

Consider Philip Larkin's use of the word 'fuck', and its derivatives. It surfaces quite often in his work, though like the fragment of tibia or surgically excised bullet the patient chooses to keep, it is both claimed and handled a touch queasily.

> When I see a couple of kids
> And guess he's fucking her and she's
> Taking pills or wearing a diaphragm,
> I know this is paradise[7]

Although there is considerable venom in these lines and in the rest of 'High Windows', for to write 'fucking' in this case is to descend to the level of the Great Unwashed of the Permissive Sixties, the poem is partly about acknowledging the toxicity in one's prejudices while striving to limit its effects as far as possible. The word is used in a way that restores to it a genuine shock-effect; Larkin's use of tone, even in this seemingly crude instance, is skilfully judged. Now a partisan afficionado of modern American poetry might argue, legitimately, that the battle for the freedom to use 'fucking' or any other 'obscenity' was won many a long year ago, and might point to Allen Ginsberg's Battle Hymn of the New Republic *Howl* for a manic, indeed Whitmanic, example. Remember Swinburne's 'one howling mass'.

> who howled on their knees in the subway and were dragged off
>   the roof waving genitals and manuscripts,
> who let themselves be fucked in the ass by saintly motorcyclists,
>   and screamed with joy,
> who blew and were blown by those human seraphim, the sailors,
>   caresses of Atlantic and Caribbean love,
> who balled in the morning in the evenings in rosegardens and the
>   grass of public parks and cemeteries scattering their semen
>   freely to whom-ever come who may[8]

The pure products of America, as William Carlos Williams asserted, go crazy. Of course some have craziness thrust upon them, and some only achieve it after a lifetime's effort. Either way, it is with Williams' crazy sons, who are also Whitman's grandchildren, that this book has to deal. Yet *Howl* for all its loudness and intensity, is not at all an unsophisticated poem. In common with many key Modernist and postmodern texts from *The Waste Land* to *The Naked Lunch*, it is simultaneously a literature and anti-art, an affirmation and a howl of defeat. Burroughs' addiction is both his curse and the basic metaphor of his satire, as fragmentation had been both the appalled diagnosis and the *modus operandi* of Eliot's greatest poem. Ginsberg's *Howl* is both a resumption of Whitman's prophetic rhetoric, and the parodic failure of that rhetoric of the hero to let itself be blown like any old second-hand saxophone. Only the first was registered when *Howl* made its mark in the late fifties, a period when the evangelical tone of McCarthyism was winding down to a sullen conservatism, and the new individualism of the jazz and art worlds had not yet become significantly marketable. At this ambiguous moment Ginsberg was taken at his word as a colourful prophet. The sixties roller-coaster denied him the opportunity to face up to the underlying problems and possibilities of his mock-heroic rhetoric, an opportunity that might have made Ginsberg a great poet, rather than the author of one great poem. Jack Kerouac's influential novel *On The Road* (1957), in some ways a prose analogue to *Howl*, shows a comparably Whitmanian patriotism in its romantic journeying by automobile in America. In and not across, because examination of a road map shows no heroic advance from sea to shining sea, but rather a series of broken loops: Kerouac's odyssey also is a howl of defeat and estrangement. Not merely the themes and literary styles but the ambiguous successes and self-images of the Beat Generation are anticipated by the poetry of William Carlos Williams. Among Williams' 'pure products' were listed, alongside his thieves and 'young slatterns':

> devil-may-care men who have taken
> to railroading
> out of sheer lust of adventure – [9]

anticipating in 1923 the later photographs of Jack Kerouac, dusty from burning up the miles with arch-hipster Neal Cassady, or perched

on Ginsberg's New York fire-escape, a brakeman's manual jammed
in the pocket of his denims.

That kind of would-be *déclassé* swagger is hardly John Ashbery's
style. Of the many tones and personae that flicker through his poems, camp or philosophical, Prufrockian or Chelsea avant-gardeist,
elegantly tracing the credences of summer or being Daffy Duck, not
one presents Ashbery as 'one of the roughs'. Probably the least likely
person in the world to grow an Old Testament beard and appear on
stage playing primitive instruments, he is nonetheless, along with
Ginsberg and O'Hara, a Whitman man. The struggle for what was
termed in the previous chapter an aesthetics of inclusion gains a
significant intensity with William Carlos Williams but it is the Great
Grey poet's struggle, first and foremost. And now that the struggle
is over, anything, *anything*, can be included – and a price is paid for
that freedom. The resistance to any kind of large-scale structure in
Ashbery's enormous, double-columned poem of the late seventies
Litany isn't part of any combative breaking of form, but proceeds
calmly from the assumption that there are no more forms to break.
While it is possible to enjoy any local effect in *Litany* it is hard to
detect any urgency in the writing of it that might therefore be summoned in the reading of it. Ashbery has never lost his enthusiasm for
the work of John Cage, and the aleatory has been felt by both British
and American readers to be his most dangerous temptation, and one
that has been there throughout. This is the price paid early on in
Ashbery's career for Whitman's insurgence:

/////////////// "I won't be very long,"/////////// she said.
(#############

(*TCO* 93)

and

???

(91)

This last – not, in all likelihood, the strongest line in Ashbery's
poetry – may bear only a distant resemblance to the 'curious abrupt
questionings' of 'Crossing Brooklyn Ferry'. About as loose as

Ashbery's poetry gets, it is nonetheless one of the offshoots of the
Whitman inheritance. I want to consider it, briefly, in relation to the
close of Philip Larkin's 'High Windows', which in terms of multi-
plicity/indeterminacy of meaning is about as loose as *his* work gets:

> And immediately

> Rather than words comes the thought of high windows:
> The sun-comprehending glass,
> And beyond it, the deep blue air, that shows
> Nothing, and is nowhere, and is endless.[10]

The underlying differences of procedure are those of a referential
and a non-referential poetry. It can be argued that such a distinction
is ultimately false, that categories of the referential and the non-
referential are wedded, *sub rosa*. The descriptive poem, determinedly
about things, is by virtue of the 'about' immediately subject to the
workings of difference, self-divided; meanwhile the allegedly non-
referential artwork can never truly emancipate itself from a social
matrix of signs and connotations. That may be true, ultimately, but
it would be agreed that one could travel quite a way in discussion of
the differences between these two poems and their poetics before
reaching that ultimate inversion. My point is that however open-
ended Larkin's poem may be, and it does close with an opening into
endlessness, it is not indeterminate in the meanings it generates.
Rather, it is *about* an indeterminacy of experience, and uses determinate significations and tones to achieve its goal. Experientially, the
sudden thought of high windows and a cloudless sky suggests both
religion, a transcendental perspective on worldly woes, and nothingness, simple blueness – just an anaesthetic moment of release
from the 'paradise', in truth the purgatory, of life. Thus Larkin
concludes in a twilight zone between two views, of the wished-for
significance and the likely insignificance of things, with a vision of
both and resolving access to neither. No doubt felt painfully by
Larkin, this kind of ironic evocation of death-in-life marks him from
a literary point of view as an heir of Thomas Hardy. Many readers
have found this poem affecting in the transitions it manages from an
ugly and self-parodying set of prejudices to a larger comprehension
that is vulnerable precisely to the extent that the self is opened up. A
more gloomy reading might find in it a transition from aggression to
masochism. Either way, Larkin's effects are inseparable from a fairly

conservative repertoire of poetic devices: rhyme and half-rhyme, the potential in enjambement for ironic dislocation, and so on. *Howl* is a painful poem, too, and as we shall see the lyrical cry in Ashbery's poetry can be at least as affecting as anything in recent British poetry. Nevertheless, it has I think to be conceded that the post-Poundian, avant-gardeist struggles to not merely break the pentameter, but heave everything else aside as so many outdated bonds and gestures, has stripped American poetry of the potential for certain kinds of artistic expression, however much it may have facilitated others.

There is in addition a combination of restlessness and intellectual hospitality about the Whitman inheritance which, if it can't quite be reduced by British impercipience to cowboy vulgarity, can still seem naive or irresponsible to a culture in which the posture of the poem is traditionally, often stiffly, moral. There are those who would find Ashbery's sincere desire to have his poems reach as wide an audience as possible, reiterated in interview, rather hard to square with, say, the performance of 'Litany' by its author and Ann Lauterbach when the two columns were read simultaneously. Even more stunning to British (and other) sensibilities would be his assertion that only 'poetry freaks' read a book of poems through from beginning to end:

> I think most people don't. I certainly don't. I'm a very scattered, disorganized kind of person. I will sit down, read a few pages of a book then put it aside, maybe take it up again, maybe read something else, maybe go out and get drunk, and go and see a friend, go to the movies . . . There is a line in my poem 'The Skaters' that seems to be the sum of my hedonistic, my seriously hedonistic philosophy, which is 'nothing but movies and love and laughter, sex and fun'. I felt very much confirmed in my careless ways by this quotation by Emerson that I read recently: it's something like 'a man should have aunts and cousins, should have a barn and a woodshed, should buy turnips and potatoes, should saunter and sleep and be inferior and silly.' Emerson is really an extraordinary writer.[11]

Ashbery is an extraordinary writer too, and often most subtle and sophisticated when apparently least so. If his tongue is not in his cheek in these interviews, it is not entirely clear where else it might be located. Those who diagnose only 'wacky sophistication' or the 'mannered . . . sumptuous high finish' of a sleek postmodernism grown fat on gullibility and the Guggenheim Foundation, those for whom Ashbery is a psychedelic-surrealist-solipsist, would doubtless be confirmed in their prejudice by the above.[12] They might be surprised by the serious discussion of spirituality that follows the above excerpt from the Warsaw interview, as they might by this poet's regular attendance at church. An apprehension of deep space, of metaphysical extension to our world of laughter, sex and turnips, alternates and intertwines at great speed in Ashbery's writing with an at times quite incredible, absorbent attention to the bits and bobs of material existence. And, as with the earlier discussion of O'Hara and Byron, we must be wary of the dangers in thinking of 'Ashbery's writing', as if there were an absolute consistency of belief and procedure stretching from *Turandot*, or even *The Double Dream of Spring* to *April Galleons* and beyond.

In the spring of 1982, in the first stages of writing *A Wave*, Ashbery was hospitalized with a spinal disorder diagnosed only belatedly, and nearly died. He has said that his brush with death had no overt influence on his writing, save for the opening lines of the title poem, 'A Wave'. ('To pass through pain and not know it,/A car door slamming in the night./To emerge on an invisible terrain.') However, the collection as a whole is perfused as never before with black jokes, *memento mori* admonitions and autumnal rumination.

> And now that the end is near
> The segments of the trip swing open like an orange.
>
> ('Just Walking Around')

> It all wears out. I keep telling myself this, but
> I can never believe me, though others do.
>
> ('Down By the Station, Early in the Morning')

> Perhaps the best that we can hope for is
>
> That we may live now with some
> Curiosity and hope
> Like pools that soon become part of the tide
>
> ('A Fly')

This is not just the movies, love and laughter, sex and fun. For a pool to become part of the tide has connotations of deep-space monism, but that 'like' yokes things utterly unlike each other, 'curiosity and hope' are so exclusively human: the pool remains shallow after all. An orange is attractive, imagistically, and to make it 'swing open' is to have it behave like so many Lewis Carrollian pictures in Ashbery: but if life is *just* an orange, then it's worth less than Joy's grape to Keats. The imaging of life as obliquely radiant, subject in Bloom's phrase to a 'near-inscrutable order', alternates vertiginously but charmingly with life as a series of loosely layered and metonymically half-connected 'rags and crystals', to borrow a formula from *A Wave*. The title of that collection points with an ambiguity worthy of Stevie Smith to matters grave, and wet. A wave is at once a fluid moment on the verge of dissolution and (feasibly) a gesture of friendship and recognition. *A Wave* is probably Ashbery's saddest book, but it is typical of the author's resourcefulness that his next book, *April Galleons*, should as it were dip behind the rhetoric of *A Wave*, deploying it while doing other things *sub rosa*. Neither book seems primed to win Ashbery a new audience in Britain, given their insistent recourse to a curious modification of the Whitman inheritance, what the Swedish poet (and translator of Ashbery) Göran Printz-Påhlson, calls 'a painfully gruff idiom, unmistakably American, crackerbarrel', just when reviewers were beginning to grant the poet baroque skills as the Houdini of conundrum and paradox.[13]

And this British-American standoff is how it stands, in 1991. I first thought about these cultural differences in 1985, for a review of Ashbery, and it is surprising how little has changed in the interim. Taking their cue perhaps from the aliens in *Invasion of the Body Snatchers*, the Martians no longer call themselves that and so have consolidated their grip; though at the time of writing ecology-consciousness appears set to make Ted Hughes the most fashionable Laureate since Tennyson. There again, a tendency towards poetic aggression and dissonance in texts like *Crow* fights the old fifties fights for freedom of expression as if the line of significant American writing from Carlos Williams to O'Hara enjoyed only the barest and most questionable existence. Hughes' Romantic deformations of sense or syntax may be rebarbative, stylistically, but they do not tend finally towards an indeterminacy of meaning. If a dish of milk were set out at night for Crow he would no doubt behave in a Hughesian way and reject it as irradiated, drown a passing kitten or see the twisted face of God reflected in it, but whatever carnage might unfold en route, the poem's drift would ultimately be determinate and clear. (Indeed, many poems in that particular volume are explicitly puzzles, and utilize the forms and furniture of the riddle, the detective story, or the religious parable.) The poetry of Hughes and Larkin is more powerful and emotionally involving than that of the younger Faber generation, but their poetic procedures are much the same. Despite the continuing Americanization of British culture, this gap does not diminish with time. There are British poets whose work has some affinities with Ashbery's: one thinks of the aptly named John Ash, and some of the excellent writers anthologized by Andrew Crozier and Tim Longville in *A Various Art*.[14] Significantly, Ash has moved to New York, and the anthology was published outside London. Of course it has still been possible for Ashbery, say, to carry the influence of two major poets, Eliot and Auden, who might be termed Anglo-American if from opposite points of departure. This chapter will investigate that influence, as it will the relationship between Ashbery's poetry and deconstruction, another American hybrid that has had to weather the blast of British scepticism.

THE OLD MAGICAL NOTIONS

In search of something more intellectually adventurous than Edgar Lee Masters and the *Spoon River Anthology*, the teenage John Ashbery came across the early poetry of W. H. Auden. This was the catalyst for his first serious attempts at writing verse. Although the two met for the first time in 1947, at a party following a Harvard poetry reading, they only became properly acquainted about four years later, through gallery owner John Bernard Myers. 1951 was also the year that Ashbery met James Schuyler, who was in fact to become Auden's secretary for a while. Ashbery and Frank O'Hara (who was so nervous at the prospect of meeting Auden that he is said to have thrown up) submitted collections of work for the Yale Younger Poets Award, for which Auden was judge, in 1955. Ashbery won, with *Some Trees*. It is important to note that the competition was judged by the 'American', and not the 'English' Auden. This was the postwar poet of 'In Praise of Limestone' and 'Homage to Clio', massively assured disquisitions on love, liberality and the cost of peace delivered with a quasi-Horatian trenchancy in every known metre, and some new ones. Like their author at this stage, these long poems go on a bit. Dubious about what the New York poets were doing, Auden was nevertheless a personal mentor of sorts. His influence over American poetry was immense at this time: its direct transmission can be seen in a forties antique such as Karl Shapiro's *Essay On Rime*, now seldom read but a paradigm of the period. Meanwhile the status of early Auden, particularly *The Orators* subtitled 'An English Study' and published in 1932) was quite uncertain. This was the work by Auden that had caused most respectful bafflement in its day, when he had been in the vanguard of English experimental writing. Auden now dismissed it as 'a case of the fair notion fatally injured', and for the Preface to a new edition in 1966 wrote as follows:

> As a rule, when I re-read something I wrote when I was younger, I can think myself back into the frame of mind in which I wrote it. *The Orators*, though, defeats me. My name on the title-page seems a pseudonym for someone else, someone talented but near the border of sanity, who might well, in a year or two, become a Nazi.[15]

'Border' is a key-term in British writing of the thirties, occurring as it does in the title of a novella by Edward Upward, political mentor of the Auden group, and in important poems such as the hortatory lyric given the number XXIX in Auden's *Poems* (1930), and reprinted as 'Consider':

> Consider this and in our time
> As the hawk sees it or the helmeted airman:
> The clouds rift suddenly – look there
> At cigarette-end smouldering on a border
> At the first garden party of the year.[16]

The border is not merely herbaceous, but carries political associations from the airman's perspective that are as ineluctable as they are inscrutable.

Borderlines of consciousness and sanity are also of repetitive interest to the Auden group, the first poetic côterie after the French Surrealists to read and use Freud. In fact, thirties writing is expressed at an almost fundamental level through the vocabulary of sickness and cure. 'What do you think about England, this country of ours where nobody is well?' asks an anonymous Orator.[17]

Notwithstanding his lexical bravura, a feature from the start, Auden was as much as a channel for as a controller of the voices of that time. Added to his anxieties was the borderline of acceptable, indeed licit, behaviour for a homosexual male, the source of the necessarily opaque melancholy in a poem such as poem VII. Politically and psychosexually this is an unstable body of work, feverish for a change of régime, and unable to stomach the torpor of the patient.

However, by the time Auden was to act as judge of John Ashbery's poems, the aesthetics of emergency and the World War itself had passed. Ashbery was too young to have served, and had not lived in a country threatened by Fascism and the possibility of invasion. To him the Oratorical voices were menacing, but as a Surrealist landscape of dream can be menacing. Auden noticed the Surrealist influence on *Some Trees*, but, by an understandable irony, missed the influence of his own early work, about which he now felt uncomfortable. Writing of the dangers inherent in a poetic attachment to 'the subjective life', Auden voiced suspicions about the manufacture of 'calculated oddities' in poetry descended from Rimbaud, 'as if the subjectively sacred were necessarily and on all accounts odd'.[18] These remarks argue a case against the poetry of the *voyant* which at a deeper level betrays a blindness on Auden's part to the value of his own early writing.

If Auden was not wild about *Some Trees*, his reservations concerning the manufacture of 'calculated oddities' were put more bluntly in his letter of rejection to Frank O'Hara:

> I'm sorry to have to tell you that, after much heart searching I chose John's poems. It's really very awkward when the only two possible candidates are both friends.
>
> This doesn't mean that I don't like your work; lots of the poems I like very much, in particular *Jane Awake*.
>
> I think you (and John too, for that matter) must watch what is always the great danger with any 'surrealistic' style, namely of confusing authentic non-logical relations which arouse wonder with accidental ones which arouse mere surprise and in the end fatigue.

Auden had never had any time for Surrealism, and as Marjorie Perloff remarks concerning this letter, it is 'hardly surprising' that he should have felt reservations about so startling a departure from the 'carefully controlled' verse orthodoxy of the early fifties. As Ashbery observed of O'Hara's work, looking back from the perspective of the seventies to those Cold War, McCarthyite years, O'Hara 'was amusing himself, another highly suspect activity'. (*CP* viii) Auden was shrewd enough to notice that, amid Ashbery's battery of devices of estrangement and allure, some juxtapositions came more naturally than others. The link with Rimbaud's preferred images that he draws here would serve as a comment on kinds of poetry by Ashbery that would only be wrought to perfection over twenty years later:

> From Rimbaud down to Mr. Ashbery, an important school of modern poets has been concerned with the discovery that, in childhood largely, in dreams and day-dreams entirely, the imaginative life of the human individual stubbornly continues to live by the old magical notions. Its world is one of sacred images and ritual acts . . . a numinous landscape inhabited by demons and strange beasts.[19]

Childhood, dreams and 'the old magical notions', the talking beasts and spellbound beauties of fable, gather in both poignancy and artificiality as Ashbery's work develops, culminating in the Nut-Brown Maid, 'grisaille shepherdesses', giant playing cards, allusions to Arthur Rackham, 'little wooden animals painted shy,/Terrific colors', cardboard castle and borborygmic giant of *Houseboat Days*. Ashbery has always, tonally speaking, written from an implied vantage slightly further on in years than he actually occupies at the time of writing; but this is not an Eliotic tic: more along the lines of Henry James's Strether, he exhibits the pathos and potential peril of an older man (re)discovering much younger things. The external, potentially invasive menaces faced by the English Auden in the thirties were transmuted by Ashbery into the troubling but ultimately reassuring voices of authority, as heard from the dark outside the nursery, and recalled to be further transformed into the strange juxtapositions of poetic artifice in much later life. This is deeply true of Ashbery and not actually relevant to O'Hara, whose absorption of early Auden is equally enthusiastic but more shallow and less transformational in the kind of imprint taken. Auden may not have noticed, or wanted to notice, but a poem from *Some Trees* is Rimbaudian, neo-Surrealist, intermittently reminiscent of Stevens, but above all Audenesque:

He is sherrier
And sherriest.
A tall thermometer
Reflects him best.

Children in the street
Watch him go by.
'Is that the thinnest shadow?'
They to one another cry.

A face looks from the mirror
As if to say,
'Be supple, young man,
Since you can't be gay.'

(ST 43)

The cracked metrics of the second stanza would be refined over the years until they reach the deviously brilliant (and very funny) McGonagallisms of 'The Songs We Know Best':

Too often when you thought you'd be showered with confetti
What they flung at you was a plate of hot spaghetti
You've put your fancy clothes and your flashy gems in hock
Yet you pause before your father's door afraid to knock

(W, p. 4)

But, beneath the light comedy of 'The Songs We Know Best' can be heard the dissonance and disappointment of the times we love least. Auden too could be adept at signalling the tragic with a sure but delicate touch, as in the painful content behind the brisk ballad form of 'As I Walked Out One Evening'. However, he was also adept at comic ballads that deal overtly with pain but really only make a black joke out of it: the glibly Freudian-cum-Groddeckian 'Miss Gee' for example. Auden's facility proved a dangerous model, not least for himself, and Ashbery's youthful effort is undone by sounding so *unbothered*. The lines that by their very brevity could have signalled the most painful matters are weakened by their own smoothness, a lack that an overlay of Surrealist crazy-paving in the metre does nothing to fill.

More successful but equally Audenesque is the opening poem, 'Two Scenes':

> This is perhaps a day of general honesty
> Without example in the world's history
> Though the fumes are not of a singular authority
> And indeed are dry as poverty.
> Terrific units are on an old man
> In the blue shadow of some paint cans
> As laughing cadets say, 'In the evening
> Everything has a schedule, if you can find out what it is.'

(9)

Those cadets are descendants of the airmen and interrogators of Auden Country, 'Dangerous, easy, in furs, in uniform', 'masked amazers', veterans of 'skyline operations', laughing now but soon to die 'beyond the border'.[20] Their utterances are as cryptic as their allegiances: no doubt they have a schedule too, if only the reader – if only Auden – could find it out. The puzzles and mysteries of poems like 'The Secret Agent' are the antithesis of 1980s Faber cleverness. The whole point is never to be able to know where 'Greenhearth' is, and why there is trouble coming while the bridges remain unbuilt; never to decode allegiances successfully. Auden's poetry *enacts*, rather than describing, the conditions of menace and trepidation that are its psycho-political base. A comment of Edward Mendelson's in relation to those early texts might have some application to early Ashbery: 'As soon as one stops looking for the key to a set of symbols, and recognizes that the poems focus on the self-enclosing patterns that bar their way to a subject in the world outside, their notorious obscurity begins to vanish.'[21] The self-enclosing pattern of end-rhymes in 'Two Scenes' is the shield of a greeting that subjectivity extends to the world only to turn away from its inaccessibility, somewhat as the hand of Parmigianino is ambivalently placed vis-à-vis the viewer in the convex self-portrait that would lend its title to Ashbery's most famous meditation.

If self-enclosing patterns of signification bar unmediated access to a shared world, the poetry is still taunted and haunted in turn by the mirage of that access: there *is* a schedule – if only it could be found. Ashbery's stronger poems from this period are shaped by the anxiety as well as the aestheticism of the Symbolist *Weltanschauung*.

More significantly however, where early Auden is frequently desperate or frustrated by his inability to break through to a world that can be trusted, Ashbery is able to be more than beguiled by the 'self-enclosing patterns' of language and perception, compensation for the breakthrough that is always impending but never arrives. As Lawrence Norfolk has said of recent work by Ashbery, the poems are forever coming closer to a new, difficult intimacy, 'and of course it's the coming closer that is his real subject'.[22] Trustworthy reality is a chimera that beckons and mocks, forever out of reach, forever alluring: hence the fairytale imagery of demons and talking beasts, which hint at a deep-space, occult 'schedule', Auden's sensing correctly Ashbery's respect for childhood's Edenic imaginings, 'the old magical notions', while simultaneously adopting a worldly, New York archness at the ceaseless fading of these insubstantial pageants.

Ashbery's writing shows an indefatigable appetite for play. This irritates critics of a moral bent, particularly in Britain. What distinguishes his work from the professional gameplaying of Borges, Calvino, Perec or other postmodernist nabobs is that their work is grounded in the reader's belated arrival on the textual scene. *Life: A User's Manual* has marvellous detail and intricacy: the ontological *trompe l'oeil* in some of Borges' magic lantern slides is undeniably brilliant. Like Ashbery, they have adapted the techniques of Chinese-box illusionism developed by Raymond Roussel in texts like *Locus Solus* (1914) and applied them to the complexities of human psychology and behaviour, where Roussel could only really offer an appealingly lunatic dandyism. Unfortunately their work is ultimately as fatiguing as Roussel's because every piece of the puzzle is in place before the reader gets there. All we can do is run to catch up, find the hidden clues, put it all together; *en fin de compte*, admire the author, in whose deific creativity we can never participate. By contrast Ashbery's work is heuristic rather than ostensive, eager to share. An apparent (at times alarming) sense that not only does he not mind where the poem is headed, but he is quite happy to turn around from the steering wheel in order to chat with us on the back seat is, at its best, a kind of generosity that allows the reader a genuinely creative role. Of course this is a risky business and it will be clear by now that whatever Ashbery learned from his predecessors tends to be the most extreme facet of their practice, whose risk he cheerfully redoubles. From Whitman he takes sprawl, and the permission to make up great lists; from Williams, the inclusion of weigela, sloppy joe on bun and general trivia; from Surrealism, a baptism by full immersion in dream; from Stevens, elaborately piped philosophical icing; from Roussel, the jack-in-a-box within a box, *ad infinitum*, and from early Auden, psychosexual enigma. To complicate matters further, it is frequently the case that what one engages with here is not an abandonment of control at all, but a simulacrum of abandon, constructed with great care by a writer whose repertoire includes an encyclopaedic knowledge of Modernism.

Ashbery's own bequests have been as dangerous. 'The Instruction Manual' from *Some Trees* has begotten a hundred progeny in books by Ron Padgett, Tom Veitch, Michael Brownstein, and other members of what I have called the second generation of the New York school.

As I sit looking out of a window of the building
I wish I did not have to write the instruction manual on the uses
 of a new metal.
I look down into the street and see people, each walking with an
 inner peace,
And envy them – they are so far away from me!
Not one of them has to worry about getting out this manual on
 schedule.
And, as my way is, I begin to dream, resting my elbows on the desk
 and leaning out of the window a little,
Of dim Guadalajara! City of rose-colored flowers!
City I wanted most to see, and most did not see, in Mexico!
But I fancy I see, under the press of having to write the
 instruction manual,
Your public square, city, with its elaborate little bandstand!

(14)

A scene unfolds in the mind, sprouting side streets and patios, incidents and speakers. The poem is descended parodically from the Romantic meditation, like Coleridge's 'Frost at Midnight', where the speaker is led on a mental voyage from which he returns and is set down at last, having gained in experience just as he might have done from a physical journey. This structure is paralleled by that of the reader, who is carried away into an extension of imaginative empathy and then returned to the normal world by the conclusion of the poem.

How limited, but how complete withal, has been our experience of
    Guadalajara!
We have seen young love, married love, and the love of an aged
    mother for her son.
We have heard the music, tasted the drinks, and looked at colored
    houses.
What more is there to do, except stay? And that we cannot do.
And as a last breeze freshens the top of the weathered old tower, I
                                      (turn my gaze
Back to the instruction manual which has made me dream of
    Guadalajara.

                                                            (18)

The openness of the Guadalajarans is a cartoon externalization of the
mind's own hospitality to creative play. The poem is also, as it
knows we well know, excruciatingly arch, the polar opposite of one
of Frank O'Hara's 'I do this, I do that' poems. Where O'Hara always
does, sees, says, makes connexions between, more things than one
might have thought possible in one day or one lyric, Ashbery opts
deliberately for an amiable, slow shamble. The reader, far from
racing to catch up with the poem's meanings, is always one step
ahead, beyond amazement at Ashbery's unerring banality. This is
one of two aspects of Ashbery's work that coincide with the poetry
of Kenneth Koch, the other being their shared fondness for the more
baroque verse-forms, pantoum or sestina. The mixture of lugubrious
elaboration in verse-form or the telling of a tale, together with a
cartoon-cum-Pop Art vividness of image is probably the nearest
thing to a New York 'house style' in poetry.

    Of the younger writers, Ron Padgett has become the master of this
kind of comic poetry that is besotted with the blindingly obvious, in
love with bathos and cliché, simple anarchy and punch-lines we see
coming a mile off. The memorial insights of *Great Balls of Fire* and
Toujours l'amour are well-represented by the following, one of 'Two
Vermont Sketches':

Autumn in the country. I am sitting on the lawn. My wife comes
up the road, hands full of beautiful leaves. As she goes by us and
into the house, she gives our son a bright red and green maple leaf.
He looks at it. 'Leaf,' I say. He looks at it. 'Isn't it pretty?' Delicate
spine glowing in green fading to yellow and burnt to deep red at

the edges, early spring to late autumn in a capsule. 'Isn't it pretty?'
He looks at it, raises it high over his head and smashes it into my
face.[23]

Padgett's decision to direct his considerable intellectual agility in the
service of an art of the cartoon and the garish may have been the
only available resolution of his particular encounter with the anxieties of poetic influence. These must operate, for any poet, whether or
not one accepts the most extensive theorization that these anxieties
have received, in the criticism of Harold Bloom. With the exception
of Auden, the young Ashbery's poetic 'parents' were safely dead
and buried by the mid-fifties, presences only through influential but
malleable text. And, as we have seen, the Auden to whom Ashbery
responded most strongly was the English Auden, buried at this
stage by his American reincarnation. Ron Padgett, like Joe Brainard,
Michael Brownstein, Jim Brodey and the rest of the younger New
Yorkers, started publishing in the early sixties when O'Hara was
very much alive and Ashbery's work was at a dramatically experimental stage. They were standing in the shadow of writers who
were personally friendly and at their most creative, a combination
both hypnotic and disabling. There is a telling poem by Ron Padgett
entitled, as so many of Frank O'Hara's lyrics had been, 'Poem', that
begins: 'Funny, I hear/Frank O'Hara's/voice tonight/in my head –
/e.g. when I/think in words/he's saying them/or his tone/is in
them./I'm glad/I heard him/when he was alive . . .'[24] To apply an
analogy explored forcefully by Hillis Miller (in 'The Critic As Host'),
who is here the host and who the parasite? Padgett's poem has the
direct rhetoric of sincerity, and such poetic tributes have helped
keep O'Hara's work alive beyond his physical death. But the experience Padgett describes is one that readers of his poetry would feel as
a constant pressure anyway, and the same is true of Ted Berrigan's
work. O'Hara is simply inescapable for that generation. To go all out
for a comic poetry as Padgett has done has meant committing himself to something hugely enjoyable that sidesteps confrontation with
the larger themes of experience and with poets to whose greater
abilities his work has openly capitulated. Padgett and Berrigan were
made as poets by their reading of and contact with Frank O'Hara. It
can't now be known – at least in Berrigan's case – whether an
alternative, perhaps more powerful poetry that they might have
written wasn't blighted out of existence by O'Hara's dominance.

It was otherwise with Ashbery. He absorbed Stevens' influence

through the non-hypnotic medium of course-work at Harvard.
Stevens gave him building-blocks: abstract nouns inside preposi-
tional phrases ('a day of general honesty') and the qualified assertion
('This is perhaps a day . . .') for example. Stevens also liked to situate
pathetic fallacies within diurnal imagery; the cool artificiality of that
would then be set against more wistful or in other ways emotional
tones. This technique Ashbery adopts wholesale:

> But as if evening found us young, still young,
>   Still walking in a present of our own.

> (Stevens, 'Martial Cadenza')[24]

> The summer demands and takes away too much,
> But night, the reserved, the reticent, gives more than it takes.

> (Ashbery, *SPCM* 2)

Ashbery's absorption of Stevens is not at all a capitulation, for the
influence enables the poems to extend themselves, rather than balk-
ing creativity or pushing the later poet's work down into minor
genres. In any case, these constructions which he found in Stevens
are often brownstone Americanizations of structures of language
that he would have discovered anyway amid the marbled columns
of Mallarmé, or other haunts of nineteenth-century Symbolism. This
double derivation renders the influence both more inescapable, and
less of a matter for anxiety. Padgett's work is immensely likeable,
and doomed to come out badly from this kind of comparative analysis, this reading with an axe to grind, by virtue in part of its own
modesty. His poetry stands in relation to Ashbery and O'Hara as the
Ashbery of 'The Instruction Manual' stood in relation to Romantic
instructors, Coleridge in structuration, Whitman in the line, Stevens
in colouring. Marjorie Perloff conjectures shrewdly that the poem
corresponds with such neatness to the neo-religious structure of the
instructional Romantic dream-meditation (as characterized by M. H.
Abrams in *Natural Supernaturalism*) that it constitutes a yawning
parody. The difference is that Ashbery can absorb and use his models, where Padgett is absorbed and used by his. That said, there came
a moment when Ashbery rejected violently the recycling of any
established genres, or traditional modes of poetic expression, seeking instead to sever his poetry almost entirely from the impetus

towards communication. That moment came with his next book, *The Tennis Court Oath*.

DREAMING OF AMERICA

After the publication of *Some Trees* Ashbery travelled to France on a Fulbright Scholarship, and found it 'very difficult to write in a foreign country without hearing American spoken around me'.[25] So prolific as a rule, he kept only 'Thoughts of a Young Girl' and the sestina 'Faust' from his first year abroad. Light, bright poems, they fail to lead the poet onward from either the successes or the limitations of his first collection. Other poems, 'Our Youth', '"How Much Longer Must I Inhabit the Divine Sepulcher ..."' and the menacingly beautiful 'White Roses' remain within the familiar constellation of influences – Auden, Stevens, Surrealism, Whitman – but are interestingly troubled, and refuse to content themselves with either an unproblematic model of referential poetry, or the equally unproblematic (though allegedly revolutionary) opposite of that, a plunge into the aleatory which produced the most experimental poems in the book. Composition of the first, more interesting group was terminated with 'Rain', written after a fairly unproductive year the poet spent in New York in 1957–8, beginning research for an aborted doctorate on the work of Raymond Roussel. Perhaps the strongest poem from that phase is also one of Ashbery's most widely-anthologized pieces, '"They Dream Only of America"';

> They dream only of America
> To be lost among the thirteen million pillars of grass:
> 'This honey is delicious
> *Though it burns the throat.'*
>
> And hiding from darkness in barns
> They can be grownups now
> And the murderer's ash tray is more easily –
> The lake a lilac cube.

(13)

That first stanza invokes a mysterious 'They', who dream, but in addition it has always seemed to me very like a dream, itself. By that

I do not mean that it is 'dreamlike', in the sense that the Dali sequence in Alfred Hitchcock's *Spellbound*, or the novels of Franz Kafka,
or the music of Ravel's *Gaspard de la nuit* have all been called dreamlike. None of them resembles a dream that I have ever had. To watch
the dream sequence endured by the Gregory Peck character in
Spellbound, where giant scissors cut through drapes painted with
eyes and Peck is harangued by a club proprietor whose face is
covered by white cloth, is to stand outside and observe an acutely
literary *representation* of dream. As in many 'dreamlike' artworks,
the intellectual framework is neo-Freudian, and we read the dream
for clues to a mystery; from the vantage of the psychoanalyst, not the
dreamer. By contrast, that sudden blaze into italics in the last line of
Ashbery's first stanza, destroying the whimsy of the line that pre-
cedes it with a surge of irrational anxiety, actually reads like a dream
feels from the inside (to me, anyway). I lay stress on this because
poems such as this one are often taken to be anti-referential, quite
rightly. But that is only half the story. A poem's disinclination to be
attached with ease to some theme or subject outside itself does not
preclude it from embodying certain experiences quite readily and
recognizably, but from a subjective angle. In other words, Ashbery is
interested in the intersubjective, the common overlap of 'private'
worlds. The most seemingly idiosyncratic or inmost corner of the
mind may be in truth a zone we can all recognize, whereas we have
not all been to Penshurst or Tintern Abbey or Appleton House, and
may be placing even more stress on the symbolic or emblematic (or
indeed non-referential) aspects of the poems of those places than we
realized.

It is the striation of anxiety, running through Ashbery's attempts
to build solid walls of poetic artifice that give the poem its force.
Who are 'they'? We do not know. Is the speaker one of 'them'? This
multiplication of instability renders ambiguous phrases that would
otherwise have made a kind of sense, such as the image of honey
burning the throat. As in an Auden poem such as 'Detective Story',
these enigmas will never be resolved at the level of narrative coherence. Instead, the poem seems to be structured at a subtle level by its
own verbal echoes and effects: *'burns'* in stanza one turns to *'barns'*
in stanza two, and the literary echo of Whitman's *Leaves of Grass* in
line two seems more important than any specifically geographical
allusion. As Veronica Forrest-Thomson argued, while using this
poem in the service of a polemic on behalf of artifice against realism:
'The phonetic solidarity of "The *lake* a *li lac* cube" asserts the domi-

nance of a formal order, its block-like resistance to empirical contexts.'[26] We cannot know whether the 'he' referred to twice in the third stanza is the same he, or whether he (or they) have anything to do with the they who dream only of America. In that sense, the poem may be viewed as a programmatically amnesiac collage of non-sequiturs, in a line of descent from Rimbaud. To revive a distinction used in previous chapters, however, the emphasis on internal connection weaves a network like a frame around deep space, an interlacing of possibly metaphysical *correspondances* that also look back to Baudelaire and Rimbaud:

> Now he cared only about signs.
> Was the cigar a sign?
> And what about the key?
> He went slowly into the bedroom.

The use of the jokily phallic cigar implies that we all know so much about *that* kind of sign that it can't really be a sign of anything. What can we trust as inadvertent self-exposure in a dream narrative if the dreamer has read a lot of Freud in his daytime life? Ashbery's ironies pre-empt the methods of psychoanalytic criticism exactly as James Schuyler's do, by building an awareness of them into the poetry's effects. (The problematic repercussions of this for deconstruction as an approach to modern poetry were explored in Chapter 1.) But this poem's playful slide into metonymic bric-a-brac, layered-space fragments of half-signs, is halted by a final outburst of emotion, related to the dream-line of stanza one. It is Ashbery's lyrical cry, to do with what life *feels* like, and not what puzzles and mysteries look like:

> 'I would not have broken my leg if I had not fallen
> Against the living room table. What is it to be back
> Beside the bed? There is nothing to do
> For our liberation, except wait in the horror of it.
>
> And I am lost without you.'

Although it is dealt with only rarely as a topic, a profound distrust of rationalization perfuses Ashbery's writing. The lines quoted give a perfectly rational account of an event in terms of cause and effect; falling-against-table-spells-broken-leg. Ironically, this statement, the

most straightforwardly coherent in the poem, has less to convey
than any other line – as the author well knows. Ashbery's tacit
suspicion, a Romantic *Empfindlichkeit* at root, finds fault with rationality for constructing explanatory narratives around events rather
than seeing into the life of things. Ashbery has written very few 'love
poems' as a separate genre, and so a poem such as the beautiful and
serene 'So Many Lives' (*A Wave*) happens only rarely: but being 'lost
without you' is what I am tempted to call his secret, constant theme.
Not that the final line of '"They Dream Only of America"' could
exactly be said to conclude with unambiguous *pathos*: its *ethos* of
programmatic dislocation is too unsettling, too insistent for that.
'Liberation' and 'horror' are so impeccably redolent of 1940s Existentialism as to make one wonder if this isn't at least to some extent a
parody of Left Bank angst, somewhat as 'The Instruction Manual'
may have been taking off the Romantic meditation, though more
solemn. Ashbery was, after all, in Paris around the time that *nouvelle
vague* films like Jean-Luc Godard's *Breathless* (1959) were first making waves.

     In an argument both too intricate and too heated to be susceptible
of adequate *précis* here, Veronica Forrest-Thomson suggests that, if
pushed far enough in the direction of conspicuous artifice, parody
can 'finally be made into something greater', the return of direct
emotion from the far side of art.[27] And so the Lady of Shalott had
passional as well as formal significance for Forrest-Thomson. Art for
her was a build-up of endlessly recessive mirrorings of experience,
whereby the artificial production of images would come to utterly
outweigh the poor chunk of life that had initially been put before the
mirror. Eventually the mirror would crack from side to side, but this
seeming calamity would come to signal a doorway to death and
Deep Space through which naked experience could step back into
the world (à la Cocteau's *Orphée*), with art now revealed as the ruse
of its occurrence. Thus it is that in an early poem Love could be 'put
to the test – the *grammatical* test', and still win every time.[28] Such a
summary does little justice to Forrest-Thomson's writing, but may
clarify our sense of what Ashbery, whose poetry she admired and
wrote about, is doing. The diverse and sometimes conflicting models
for poetic practice that she tried to wrench into working order –
Parisian structuralism, Pre-Raphaelite stylization, a witty
confessionalism influenced by Frank O'Hara – are often very close,
even in their greatest diversity, to Ashbery's tastes and interests, but
there are vital differences of approach. Forrest-Thomson was deter-

mined to theorize, that is to rationalize the creation of the poem as autotelic construct, while still being haunted by 'the quest for another human being', with all the un-cool, non-autotelic ties to a world of mess and passion and vulnerability outside the poem that completion of that quest implies.[29] If Ashbery resists theorization, that is not because of any prelapsarian faith in the possibility of unmediated experience, or the solidity of empirical reality: 'Just living won't do.' (W 34) He is suspicious of rational formulation in part because he is adept at constructing it, and gives proof that words never touch their intended target of non-verbal experience, be it the loved one or anything else. They skid off, proliferating meanings as they go, meanings that the poem can build into itself as a simulacrum of independence with a space in the centre which is the extra-linguistic reality words never can reach. It is as if Forrest-Thomson (and the whole Symbolist tradition, back into the nineteenth century) wanted the poem to be its own world, a carved ivory ball, in which the only spaces and intervals would be put there for aesthetic relief. It is Ashbery's perception that those intervals lead to the emptiness at the heart of the ball, an emptiness related to the world outside the artefact against whose inaccessibility its carving had been turned in self-defence. To repeat Mendelson's comment on the early poems of Auden: 'As soon as one stops looking for the key to a set of symbols, and recognizes that the poems focus on the self-enclosing patterns that bar their way to a subject in the world outside, their notorious obscurity begins to vanish.' That is to look at the world outside from the hollow centre of the ball, lamenting the inaccessibility of an outside subject, and investing attention in the leaves and vines and squirrels that make up the patterns in the carving. That is (intermittently) the Auden-Forrest-Thomson position. Ashbery moves effortlessly from inside to the outside and back, more wry and sceptical and disbelieving in the reliability of either art or love, but also more ready to be taken up by the accidentalism of either:

> And it ends up
> Nobody's, there is nothing for any of us
> Except that fretful vacillating around the central
> Question that brings us closer,
> For better and worse, for all this time.

> (W 34)

But that is the attitude of the poet's recent, most fully developed work. *The Tennis Court Oath* is not on such steady terms with 'the central question'. In the stronger poems, '"They Dream Only of America"' for example, Ashbery is more fearful. In the less successful and more experimental poems in the collection, 'Europe' or 'Idaho', he tries to pre-empt pain, and, for the only time in his writing, to get on top of it as an intellectual problem that, solved by art, would leave play as reward.

Those experimental poems have been so savagely mauled by critics that one's instinctive desire is to find them more interesting than they are; to think that if Harold Bloom dislikes them so intensely, there must be something in them. To Bloom the majority of poems in Ashbery's second collection are 'a fearful disaster', wherein 'a great mass of egregious disjunctiveness is accumulated to very little effect', offensive to 'the dismayed admirers of his earliest work', and appealing only to 'the rabblement of poetasters who proclaim themselves anti-academic while preaching in the academies, and who lack consciousness sufficient to feel the genuine (because necessary) heaviness of the poetic past's burden of richness'.[30] It is this last factor which is the real outrage, to the Yale professor. Ashbery's reputation as a poet has, for good or ill, been bound up with what Bloom has had to say: the one is the most esteemed poet and the other the best-known critic writing on America's East Coast. The Bloom factor, and the direct but vexed relationship between Ashbery and deconstruction that has developed through his encomiums, form the next context with which I want to deal.

Before moving on to Bloom, however, it is worth noting that Ashbery doesn't like *The Tennis Court Oath* much either, but some of the younger Language poets like parts of it exceedingly and have co-opted the 'French' Ashbery as poetic godfather to their own offspring. This early collection from 1962, popular with no-one in its entirety (including its author) still touches a nerve in the most intense current debates about poetics in and outside the academy, for deconstructionists and for the poetic avant-garde:

> I don't know if you've seen my book *The Tennis Court Oath*? It's the second one, and it's the one that most people have the most difficulty with, and I don't really blame them, because I was experimenting – I would just throw a few words that really didn't make any sense, I don't think. I have a long poem in that book called *Europe* which is not about Europe or about anything else

. . . Deconstruction is now a popular word; it's not what I would apply to my work, not in the accepted sense, but I was actually deconstructing my poetry in the sense of taking it apart, and the pieces were lying around without any coherent connection . . .[31]

If Ashbery can be taken at his word, this would then form a poetry with a different orientation to any discussed up to this point. A poem like 'Europe' would be neither innocent of self-criticism, nor knowingly braced to meet Freudian and deconstructive approaches as a poem by James Schuyler like 'The Dog Wants His Dinner' was shown to be, in Chapter 1. Instead the poem would have disintricated and laid bare all its internal workings, not unlike those 'high tech' buildings – the Centre Georges Pompidou would be an aptly Parisian example – whose pipes and stairs and rails are exposed on the outside.

Something like this must have gone into Ashbery's choice of title. *The Tennis Court Oath* refers to a picture by Louis David, whose Revolutionary figures have only been partially painted, and so remain nude in the sketch. As David Shapiro tells us, this nudity 'does not vitiate the very fully dressed nature of their smug classic gestures and posings, and the whole effect is thus a typical dreamlike embarrassment: To be caught with one's pants down, while initiating a great revolution with one's peers.'[32] Shapiro reads metaphysics into this, concluding not only that the painting is unfinished but that Time in Ashbery's view 'leaves us unfinished' (as well as polishing us off). Unfortunately for all these grand possibilities, what we actually get in the experimental pieces is a lot of lines like 'The sky hopes the vanilla bastard/Axle busted over fifth dimwit slump' (p. 52), a casual Surrealist pile-up of decontextualized bits and pieces that is partly responsible for the New York-poetry-by-the-yard turned out by magazines like *The World* or *Adventures In Poetry* during the Sixties and early Seventies.

Those magazines have been supplanted by the Language group, Bloom's 'rabblement of poetasters'. Their house has many mansions, very differently furnished. For now, it might be said that while the kind of scatter-gun effect I quote forms part of the armoury broken into by Charles Bernstein, by Craig Watson in a book like *After Calculus* and, alongside more considered techniques, in the often brilliant work of Diane Ward, it is only one among a large number of influences affecting Language poetry at its best (Ron Silliman, Steve Benson), and for that matter its weakest. The currently esteemed

Michael Palmer, who writes scrupulously 'European' poems, like a
mature student trying to rack up credits in the Paul Celan Summer
School, might in fact have benefited from attention to Ashbery's
'Europe' which whatever its deficiencies, is never slick.

Living in France 'a place where the language was not spoken', the
American Ashbery's attention was shifted away from discourse and
conversation towards an awareness of the single word.[33] This shift
was assisted not only by words, but by the example of music. The
poet 'used to go to the Domaine Musicale concerts in Paris regularly', and was particularly interested in the music of Webern's 'very
sparse works', alongside work by Luciano Berio and other modern
composers.[34]

> And I was tremendously moved by these isolated notes . . . you
> hear a note plucked on a violin and it seems as though you're
> hearing that note for the first time – he has the power to produce
> this atmosphere where everything takes on a heightened signifi-
> cance . . .[35]

It might be said that what Ashbery heard in Webern and tried to
reproduce in poetry was the equivalent in art of the aims and discoveries of phenomenology, from a perspective more like that of
Merleau-Ponty's writing, rather than Heidegger's essentialism or
the transcendental subjectivism of Husserl. The implications of such
a phenomenology for so-called ordinary life are explored in the
work of Ashbery's contemporary, the poet Robert Creeley. His work
has always shown an intense fidelity to the moment of experience, a
'constant concern' not with any idea of constancy, but with the
'sudden instance' of felt life. In the words of the Preface to *For Love*
(1962), 'I want the poem as close to this fact as I can bring it; or it,
me'.[36] Creeley's homing in on the single word through the brief line
are the visible embodiment of this attention. Ashbery may have
thought he was doing something like this, but his early sixties poetry
is actually more in consonance with the Parisian structuralism also
gaining impetus at this time, and in that place. Far from focussing
attention on the single word, poems such as 'Europe' treat words as
examples – of discourse, of genres, of literary codes. The opening of
'Idaho' is a case in point: 'During the past few months, Biff had
become quite a frequent visitor to Carol's apartment' (91) We can tell
at once that 'Biff' and 'Carol' are not going to be individuated and
characterized in depth, as they might in a realist novel. They are

types, Roy Lichtenstein cartoons. More accurately, the writing is a type, the type that generates that kind of sentence. And when the writing opts for a different strategy, it is often the related one of talking about the dismantling of discourse and genres and codes: 'You knew those square doctrines had – /Come apart . . . the paper lining had gotten/Unpinned, or unstuck' (55) The effect is not unlike a Pop-art painting where an aspect of comic book printing, the dot-matrix effect caused by the stippling of colour on grainy paper, is blown up to huge proportions by the size of the canvas. Everything deconstructs itself in a blast of coloured ironies.

ANXIETIES OF INFLUENCE

This must be the source of Harold Bloom's intense dislike of the book. To Bloom, all poetry is about poetry, and a poetry that does not consciously know this is still caught in its toils. Ashbery's early writing replicates those convictions (and may have helped form them). But his second collection is an exceedingly deliberate affair, cool (if not icy) over matters of procedure, whereas Bloom's model is fundamentally heated, conflictual: the formation of poetic style is a struggle for authority among competing titans. These titans are generally dead, and famous: Milton, Wordsworth, Whitman, Stevens. Bloom's local insights startle frequently, but the names do not: he is stern in defence of the canon. For reasons never made entirely clear in his work to date, Bloom believes that our time is somehow smaller than other periods of history – 'belated' is his favourite term both for our time, and for the unpropitious conditions set to daunt the neophyte in poetry. The pressure of the past grows ever greater, the likelihood of an emerging voice strong enough for the struggle, ever less. For some years now John Ashbery's has seemed to Bloom to be the last strong voice. Indeed, Bloom has 'followed' Ashbery with a persistence that no critic ever showed to Eliot, or Auden, or Stevens. As a result, the poetry is in some minds not to be separated from the vogue for deconstruction: Ashbery's rise to fame coincides in time with the rise of deconstruction in the academy.

However, Bloom's writing in the late seventies and eighties surfaced in dialogue, rather than in tandem, with that of the 'boa-deconstructors' Derrida and de Man.[37] Curiously, Bloom is a more conservative reader of Ashbery than he is of Emerson or Elizabeth Bishop. His fusion of pessimism in the face of a culture alleged to be in decline, and a belief that when the rare new voice does emerge, the monumental order of the past will be shifted at once and in its entirety, shows a more harmonious convergence with Eliot's essay 'Tradition and the Individual Talent' (1919) than Bloom would ever wish to concede publicly. In interview, he has described the atmosphere at Yale in the late fifties as 'an Anglo-Catholic nightmare':

> Everyone was on their knees to Mr. T. S. Eliot and, no matter what you read or how you taught it or how you wrote, you were always supposed to gravely incline the head and genuflect to the spirit of Mr Thomas Stearns Eliot, God's vicar upon earth, the true custodian of Western tradition.[38]

In the previous chapter I argued that the massiveness of Eliot's reputation was as unscaleable a height for the emerging avant-garde of this time as I am now saying was the case for Bloom in the academy. I suggested that this is part of the motivation for the filial interest in Pound shown by Olson, Creeley, Ginsberg, Wieners et al. Here was a way to make manageable and useable techniques and atmospheres deriving at least as much from Eliot, but without encountering Eliot's unassailability, together with his more awkwardly intimidating involvements: religion (the numinous touches in Pound are vague and charming), or the influence of Baudelaire and continental Symbolism, with which American poets outside the East Coast do not tend to feel comfortable. It would be glib to turn Bloom's own methods, the de/reconstruction of a particular poet's or poem's family romance (in Freud's phrase), onto his own work. Glib, at any rate, to offer that as the whole story: but there is in Bloom's studied aversion from Eliot, and his respect for the more homely mythologist Northrop Frye, a recognition of Eliot as begetter that has to show more of a shield than a greeting for Bloom's own identity to emerge freely. Frye was Bloom's Pound. He replaced the Anglo-Catholic nightmare with the doctrines of the United Church of Canada, what *The Waste Land* calls the awful daring of a moment's surrender to belief with an 'Inner Light' modification of seventeenth-century Protestantism. As Imre Salusinszky points out, Fryean phrases about 'autonomous imagination' or Romanticism as 'displaced Protestantism' recur in Bloom's first books. Eliot, of course, had little interest in the English Romantics, whereas Bloom has been along with Geoffrey Hartman the most important agent in their retrieval as dominant figures. And there is also the vital factor of Bloom's

Jewishness, so intensely productive an identification for him: he is the first American critic to make Jewishness the central fact of his self-presentation on the page. I still lay stress on Bloom's swerve away from Eliot, because I believe it to be a distorting factor in his writing on John Ashbery. It cuts him off from three important factors in Ashbery's work: the relationship between his poetry and Eliot's, the whole procedural influence on Ashbery of French poetry from Baudelaire to Surrealism, and most surprisingly, Ashbery's wit. I shall deal with these in reverse order.

Harold Bloom's theorizing of poetic influence is without doubt the most persuasive model for an understanding of its subject to have emerged in the last thirty years. Reading structuralist and post-structuralist theory one's repeated sensation is that the work in hand might usefully apply to the novel (Barthes, Eagleton, Sollers, Genette), or to examples of discourses which, often unconsciously, use literary procedures without being necessarily artistic (Faucault, Lacan, Derrida). But for the student or other reader whose main intellectual interest lies in poetry, there can arise a feeling of dissatisfaction that all this theory can only be applied by an effort of analogy, or contiguously, to specific poems. This is particularly true when, as in my case, the reader of theory maintains a recalcitrant perception of poetic language as in certain identifiable ways separate from, even antagonistic to, customary language. It is possible to ground that position in a reading of modern, recent and contemporary poetry without tumbling unselfconsciously into a belated revival of Russian Formalism. The reading of Baudelaire's 'Les Chats' proffered by Jakobson and Lévi-Strauss may indeed seem naive today in its aversion from all historicization, and in the idealism with which it attempts to cover its topic entirely. But there is a meticulousness in close reading at work in that essay which is apt for the impacted, patterned intensities of the lyric poem, and which is simply not there in Barthes or Foucault. Meanwhile the New Criticism could only answer these omissions within the terms of its time, and seems to us now to oscillate between a too-simple account of the autonomous imagination – innocent of theory – and an excessive moralizing in the train of F. R. Leavis, whose hypnotic tones have more to do with a specific cultural elitism than with close textual analysis. So it is that one might turn to deconstruction.

Hartman and Hillis Miller both offer powerful close readings of particular texts, but with magnificent exceptions – 'The Voice of the Shuttle' and 'The Critic As Host' respectively – their essays tend not

to offer a theorization of poetry which is, so to speak, large enough
to be portable – a theory of poetry one could try out with many other
poems than those under debate. And of all these writer/teachers,
Paul de Man was most the essayist. The sight of his own pieces, laid
out in chronological order as *The Rhetoric of Romanticism* seemed to
him 'a somewhat melancholy spectacle'; 'coherence *within* each essay is not matched by a corresponding coherence *between* them . . .
Rather it seems that they always start again from scratch and that
their conclusions fail to add up to anything.'[39] De Man's last writings
on aesthetic ideology promise a theorization of larger matters, but
they remain fragmented by his death as well as by these ingrained
factors of temperament and method. Within literary theory, only
Bloom has a theory of poetry.

To many, the very conception of a theory of poetry is ahistorical,
and therefore unreal. Harold Bloom's thesis, laid down first in *The
Anxiety of Influence* (1973) and developed in a series of books from *A
Map of Misreading* (1975) to *Agon* (1982), is not ahistorical, but historical in a special sense. It prioritizes poetic history as an arena of
combat that is creative and dignifying, in relation to the wider but
darker mass of History. Certain essays by Bloom are sharply historical in the usual sense, for example 'Free and Broken Tablets: The
Cultural Prospects of American Jewry' in *Agon*, but as a rule he
shows a dual sense of history, neither aspect of which engenders
historical criticism. First there is Bloom's personal narrative: he is
'the son of a New York garment worker, who was an unwilling
member of the International Ladies Garment Workers' Union, which
he always despised'. In consequence Bloom displays a lucid con-
tempt for American 'Marxist' critics whose subversions would never,
if the crunch came, extend from the page into the street, and whose
rhetoric is merely a displacement of middle-class guilt at their own
easy rise through a system of privilege they have no real wish to
dismantle. The spectacle of university radicalism is understood by
Bloom to be 'the high bourgeoisie being unable to stand its status as
the high bourgeoisie, while continuing to enjoy it in every possible
respect'. The urgency of Bloom's theory of poetry does stem in part
from his personal knowledge of a full-time absorption in poetry
being a hard-won freedom, about whose privileging of introspection
and individualism one ought to be neither ashamed nor deluded.
But what about the critic's alleged responsibility towards the social?
'Forget it; it is not your function; you deal with a solitary pleasure
which it is immensely difficult to impart usefully to others.'[40] This

pugnacity comes from the working-class, and Jewish, understanding that one must always be in readiness to defend what can always be taken away. Bloom's is a self-made man's theory of the poet as a self-made man, or at least a would-be self-made man burdened by anxieties of origin.

The keynote is personal struggle: 'Battle between strong equals, father and son as mighty opposites, Laius and Oedipus at the crossroads; only this is my subject here, though some of the fathers, as will be seen, are composite figures . . . my concern is only with *the poet in a poet*, or the aboriginal poetic self.' This doubleness is typical: just as the unique self is stressed, the forging (in two senses) of that self comes under scrutiny. 'Poets, who congenitally lie about so many matters, *never* tell the truth about poetic influence.' Thus it is that Milton had to struggle with Spenser, ending up 'formed and malformed' in the process.[41] Tennyson struggled with the aestheticism of Keats and the radicalism of Shelley, absorbing (and thus perpetuating) the first, while trumping both with his marmoreally thanatropic lusciousness. Hardy has to argue against Shelley, his 'Darkling Thrush' questioning the soaring skylark. Wordsworth's line twines around, draws sustenance from, supplants and yet perpetuates Milton's line. And so on. Some of these examples are drawn from Bloom, and some are my own. Pedagogically, the usefulness of Bloom's model is its immediate applicability. It is that rare thing, a piece of literary theory which works in practice, that is, which can lead a modified but undiminished life outside the experience of reading the text in which it was articulated. The model has complicated variants. Sometimes the precursor is so strong as to disable later writing; witness the long shadow cast by Shakespeare over the possibilities for verse drama. And at times the ephebe can wring a submission from the precursor in round one: Shakespeare vs. Marlowe. Most readers of Bloom have been impressed but unconvinced by the rhetorical subdivision of the anxiety of influence into *clinamen, tessera, kenosis, daemonization, askesis* and *apophrades*. They tend to turn into each other. The force of his case lies in its application of Freudian psychodrama to the dynamics of poetic influence.

The other, irrefutable contribution Bloom has to offer lies in his ability to blow the dust off the canon. This he does not so much by close as by empathetic reading: all his pieces on Whitman and Emerson fall into this category, particularly his moving account of Whitman's 'As I Ebb'd with the Ocean of Life' in *A Map of Misreading*, and the wonderful and outrageously partisan essay on Emerson's

philosophy as 'The American Religion', collected in *Agon*. Bloom is
(by his own admission) a comic critic, just as de Man was a tragic
one. Bloom's gloom, a prophetic apprehension of the immanence of
catastrophe and the shoddiness of culture, seems to belong with
equal profundity to the experience of Judaism and an engagement
with Eliot, a combination as potent as it is unrepeatable. Yet the
tendency of his criticism is always towards redemption of the material in hand, an unsealing of poems entombed by familiarity and
academic platitude, in the service of a fiercely judgmental but, in the
end, liberating criticism. Reading de Man, one feels sucked into a
vortex, as his refusal to be seduced by the consolations of metaphysics or any kind of faith gnaws with rigorous nihilism at all ties of
sense, of connectedness, of any but the most mournful pleasure,
leaving him alone at last in the pure zone of existential darkness.

And of course there is something alluring in that refusal to be
seduced, something beckoning in that aloneness. De Man detected
exactly these paradoxes in the self-presentation and influence of T. S.
Eliot. Particularly in the light of revelations concerning de Man's
collaborationist past, his vignette of Eliot looks increasingly like a
self-portrait:

> The perfect embodiment of the New Criticism remains, in many
> respects, the personality and the ideology of T. S. Eliot, a combina-
> tion of original talent, traditional learning, verbal wit and moral
> earnestness, an Anglo-American blend of intellectual gentility not
> so repressed as not to afford tantalizing glimpses of darker psy-
> chic and political depths, but without breaking the surface of an
> ambivalent decorum that has its own complacencies and seduc-
> tions. The normative principles of such a literary ambiance are
> cultural and ideological rather than theoretical, oriented towards
> the integrity of a social and historical self rather than towards the
> impersonal consistency that theory requires.[42]

But of course (to paraphrase the ambivalences of Eliot's 1919 essay)
only those who have personality know what it means to want to
escape such things, and those whose cultural ambience once con-
doned a lack of integrity in 'the social and historical self' might have
private cause to be especially rigorous in the pursuit of a cloaking
impersonality. A distinctively Romantic constellation of anxiety, solitude and mystique ought to be visible, twinkling through the sable
rhetoric adopted by Eliot and by de Man. Bloom is more overtly,
more honestly Romantic:

Reading, writing, teaching, being taught: the experience of literature is the experience of an isolate and solipsizing glory . . . It is the
greatest and most superb of narcissistic self-indulgences: *and why
should it not be?* . . . It restitutes our wounded narcissism . . . It is a
solitary and inward joy. It is an overwhelming joy. It is indeed a
gnosticizing joy. It surely is our most authentic experience of
poetry. It is down to the person alone. That is what Dickinson's
poetry is all about, which is why it is so superb and honest. It's a
solitary transport, which in the end we desperately try to communicate to others. But we can no more communicate it to others than
we can communicate our love for others to them.[43]

This is all rather ironic, given that out of all the theorists cited here it
is Harold Bloom whose work communicates most straightforwardly
and immediately. However, Paul de Man does argue with some
persuasiveness that the struggle of titans that Bloom paints as a
history of poetry is at bottom a psychodrama of the single mind,
facing the otherness of the silent page:

> We can forget about the temporal scheme and about the pathos of
> the oedipal son; underneath, the book (*Anxiety of Influence*) deals
> with the difficulty or, rather, the impossibility of reading and, by
> inference, with the indeterminacy of literary meaning. If we are
> willing to set aside the trappings of psychology, Bloom's essay has
> much to say on the encounter between latecomer and precursor as
> a displaced version of the paradigmatic encounter between reader
> and text.[44]

Bloom frequently writes of poetry as 'the lie against time', and his
picturing of history is really a sense of time, an anxiety born of
mortality. The 'scheme' of which de Man speaks in this review can
so readily be shifted around, leading for example to what de Man
calls the 'surrealistic' perception by Bloom of Wordsworth's having
influenced Milton. De Man's scepticism is, as usual, instructive, and
it would divert this discussion from Ashbery's contexts to build up
the objections that might be raised to it. Suffice it to say that Bloom
has a double sense of history: the first is his own self-perception and
sense of origins, bearing on but only occasionally written into his
criticism. His second understanding of history is a literary history
only, and even that may be seen as subjected to a deconstruction
that exposes it as either a solipsistic and Romantic 'glory', and/or
a characteristically Western flight from Time. In this it coincides

exactly with John Ashbery's sense of history. There is a personal narrative, not excluded from, but certainly not foregrounded in, the poems.

There is also Ashbery's delight in constructing 'the other tradition', to use a phrase drawn from *Three Poems* that was also the title of the first poem in *Houseboat Days*, and more recently of his Charles Eliot Norton lectures at Harvard. Ashbery likes to draw attention to lost Modernists such as the English novelist Mary Butts, the once popular poet, Nicholas Moore, neglected American poets such as David Schubert, and from a slightly earlier generation John Wheelwright. This is done partly in order to conjure what looks like a more friendly but also more Surrealistic gallery of literary aunts and uncles than cultivators of the family tree, such as Bloom, tend to offer. Ashbery speaks and writes more enthusiastically about Schubert or Wheelwright than he does about virtually any major poet. Yet neither I, nor any reader I have spoken to, can detect any trace of their influence on his work; meanwhile the influence of Whitman, Stevens, Auden, Rilke and Surrealism is ubiquitous. Bloom's model of an anxiety of influence is straightforwardly helpful here, in showing how the necessary engagement with a precursor involves swerving away, as well as confrontation: in this case, avuncular celebration of minor figures in preference to a more vexed relationship with major ones. And, ultimately, Ashbery would agree that all of this, whether it be subscribing to a republication of Nicholas Moore, or teaching 'creative writing' in Brooklyn, or remembering getting excited about Schubert's *Initial A*, or writing 'Forties Flick', is all an indulgent and vital flight against time:

> As you find you had never left off laughing at death,
> The background, dark vine at the edge of the porch.

> (*SPCM* 5)

HEANEY WAVES THE BIG STICK

An anecdote. Some years ago I helped organize a visit to the University of Liverpool by the poet Seamus Heaney. His lecture, published afterwards in pamphlet form as *The Making of a Music*, concerned the nature of poetic influence, and the dominance within nineteenth- and twentieth-century poetry of the Wordworthian and the Yeatsian strain.[45] Unsurprisingly, Heaney presented his own poetry as emerging from a dialectical negotiation between the two. This was not precisely a Bloomian account of poetic lines of descent, for to Bloom poets are never candid about these matters; but it was squarely on the topic of poetic influence, imaged as a passing of skills from fathers to sons who must wrestle with, as well as listen to, their begettors. With a characteristic generosity Heaney agreed that on the day following the lecture, he would be available in a seminar room for an *ad hoc* question and answer session with students. On that occasion he talked at length about the poetic line, in Wordsworth's case a steady walker's line, built for negotiation of long stretches of blank verse, in Yeats' case a more tautly equestrian measure. Heaney used the word 'masculine' to characterize both, contrasted with the 'feminine' line of Mallarmé in particular, and French Symbolism in general. In Heaney's vocal delivery, the last syllable of 'masculine' and 'feminine' rhymed emphatically with 'line'. It is relevant to note that the poet had hurt his foot, and managed his own walker's line only with the aid of a stick. With whatever mixture of conscious and unconscious motivation and humour he would, on using the word 'mascu*line*', jerk his cane proudly into the air. On mentioning the feminine line of the Frenchman Mallarmé, his prop would droop coyly to the floor.

There is something in this. Bloom's model for poetic begetting is also 'mascu*line*', quite rigidly so. ('Battle between strong equals, father and son as mighty opposites, Laius and Oedipus at the crossroads; only this is my subject here . . .') Women are excluded, with the token exception of Emily Dickinson. Neither a Jocasta, nor mother in the main to modern poetesses, she possesses in Bloom's eyes that 'solipsizing glory' that grants poets potent pens. Bloom is also resistant to any *school* of writing, any collaborative practice. His poet is a proud solitary. Ironically, the poets about whom Harold Bloom has written most regularly, from Whitman through to Hart Crane and Ashbery, do not fit the heterosexual mould unequivocally. A relatively recent essay by Bloom on 'Whitman's Image of Voice' (in *Agon*) draws attention away from homoerotic desires and attachments, focussing instead on that most solipsizing glory, masturbation. There are aspects of the sensibility operative among his prized poets which Bloom has neglected to investigate beyond the Freudian suggestion of narcissism in a creative aspect. Meanwhile, the fear of homosexual taint among heterosexual male poets is strong in a culture which still schools its boy-children to believe that writing

poems is for sissies (as opposed to playing rugby or American foot-
ball, with the ample opportunities they afford to knead and be
kneaded by male muscle). The modern cliché of the Poet as Maker,
artisan of words, that runs from Pound and Bunting through to
Heaney and Hughes, combines strategies for dealing with two anxieties. The first is that writing poems could be thought effete in a
sexualized sense; the second is the related fear that to write poems is
not to be at *work*, in the usual male provinces. We hear often about
the 'granite' quiddities in Hughes, the 'sinew' of Heaney's verse.
There are specific historical threads that have led to this knot of
anxieties, beyond the general fear of homosexuality prevalent in
society, so inflamed at the time of writing by the Aids crisis.

I would suggest that the critical moment, even after the lapse of a
century, is the trial of Oscar Wilde. Its identification of the Homosexual with the Artist still resonates. The fear of being thought one-
of-them had an immediate part to play in the 'cult of beer and
Sussex, of walking and simplicity' that Cyril Connolly so scorned in
the Georgian poets.[46] Of course other forces were at work in the
twenty-year flight from aestheticism that followed Wilde's trial, but
homophobia has been underrated as a factor in the self-imaging of
the artist at this time. It is responsible, for example, for the sometimes hysterical behaviour of the so-called 'Men of 1914'. T. E. Hulme
got acquainted with Wyndham Lewis by way of a fistfight that left
Lewis happy, but hanging upside down from a set of railings. Hulme
possessed knuckledusters sculpted for him by Henri Gaudier-Brzeska:
the artist as maker, with a vengeance. Some psychosexual ambivalence in the determinedly macho figure of Hemingway has been
documented. Anxiety about sexuality and gender may have been
particularly strong among English poets, because the stereotyping of
the Lake Poets as ecstatic Nature-lovers, together with the shrillness
of Shelley and the aestheticism of Keats, had already compromised
the social normality of the Poet before first Swinburne and then
Arthur Symons' 1890s Decadents dished it entirely. T. S. Eliot, of
course, never got into fistfights: but then Eliot drew directly on *fin de
siècle* Dandyism, and had been corrupted by exposure to the femi-
nine Frenchness of Baudelaire and Mallarmé.

The influence of Symbolist and 1890s aesthetic debates on poetry
up to and including the present day is still significantly underrated:
the important recent studies of Baudelaire, Symons, Wilde and Eliot
have all been biographies, critical only in a secondary way. To build
up a detailed argument here would be relevant to the modes of self-

figuration in Ashbery's poetry, but would digress in other respects. Some brief remarks must suffice. That unitary term 'The Nineties' disguises both a series and a juxtaposition of differing attitudes. This may seem not to be the case initially because the nineties was indeed the first decade to see itself as a distinct period, at the time. It is the model for the building blocks in a cultural understanding of the twentieth century. The Roaring Twenties or the Swinging Sixties are catch-phrases of cultural summary initiated by the self-conscious reflections of the Beardsley Period. But the trial of Oscar Wilde in 1895 drives a wedge down the centre of the decade. Prior to that moment, the posturings of the Decadents were tolerable eccentricities, fodder for the cartoonists of *Punch*, both defused and rendered immune to attack by the *cordon sanitaire* of class. After the trial, the artist was exiled to the social periphery: this was the queer birth of the English *avant-garde*, the artist as cryptic, deviant, misunderstood, comparable to the criminal and the anarchist. Consider for example the new Preface to Arthur Symons' collection *Silhouettes* (1896) with its deliberate echoes of phrases from *The Picture of Dorian Gray* quoted against Wilde at his trial. Even by Victorian standards, a right-wing jingoism was also particularly strong in the nineties, and the verdict of 'Guilty' at the Old Bailey allowed the discharge of sentiments that had been waiting for an outlet. Even so, a judgment such as this from the *National Observer* surprises, not only by its ferocity, but by the neatness with which it allows a whole series of identifications to interlock in condemnation of the artist. Sexual deviance, social marginality and semantic obscurity are superimposed with a vigour and clarity that anticipate Dr Goebbels.

> There is not a man or woman in the English-speaking world possessed of the treasure of a wholesome mind who is not under a deep debt of gratitude to the Marquess of Queensberry for destroying the High Priest of the Decadents. The obscene imposter . . . has been exposed, and that thoroughly at last. But to the exposure there must be legal and social sequels. There must be another trial at the Old Bailey, or a coroner's inquest – the latter for choice; and of the Decadents, of their hideous conceptions of the meaning of Art, of their worse than Eleusinian mysteries, there must be an absolute end.[47]

The art of the Modernists, Eliot, Joyce and Lewis would be founded in many ways on the progressive tendencies in the later nineteenth century – Symbolism in Eliot's case, a Paterian aesthetic in Joyce's, both grounded in the cult of the moment – but their own self-image as artists had to swerve away from anything interpretable as Bohemian in a Wildean way. Joyce and Eliot condemned Romanticism and cultivated impersonality: Lewis became 'the Tyro' and 'the Enemy', but an outrageously macho, hetero Tyro. I am not arguing the wholesale containment of Modernism by the Wilde case, merely suggesting that the shock-waves from his trial may well have carried further, and muddied the waters for longer, than has generally been argued.

We have seen therefore how homosexuality, wit and artistic obscurity could come to be associated through the maltreatment of Wilde by the establishment. These are elements which homosexual writers of this century have built into their own art and self-imaging, sometimes in self-doubt or laceration, more often constructively or ironically ('camp'). Here is Charlie Shively, talking about the homosexual, and black, poet Steve Jonas, who died in 1970 but who was of the same generation as the New York Poets:

> Jonas mastered and everywhere displayed a gay sensibility sometimes called 'camp', although that overused term hardly describes more than a few artifices. Gay 'camp' might be closer to jazz (especially a jazz rendition of some conventional song like 'Autumn Leaves') where new values (quite contrary values) subvert the melody. Gay people have done that so often – teasing, caressing their sexuality against the grain of society.[46]

The negro, like the homosexual, is consigned to the margins of society's self-image, and his/her art is often in consequence a cleansing subversion, a straightfaced mockery where the joke may be coded, *sub rosa*, for the benefit of those made vulnerable by living on the edge. So it is that the paradigmatic image of acceptable all-American maleness for the fifties, Frank Sinatra, is mocked, subverted, ingested and used by Frank O'Hara and by Miles Davis, respectively the great homosexual and black artists of that time. O'Hara takes the literal *image* of Sinatra, the alternately yearning and cynical figure behind a highball on a Manhattan bar-stool, tie loosened, ashtray slowly filling. Davis takes the tunes Sinatra made popular, *I Thought About You, Old Devil Moon*, and inverts and parodies and complicates them, perfecting them to destruction through 'quite contrary values', to pick up Shively's phrase. There is a very obvious overlap of secret codes between the worlds of gay nightlife, black jazzmen, white hipsters and drug-related crime encrypted, with different emphases, by a number of key fifties texts: William Burroughs' *The Naked Lunch* (1959), John Wieners' *The Hotel Wentley Poems* (1958), (praised by O'Hara), and a once celebrated play by Jack Gelber, *The Connection*, first staged by New York's Living Theater in 1959. The burgeoning influence of Jean Genet on New York gay writing at this time is also pertinent.

On the face of it, this has virtually nothing to do with John Ashbery. His origins, education and professional involvements have all been straightforwardly and successfully middle-class. His interests on or off the page are a world away from the kind of life that, say, Steve Jonas or William Burroughs lived. He doesn't even care for jazz much. Nor are there any vivid self-portraits in his poetry, unlike O'Hara's, at least not consistently. He is as much to be identified with Daffy Duck as Parmigianino. Nor is he a 'gay poet': to an even greater extent than Auden's, the pronouns of his poetry are eminently transferable, in recognition and acceptance of whatever experience a reader might breathe into the writing so as to help bring it to life. Perhaps more than any other modern poet, he stretches the perimeter of what the poem might include in terms of empathy as wide as may be achieved before it flies apart entirely. Curious to follow lines of connexion, the reader enters the poem to have its doors close behind him or her. A poem by Ashbery will often adopt a bland expression, as if it made perfect sense *to itself* and wanted very badly to get on with the reader: so what's the problem? ('Paradoxes and Oxymorons' from *Shadow Train* does this brilliantly). He is the master of the loose embrace. However, I want to suggest that despite the bourgeois social matrix of his writing, and alongside its emotional and procedural attributes of selflessness, deep inside the largeness of imagination inhabiting great poems like 'Pyrography' and 'A Wave', there does exist a repertoire of attitudes and devices which, while not belonging exclusively to gay writers, does have to do with seeing from the edge of things where the excluded go. The use of this repertoire of devices is quiet, but crucial. It cannot be squared with Bloom's account of the canon, or with Seamus Heaney's account of the proper influences in nineteenth and twentieth century poetry. In a moment I will examine Ashbery's poem 'Wet Casements', and Bloom's instructive misreading of it. But there is one last factor to be cited in relation to the kinds of wit, irony, surrealism and erotic sensibility present in the poetry. It is Ashbery's interest in collaboration.

COLLABORATION AND ITS SUB-TEXT

The amount of collaborative work done by the New York poets is large. In addition to joint projects with painters, such as the *Stones* lithographs done with Larry Rivers, O'Hara was the co-author of a number of poems: between 1960 and 1962, he wrote a series of collaborations with Bill Berkson, some of which are in *The Collected Poems* and some assembled thereafter as *Hymns of St. Bridget* (1974). James Schuyler collaborated with novelist and composer Paul Bowles to produce 'A Picnic Cantata', and with John Ashbery on a novel, *A Nest of Ninnies* (1969). Ashbery's other collaborative work includes the *Vermont Notebook* with its facing-page illustrations by Joe Brainard, who had also worked with O'Hara on poem-cartoons. It is a practice carried on by other 'second generation' New Yorkers: Ron Padgett, for example, has collaborated with Tom Veitch to produce the anarchic novel *Antlers in the Treetops* (1973) with artist Jim Dine, and with Ted Berrigan and Joe Brainard once again on *Bean Spasms* (1967) The list could go on.

As early as 1961, Kenneth Koch edited an issue of *Locus Solus* entirely on collaborations. The usual editorial board of *Locus Solus* consisted of Koch, Ashbery, Schuyler and Harry Matthews, (who might best be thought of as a New York poet who usually writes novels). O'Hara was among the contributors. What is surprising is not only the sheer quantity of collaborative work but the degree to which the practice of collaborative writing is theorized and historicized with scholarly detail. If this was a côterie practice, it was one that received an immense amount of thought and labour to ready it for public consumption. Koch includes commentary on Chinese, Japanese, Troubadour, Metaphysical, Cavalier, Surrealist, modern Australian and Burroughsian cut-up collaborations together with contemporary New York efforts, most baroque of which is a poem by himself and Ashbery entitled 'Crone Rhapsody', written according to the following formal requirements: 'that every line contain the name of a flower, a tree, a fruit, a game, and a famous old lady, as well as the word *bathtub*; furthermore, the poem is a sestina and all the end-words are pieces of office-furniture.' (This catalogue of constrictions engenders vignettes of surprising elegance: 'The maple gladioli watched Emily Post playing May I? in the persimmon bathtub with the fan.') The fanfare to the collection, 'To a Waterfowl' is a concatenation of sound bites from the Western lyric tradition, 'by John Ashbery':

> Go, lovely rose,
> This is no country for old men. The young
> Midwinter spring is its own season
> And a few lilies blow. They that have power to hurt,
> and will do none.[49]

Sardonic as this pillaging of Waller, Yeats, Eliot and Shakespeare may be, its facetiousness doesn't devalue one serious implication: that a collaboration can be not only the work of two writers, but the contestation and collaboration of any number of different writings, set in motion but not controlled by a single writer. Here (1961) Ashbery was working in proximity to the 'cut-ups' of Burroughs and Gysin, developed in Paris, and structuralist analyses of what would become taught in the universities as intertextuality. At this stage too Ashbery was translating Surrealist poetry, translation being another form of literary collaboration, including texts such as *L'Immaculée Conception* (1930) itself an example of co-authorship between André Breton and Paul Eluard. In short, collaboration has been a vital factor in Ashbery's tastes in poetry, his own writing, and his literary milieu.

It may be worth sketching in some of the qualities that literary collaborations have tended to share, so as to be able to place more exactly the fascination and the functions of this practice for Ashbery. I believe its implications to be absolutely central to his work, yet they subvert not only Bloom's version of the canon, but all models of an *integrity* of writing.

Collaboration in poetry and the novel has become a somewhat marginal activity, which, however paradoxically, is why writers like Ashbery who are attracted to the margins in other respects have been interested in trying it. The situation was very different earlier in the century, for example when Joseph Conrad and Ford Madox Ford sat down to collaborate on their shared productions *The Inheritors*

(1901), *Romance* (1903) and a novella, *The Nature of a Crime* (1924). None of those books did particularly well, and conditions attaching to the collaboration were unpropitious from the start. Ford was later to recall that H. G. Wells journeyed seven miles by bicycle solely to dissuade him from working with Conrad. Yet the reservations felt by Wells (and Henry James) are no less strong than some of the doubts experienced by the two collaborators before, during and after collaboration. In the Preface to the first book edition of *The Nature of a Crime*, Ford called it a 'dark, blind spot on the brain', and claimed not to remember writing it.[50] He called *The Inheritors* 'a thin collaboration with no plot in particular', and referred in his *Personal Remembrance* of Conrad to its 'juvenile prose'.[51] Conrad was hardly more sanguine at the outset. He would rather have worked with Edward Garnett. 'Why didn't you come?' he wrote. 'I expected you and fate has sent Hueffer. Let this be written on my tombstone.'[52] Why, then, did Conrad and Ford (or Hueffer, as he was then) launch into a mode of authorship that seemed so unpropitious, not once but three times? There are a number of reasons, ranging from Hueffer's difficulties in finding a publisher for his solo ventures, to the fact that Hueffer was half-German, Conrad Polish, and both influenced by Flaubert and Maupassant at a time when to the British everything continental spelled moral decay. But these are exactly the sort of reasons that would surely have been cancelled out by the bad notices their efforts received from the start. In collaborating, they were persevering in a practice that they found awkward (work on *Romance* broke down frequently), which their friends had advised against, which the public resisted, and this at a time when both novelists were hard up.

It is worth recalling that collaborations were fairly common at this time, at least in prose. Walter Besant and James Rice had a dozen successes in the genre. Kipling had collaborated with Wolcott Balestier on *The Naulakha* (1892), and before them Robert Louis Stevenson and Lloyd Osbourne had constructed *The Wrong Box* (1889). There is therefore a sense in which, at the turn of this century, an up-and-coming novelist like Ford might have wanted to take on collaboration as he took on the tale of adventure or the domestic drama, to show that he could do it. To undertake this kind of writing was a sign of professionalism, not the cultivated eccentricity it might seem now. That said, it is significant that the two collaborators were Polish and part-German in origin, outsiders by virtue of their foreignness. The longstanding canonization of Conrad and Henry James obscures their status at the time as writer's writers: Conrad didn't sell, and the late fictions of Henry James were perceived to have abandoned conventional intelligibility for a retreat into convolution and solipsism. The group that gathered geographically within cycling distance of the Master were, however marked by diffidence and depression, the avant-garde of the English novel, its stylists; and to collaborate was to be *par excellence* the outsider on the margins, or the côterie within a côterie.

There are kinds of seriousness in writing, for example the sustained pursuit of a train of thought into the depths of feeling or memory, which may well be inhibited by the hovering presence of a collaborator even when two writers are not literally close neighbours, as Ford and Conrad were. The corollary of that inhibition is the recurrent surfacing of comedy, private jokes, and the weird – more likely to emerge when two writers, friends most probably, attempt to please themselves before pleasing a wider public. In confirmation of this, one notices how the facetious and bizarre elements in Auden's and Isherwood's writing come to the fore in their collaborations. The avowed political seriousness of such plays as *The Dog Beneath the Skin* (1935) and *The Ascent of F6* (1936) is outweighed by their pantomime effects. In their novel *A Nest of Ninnies* Ashbery's inwardness and Schuyler's use of intense observation are there, but tend towards whimsy. This had been even more the case in Surrealist collaboration, and the *Locus Solus* collection gives ample evidence of a general tendency towards Surrealist fantasy in modern collaboration. (Consequently, second-generation writers such as Padgett, Veitch and Berrigan have been able to produce collaborations which exploit the oneiric and farcical possibilities *ab initio*, rather than experiencing them as a side-effect of the experiment.) But certain continuities might be posited for literary collaboration over the last hundred years, if not longer. As a rule, I would suggest that the thematic drift of a collaboration will be dictated by that genre which, from the period in question, speaks most clearly of *escape*.

For Kipling and Wolcott Balestier, escape meant tales of adventure. Now it is the turn of dream and the absurd. Conrad and Ford's *The Inheritors* (1901) shows something of both, hardly surprising in a work neither Victorian nor Modern. Collaboration is bound to tend towards escape because of its method: by collaborating, a writer steps for a while outside that singularity which Auden called 'the cell of himself'.[53] Analogies for 'collaboration' in the overlapping spheres of espionage, writing and Thirties Leftism will hold, and are implicated in a politics of dream and escape. In the thermal lock of the Cold War, there was no escape, except through dream. The editors of *Locus Solus* turned away from the potential of literature for social analysis, in order to play. They used techniques which, when pioneered by the Surrealists, had carried subversive intent but which now paraded their own uselessness; with comic effect, to be sure, but to cover a range of political opinion that can only have ranged from the complacent to the pessimistic.

A Nest of Ninnies (1969) was first published at a time when attitudes that had surfaced first with the Beat generation were reaching their maximum point of diffusion throughout society, making such a comedy of manners seem like a relic from a lost world:

> A light of kinship gleamed in Alice's eye. Before she could speak, something like an explosion shook the room. It was the bagpipes of the Ayrshire Rifles. A general rush to the dining room ensued.
>
> 'Women and children first', Irving cried as he whisked the lid from a steaming casserole.
>
> 'A New England boiled dinner!' Mrs. Turpin exclaimed shrilly. 'I haven't had one since we left Honolulu.'
>
> (*NN* 72–3)

An entertainment first and last, Ashbery's and Schuyler's novel is not merely a collaboration between the two poets, but between such varied influences as Ivy Compton-Burnett, the late novels of Henry Green, E. F. Benson's tiresome 'Lucia' books, and the Glen Baxter side of Surrealism. Yet in another sense all writing is collaborative. All texts are reworkings of other writings with which their relationship may be filial, fraternal, nurturing, destructive. Texts overlap.

'WET CASEMENTS'

Up to now, this chapter has not been based on close readings of particular poems by John Ashbery. Numerous analyses by divers voices are now available, but as the anthology *Beyond Amazement* makes clear, there is little to be learned from competing interpretations of, say, 'The Skaters'. The poems generate interpretations very readily. Instead, I have tried to sketch some contexts for reading Ashbery. These have included his profound allegiance to models that are not merely American and not British but positively anti-British, in particular Whitman and Williams. Other models are British, for example the early poems of Auden, which stimulated Ashbery to write in his teens. Auden's homosexuality ran counter to the laws prevailing for most of his lifetime, and could not be given direct expression in his poetry. Obliquity, menace, anxiety and a forlorn self-consciousness are hallmarks, made emphatic by the Depression and danger on the political horizon at the end of the twenties. The stylistic consequences of these pressures have helped shape Ashbery's writing, though the latter has emerged in a different climate, with less direct menace on either the personal or the political front. An abrading and ironizing touch, characteristic of homosexual and other minority coigns of vantage in a WASP culture, is another part of Ashbery's repertoire. His ability to playfully deconstruct orthodox discourses, to let those 'square doctrines' come 'apart' and 'unstuck' (*TCO* 55), had been sponsored already by other influences, such as Surrealism. All of these tendencies can be seen to combine and confirm each other through the practice of collaboration, which in this final section I hope to show to be central to Ashbery's practice.

I take as my text the poem 'Wet Casements' (*HD* 28), lent a prominence above that of its neighbours in *Houseboat Days* by the laurels bestowed on it by Harold Bloom, in an essay collected in *Agon*. Solipsizing glory is once more the order of the day, and Bloom's argument is not merely one that makes no room for literary collaboration. Its existence is denied. Perhaps here more than anywhere else in his work, Bloom makes a case for the act of writing as a psychodrama of essential solitude. 'Indeed, no American feels free when she or he is not alone, and it may be the eloquent sorrow of American that it must continue, in its best poems, to equate freedom with solitude.' The poem as an action of supreme and lonely individualism is archetypally American, in Bloom's (highly debatable) view.

It is not surprising that 'Wet Casements' should urge Bloom to heights of portentousness that reach self-parody. On hearing the poet read this piece at a Yale gathering, Bloom notes: 'Only the pathos of the traditional phrase "immortal wound" seems to me adequate to my response, both immediate and continuing. For me, it had joined the canon, directly I had heard it . . .'.[54] This is a poem liable to confirm any reader in the view they already held of Ashbery's work. The epigraph, from Franz Kafka's *Wedding Preparations in the Country*, could in its drollery and self-qualification have come from *A Nest of Ninnies*, if 'snowing' were to replace 'raining':

> When Eduard Raban, coming along the passage, walked into the
> open doorway, he saw that it was raining. It was not raining
> much.

The poem's opening confirms the note of drollery, while hinting in
a faintly Jamesian way at reserves of deeper or more cutting emotion
that might precisely be the reason for tone to keep itself moderate:

> The conception is interesting: to see, as though reflected
> In streaming windowpanes, the look of others through
> Their own eyes. A digest of their correct impressions of
> Their self-analytical attitudes overlaid by your
> Ghostly transparent face.

Yes, such a conception is 'interesting', and that adjective may be, as
Bloom argues, a dry substitute for some more powerful term: 'desperate', perhaps. But it is, undoubtedly, all rather weird. I would
hesitate, as Bloom all too clearly does not, in categorizing this
phenomenological flickerbook of what is Self and what is Other as a
blow for America and freedom. It is too weird – but also, surely, too
funny. There follows the extraordinary thirteen-line sentence that is
the base of the poem:

> You in falbalas
> Of some distant but not too distant era, the cosmetics,
> The shoes perfectly pointed, drifting (how long you
> Have been drifting; how long I have too for that matter)
> Like a bottle-imp toward a surface which can never be approached,
> Never pierced through into the timeless energy of a present
> Which would have its own opinions on these matters,
> Are an epistomological snapshot of the processes
> That first mentioned your name at some crowded cocktail
> Party long ago, and someone (not the person addressed)
> Overheard it and carried that name around in his wallet
> For years as the wallet crumbled and bills slid in
> And out of it.

Like the twenty-seven line sentence in the middle of 'A Wave', this
strikes the reader as a wave, that crests in each image as it dissolves,
so that the whole is both rollingly impressive and yet filled with
existential pathos, its flourishing of images perhaps not a waving so

much as a near-drowning. In the midst of the archness and cartoon
strangeness there is a lyrical cry, typical of Ashbery in being the
inextricable partner to abstraction. We see here the 'wacky sophistication' that Stephen Fredman diagnoses in Ashbery's writing and of
which so many have been suspicious, including at times his admirers. There is here a mixture of bizarre construction and 'sleek argu-
mentative exercise' (in Lawrence Norfolk's phrase), 'coolly witty,
decorous and aloof' to be sure, animated by an 'eel-like darting' of
mind (in Helen Vendler's phrase), but as firm as Robert Creeley in
holding to a moral essentialism of the moment.[55] David Shapiro saw
'parodies of spiritual progress' in *Three Poems*, and perhaps they are
here too, though with a striation of anxiety in the parody that makes
it something else.[56] Whatever one tends to feel about Ashbery will be
confirmed by this sentence.

The 'you' wearing falbalas is a Modernist you, the you of
Apollinaire's *Zone* and Eliot's 'Rhapsody on a Windy Night', a divided self conjured through the rhetorics of comedy and madness.
The 'name' for which it itches and yearns is the signifier which we all
always miss, just as 'the timeless energy' of a perfect present is the
state we never attain. Both imply a human condition which is basically, originally flawed, in which names never fit things and both
dissolve, yet the ceaseless 'drifting' of things seems always to point
to the clarifying resolution which (as for Eliot's voices) never comes.
The formal structures of language promise it: 'how long you/Have
been drifting; how long I have too for that matter' is Romantic cliché,
Brief Encounter-type stuff, tantalizingly promising a coincidence of
lips on lips, of lips on words, of words on things, that never comes
to rights, but is only supplanted in difference by new images, part of
the rolling wave.

So it appears somewhat naive of Bloom to reduce these lines to the
record of 'the loss of a beloved name, or perhaps just the name of
someone once loved'. (Wearing *falbalas*?) He may be right to go on to
argue that the poem's closing lines express 'the creative anger of a
consciousness condemned to a solitude of lost information, or a
world of books':

> I want that information very much today,

> Can't have it, and this makes me angry.
> I shall use my anger to build a bridge like that
> Of Avignon, on which people may dance for the feeling

Of dancing on a bridge. I shall at last see my complete face
Reflected not in the water but in the worn stone floor of my bridge.

I shall keep to myself.
I shall not repeat others' comments about me.

Irritable, slightly mad, unintentionally comic, what this voice wants
is to see 'my complete face', my whole, distinct identity, in the
mirror of worn stone of a bridge like that in the children's round 'Sur
le Pont D'Avignon', which repeats in mindless and eternal circularity that here is a bridge on which there is dancing. It is a mad parody
of the urge to have one's discrete identity as a subjectivity confirmed
by an obliging world. What Bloom sees as the poem's heroic project
is exactly the false idealism it most mocks: Bloom fails to see this,
because he fails to see the wit in 'Wet Casements'. Indeed, he fails
entirely to see the wit in any of Ashbery's work. (Ashbery's detrac-
tors generally see the wit and can't see anything else.) The reason,
one must assume, is that Bloom feels a deeply Puritan suspicion of
levity as compromising the prophetic power of poetry. Helen Vendler
appears to share this regrettable blindness. It is ludicrous to say, as
Bloom does of this poem's last two lines, that they are an Emersonian
exaltation of the divine solitude 'that Montaigne both praised and
warned against'.[57] They are a comic and paranoid assertion of
selfhood. Comic and paranoid because, Ashbery is saying, *you have
no complete face*. There is no single, discrete self, be you reader or
writer. The worn bridge of words reflects not one face, but the
multitude of faces – Kafka's, Eliot's, Keats's, the faces of Breton and
Eluard whose *L'Immaculée Conception* helps underpin the bridge –
that made up the collaboration of this writing. They had been, in
their time, composite and shifting faces. The power of the writer is
not the closing of doors and windows, so that he may retire from the
world à la Roderick Usher, but an opening outward of the casement
to the other airs and voices without which our own would not exist.

4

Lyric Poets in the Era of Late Capitalism

In a capitalist country fun is everything.

Frank O'Hara, *Art Chronicles*

BOTANIZING ON THE ASPHALT

This is the second movement of a poem by Ron Padgett entitled 'How to Be a Woodpecker':

I would rather not participate in this society anymore, hello, but I must because I do not have the money to live outside it, *on my yacht*. This paragraph is a verbal checkerboard. It's your move. You jump around the board until my consciousness gradually disappears into yours. Now when *I* tell a joke you laugh your long gray wooden laugh, woodpeckers in its future, woodpeckers who have decided they definitely will not participate in their woodpecker society.[1]

Although this characteristically amusing piece is taken from a 1990 collection (*The Big Something*), its procedures show no significant difference from those in poems of the sixties by Padgett, Ted Berrigan, Dick Gallup and others offering a poetry of cartoon comedy in O'Hara's wake. Like the talking alsatian dogs and grasshoppers in the collaborative collages produced by O'Hara and Joe Brainard in 1964, Padgett's joky woodpeckers have stepped out of Walt Disney via the psychedelic sensibility, and via the movement when Pop Art made its transition from New York gallery phenomenon to common cultural currency. During what I. F. Stone called 'the haunted Fifties', it had seemed important not to be caught holding the wrong set of convictions in the wrong place at the wrong time, be it on race, politics or sexuality. But as America emerged blinking into the sixties and the new cultural primacy of images celebrating glamour and youth, it became imperative not to get caught holding any attitude at all. Knowingly aware of everything, committed to nothing, cultural consciousness became a 'checkerboard', where, as in Padgett's woodpecker society, grand gestures of social disaffection became so frequent as to be meaningless, neutralized by the 'long gray wooden laugh', the hollow laugh of Cold War liberalism. In a capitalist country, as O'Hara warned, fun is everything; and even fun can be totalitarian.

Like many productions of Pop culture and the New York school, Padgett's poem is kept alive by the rapidity of its transitions. Faced by his or O'Hara's comic fluency, criticism will always be late, forever lumbering to catch up with the text, missing the point and making heavy weather. It is always 'your move', as the poet escapes capture, Houdini-like in his ability to wriggle free from any critical, or credal, pressures. In a literary obituary for *Book Week*, John Ashbery offers a blithe résumé of this aspect of O'Hara's work:

> Frank O'Hara's poetry has no program and therefore cannot be joined. It does not advocate sex and dope as a panacea for the ills of modern society; it does not speak out against the war in Viet Nam or in favor of civil rights; it does not paint Gothic vignettes of the post-Atomic Age: in a word, it does not attack the establishment. It merely ignores its right to exist, and is thus a source of annoyance for partisans of every stripe.[2]

Although Ashbery captures the mercurial, hipper-than-thou face of what he rightly terms this poet's *culte du moi*, a number of things are not quite right here. There are innumerable, pointedly favourable references in O'Hara's poetry to black friends and artists, most famously in his elegy to Billie Holiday, 'The Day Lady Died'. In 'Personal Poem' he draws attention to the disgraceful incident when jazz trumpeter Miles Davis was clubbed by the police (outside Birdland, ironically enough) and pictures himself shaking hands with another black artist, Le Roi Jones. He wrote one of his most successful Odes as a 'Salute to the French Negro Poets'. O'Hara was no polemicist, but it is hard to see what political line could be implicit in these poems other than one in favour of black style and self-expression, social equality and 'civil rights'. In general, the poems are insistently libertarian precisely because of their basis in personal encounters, feelings, friendships and tastes. If the poems do not finally succeed in the 'attacks' they mount, that may be a result not of the apolitical stance alleged by Ashbery, but of the social impotence of poetry *ab initio*, a possibility to be explored in this chapter.

I would suggest that, precisely to the extent that his poems show him to be the master of fast transitions, O'Hara was troubled by the ethical consequences. His last poems, particularly *The End of the Far West*, nine poems for a projected collaboration with artist Jan Cremer, do attempt to work up an interest in rapid-fire, two-dimensional images derived from Pop. But those poems are not as funny as they needed to be, and indeed O'Hara's death in 1966 pre-empted a debate within his poetry which might equally have resulted in a reassessment of the Pop influence, or silence. O'Hara was in any case drying up at this point, and only composed two or three poems in the whole of 1965. Alcohol was undoubtedly a factor, but so was his displacement from the role of critical intermediary for the most significant avant-garde art of his time. The position of junior and jester to the monumental severity of Abstract Expressionism had in fact liberated his poetry. The new sixties celebrations of the light-weight took the antithetical edge off his insistent use of wit, as it were stealing O'Hara's firepower only to declare that the weapons were plastic.

A typically flip epigram of Andy Warhol, 'Beauty in danger becomes more beautiful, but beauty in dirt becomes ugly', dips into the lexicon of urban paradox trawled by O'Hara's poem 'Song', to a comparable but significantly divergent end.[3]

> Is it dirty
> does it look dirty
> that's what you think of in the city
>
> does it just seem dirty
> that's what you think of in the city
> you don't refuse to breathe do you

(CP 327)

J'ai pétri de la boue et j'en ai fait de l'or. Baudelaire had been the first urban dandy in modern poetry, alchemist of dirt. But the Second Empire public were reluctant to subsidise his Bohemianism, and the poet wrote in his journal of being unable to make spontaneous movements, for fear of tearing clothes already threadbare. Neither O'Hara nor Warhol ever had to suffer anything like these privations. We have to ask whether O'Hara's refusal not to breathe in the carbon monoxide of the city's mixed morals, shares the unflinching consciousness of *Les Fleurs du Mal*, or the stale air of Andy Warhol's Factory. Is O'Hara's taste in paintings and poetry and people, paraded so insistently in the *Collected Poems*, merely a dandified training in consumerism, complicit at last with the bourgeois appetites it pretends to have superseded? O'Hara's inscription of his own largely brilliant career in the *Collected Poems* begs the question as to whether a beeline might be traced from his artistic *culte du moi*, to the appetites of the Me Generation in the Yuppie 1980s.

Warhol wanted to paint his portrait, but O'Hara refused. (The artist is then said to have badgered him for a partial portrait: the head, then – or just a foot? – with predictable anatomical variants.) The poet did sit for many painters, the more successful results (Larry Rivers, Jane Freilicher) being those that give up the attempt to capture any fixed expression. In Elaine de Kooning's 1962 portrait, the face was originally painted, then wiped out entirely; 'and when the face was gone, it was more Frank than when the face was there'.[4] There are analogies with the poetry. O'Hara might well have viewed with sardonic disquiet the petrification of his own poetic 'face' into a school, particularly one whose addiction to cartoon fosters such an airbrushed, partial portrait of the breathing city. Then again, he was kind to Berrigan and the rest, and thought it was a marvellous thing that the Warhol crowd should have the run of a Cinémateque on Lafayette Street just to show their movies.[5] Ever the facilitator, O'Hara was generous with his time in a variety of causes that may arguably have diluted, while they fed, his own writing. The fact of early death casts a formidable shadow over his work, one that, as we still live in a Romantic age, proposes itself as tragic, with a consequent elevation of the poetry. Yet that darkness may be misleading, like the distracting shadow cast by objects in cinema that shows the director to have used the illusionary technique known as Day For Night, or *la nuit Américaine*:

> lying in a hammock on St. Mark's Place sorting my poems
> in the rancid nourishment of this mountainous island
> they are coming and we holy ones must go

is Tibet historically a part of China? as I historically
belong to the enormous bliss of American death

(CP 326)

A poem such as 'Rhapsody' seems far from offering immediate
evidence of a sensibility ready to be bought off at the hoisting of a
flag. In that paradox of New York as purveyor of 'rancid nourishment', inextricable terms in which rancidity promotes rather than
poisoning nourishment, the distinctive note in O'Hara's poetry may
be heard, one that sets him apart from the mass of his generation. It
might recall the savage paradoxes of Baudelaire, in a comparison
from which O'Hara would not emerge with dishonour. Yet it does
have to be asked more precisely where O'Hara stood, 'historically'
and politically, and to what extent his confinement on that spit of
land made 'mountainous' by the soaring architecture of modern
capitalism, set strict limits to his botanizing on the asphalt.

This last phrase is drawn from Walter Benjamin's book on
Baudelaire, subtitled 'A Lyric Poet in the Era of High Capitalism'.
There Benjamin draws explicit and detailed links between the evolution of a poetry of the city, and moments in the metanarrative of
capitalist development. The leisured style of the Bohemian, for example, is shown to have been forced on writing at certain moments
by a combination of a governmental ban on political satire, operat-
ing through the newspapers, and the technology of night, with its
newly-illuminated arcades built for strolling.[6] But by the time of
Frank O'Hara, the explosion of communications networks, fashion,
publicity, the leisure industries – everything that Marx had termed
with a legendary want of prescience the 'non-essential' sectors of
capitalism – was remaking Western culture at the level of the reproducible image.

According to Jean Baudrillard, the most influential current com-
mentator on these changes, we are living through a triumph of the
image, an Age of Simulacra, where 'the map engenders the territory', where what is real is now a question of flickering vestiges,
where indeed 'the real is no longer real'. 'The very definition of the
real becomes: *that of which it is possible to give an equivalent reproduc-
tion.*' Such a scenario of reduplication has vertiginous implications
for artistic practice. Warhol's Marilyn Monroes (discussed by
Baudrillard) and other serialized portraits now join the self-replicat-

ing, needlessly twinned towers of New York's World Trade Center
to proclaim 'the death of the original and the end of representation'.[7]
Indeed, New York is now no longer a city in the civic sense, but the
world trade centre for the marketing of imagery; the enormous bliss
of American death. Poetry hardly signifies in this debate: Baudrillard
is a theorist of mass culture, and so ignores it. Yet it might reason-
ably be asked if the conditions of so-called late capitalism (a phrase
coined by the Marxist economist Ernest Mandel, and one turned at
the time of writing into an oxymoron by events in Eastern Europe)
offer a critical loss or gain to an art already marginalized in the age
of the novel, let alone the computer. The burden of the remainder of
this book will be the asking of a question: whether the small space
occupied by a lyric poetry such as O'Hara's in the present epoch
signifies a zone of irrelevance, anachronism, or resistance. The notion of endlessly reproducible simulacra carries some interestingly
questionable ironies given the limited print runs of O'Hara's books
of poetry.

And what of John Ashbery, in this context? Between 1962 and 1966,
the year of O'Hara's death, he was assembling the contents of his
third collection, *Rivers and Mountains*. This volume would establish
not only some of the characteristic tones and styles, but also the
format of an Ashbery book. A series of shorter pieces, commencing
with a poem about origins, culminate in what is by the standards of
the late twentieth century an immensely long poem, in this case 'The
Skaters'. The latter is as rhetorically grand, but a deal more arch,
than comparably long poems of more recent date, such as 'Self-
Portrait in a Convex Mirror', or 'A Wave'. Carnivalesque and ceaselessly mobile, it seems at first to share common ground with a
culture of the disposable, and Warhol's trash aesthetic:

> The films have changed –
> The great titles on the scalloped awning have turned dry and
>   blight-colored.
> No wind that does not penetrate a man's house, into the very
>   bowels of the furnace,
> Scratching in dust a name on the mirror – say, and what
>   about letters,

The dried grasses, fruits of the winter – gosh! Everything
     is trash!
The wind points to the advantages of decay
At the same time as removing them far from the sight of men.

                                                    (*RM* 37)

As usual, the animus of the poetic voice is against time, rather than
history. The end of metanarratives proclaimed lately by Jean-François
Lyotard as the decisive characteristic of Postmodernity, is taken as
read by Ashbery's poetry of the 1960s. Another alleged hallmark of
postmodernist writing, textual play, is freely and windily indulged.
Imagistically lavish, at times gloriously Romantic, 'The Skaters' is
still troubled by the evanescence of the things it brings into play. As
always with this poet, the aesthetic of inclusion erases as freely as it
introduces. This, Ashbery's method, is in fact identified by him as
the uncaring lack of method in time's sway over us: things vanish,
leaving only the chill fear of mortality which forms the enduring
core of his concern. A later poem, 'Grand Galop', is among other
things a parody of *The Waste Land*, the Chapel Perilous cum Dark
Tower of its finale adorned with an advertisement for Van Camp's
Pork and Beans. And even in 'The Skaters' Ashbery shows himself to
be Eliot's prodigal son, smilingly showing us trash, in a handful of
dust.
     Despite the breathtaking array of vocabulary and formulation in
Ashbery's poetry of the sixties and seventies, there are certain terms
commonly heard at the time for which one would comb his poems in
vain: 'Vietnam', say. 'The Skaters' is virtually unique in its inclusion
of recognizably political material. But then the treatment of that
material is guaranteed to set teeth on edge:

In reality of course the middle-class apartment I live in is nothing
     like a desert island.
Cozy and warm it is, with a good library and record collection.
Yet I feel cut off from the life in the streets.
Automobiles and trucks plow by, spattering me with filthy slush.
The man in the street turns his face away. Another island-dweller,
     no doubt . . .
                                                    The head-
     lines offer you

News that is so new you can't realize it yet. A revolution
    in Argentina! Think of it! Bullets flying through
    the air, men on the move;
Great passions inciting to massive expenditures of energy,
    changing the lives of many individuals.
Yet it is all offered as "today's news", as if we somehow
    had a right to it, as though it were a part of our lives
That we'd be silly to refuse. Here, have another – crime or
    revolution? Take your pick.

(RM 56–7)

That word 'Cozy' is revealingly Audenesque, and recalls not the
anxieties of thirties politics and psychology, nor even the Horatian
Auden of the post-war phase, but the years of decline, when the
poetry was smothered in its own self-assurance. And Ashbery knows
that he is facing questions of political commitment and escapism, the
basis of reality in personal or collective experience, with a gratingly
guileless wit. Yet, teetering on the brink of a fall into solipsism which
would leave this monologic consciousness only too delighted to
retire to a Segal-locked apartment well sandbagged with books and
records, the poem still sends signals in two, interestingly contrary
directions. One direction, that phrase about a geographically distant
conflict, 'as if we somehow/had a right to it', recalls a profoundly
American philosophy shocking (at least until recently) to European
ears, even though its origins were in part European and Romantic:

> Nothing is at last sacred but the integrity of your own mind.
> Absolve you to yourself, and you shall have the suffrage of the
> world . . . Good and bad are but names very readily transferable to
> that or this; the only right is what is after my constitution; the only
> wrong what is against it . . . I am ashamed to think how easily we
> capitulate to badges and names, to large societies and dead insti-
> tutions . . . Then again, do not tell me, as a good man did to-day,
> of my obligation to put all poor men in good situations. Are they
> *my* poor?[8]

The ambiguous political and ethical consequences of Emerson's philosophy of Self-Reliance are played out at all levels of American
social behaviour, and have grown no less debatable with the passage
of time. That philosophy is a part of Ashbery's intellectual back-

ground, and absolutely to the fore in the high valuation that Harold Bloom sets on his poetry, and the ways in which he interprets it. However, what Emerson's prose argues with clarity and fire is in Ashbery's poem one more possible drift of expression among the shifting signifiers. Rather than signalling a rigorous individualism, that regards the immediate digestion of revolution in South America through the news media as itself a subtle form of tyranny, a lack of acknowledgment of otherness, it may be that Ashbery – for all his agility, and layers of irony – has retreated at last into liberal quietism. One could argue that to isolate one phrase as I have is to make heavy weather, that this is only a poem, not a draft Constitution: but in that 'only' the intense ambitions for poetry held by Whitman, and Emerson, and Williams, would crash down to zero.

American poetry, particularly in its most risky invention, the epic of improvisation, has ached to turn Shelley's nomination of poets as the world's unacknowledged legislators into a real political intervention. This urge to negotiate the gap between questions of poetic diction and political edict has been a substantial theme and motivation to Whitman, to Pound in *The Cantos*, Williams in *Paterson*, Charles Olson in *The Maximus Poems*, and more recently John Wieners, in that most unacknowledged and painfully brilliant revision of the statutes, *Behind the State Capitol* (1975). Yet all these works of extraverted political attention have had to fall back on the ambiguous consolations of a dramatized subjectivity, in part because the commercial world, itself fired by a variation on Emersonian principles, has no place for poetry. The spendour of the subject, as Baudrillard remarks in another context, is our consolation for the poverty of objects, a poverty that can in reality only be increased by the endless reduplications of commodity capitalism. Such traditions were firmly in place by the mid-sixties, and although Bloom's particular theories may be perfectly irrelevant to Ashbery's sense of his own practice, other anxieties of influence may be traced in his work that do issue from these pressures. The quietly garrulous nature of Ashbery's poetry, diffident and sadly witty, may have been able to produce long poems through a recognition *ab initio* of the political irrelevance of poetry: in consequence a relaxed capitulation to the consolations of the market and the subject become possible. 'Out here on Cottage Grove it matters': this is the urgent beginning of Ashbery's 'Pyrography'. (*HD* 8) This is very definitely a poem of the United States, commissioned by the Department of the Interior for its Bicentennial Exhibition *America 1976*, an occasion on which Warhol's self-portraits were also winged around the world's major galleries to represent their country's achievements. But the ambiguity of the crucial pronoun, Ashbery's infamously evasive 'it', undercuts the possibility of the poem's mattering publicly at all.

We have seen, then, how Ashbery's poetry resembles Warhol's trash aesthetic but is too imbued with the pathos of mortality to collude with Warhol's coolness and emptiness. The winds that bring decay bring *timor mortis*. This leaves him with an inherited, Emersonian individualism into which to retreat from poetry's struggles to re-enter the world, competing with an inclination to give in to the blandishments offering relief from the threats of death and social conflict. Of course Ashbery knows all this, knows it backwards, and knows that we know he knows; all of which is at work in the poetry. The political cartoons of 'The Skaters' are to be read within the frame of that poem's allusions to the Symbolist past, its echoes of Wordsworth and Whitman, Rimbaudian 'bâteau', and parody of the opening to Baudelaire's 'Le Voyage', a parody that finally restates Ashbery's ironic and self-conscious allegiance to art as buffer against time: 'But how is it that you are always indoors, peering at too/ heavily canceled stamps through a greasy magnifying/glass?' (*RM* 42)

And so it is to Baudelaire that we return, and to the problems for art in a capitalist culture which he foresaw with a prescience exceeding that of Marx:

> He proposed the creation of a commodity somehow absolute, in which the process of fetishization would be pushed to the point of annihilating the very reality of commodification as such; he conceived of commodities in which use-value and exchange-value would abolish each other mutually, whose value consists, therefore, in its inutility . . . Baudelaire understood that to ensure the survival of art in industrial civilization, the artist would have to seek the reproduction in his work of this destruction of use-value and traditional intelligibility.[9]

We may now be in a position to understand both O'Hara's recourse to a poetry animated by rapid transitions, and Ashbery's alleged 'difficulty', as developed strategies for dealing with poetry's 'inutility', a gratuitousness which as Baudelaire foresaw would have to be made brazen rather than disguised. Here lies the basis for the acceptability of rhyme, metre and classical allusion, supposedly conservative devices that have puzzled commentators on the radical Baudelaire, from André Breton to Jonathan Culler. What could be more flagrantly, even stupidly distant from normal exigencies of communication than rhyme? The chiming ornamentation of these devices carries the authentic rattle of mass-produced jewellery. Meanwhile shock is built into the poetry at other levels, charging objects ('Le Pipe', 'Les Bijoux') with strangeness as their use-value is forced to cede to what Giorgio Agamden calls 'the aura of cold materiality', metamorphosis of commodity into fetish.[10] Here lie Baudelaire's bequests to Surrealism, whose interest in *objets trouvés* and those made in dreams attempts to push fetishism towards political delirium.

The boxes of Joseph Cornell, much admired by Ashbery, are their contemporary descendants. 'For Cornell's boxes embody the substance of dreams so powerfully that it seems that these eminently palpable bits of wood, cloth, glass and metal must vanish the next moment, as when the atmosphere of a dream becomes so intensely realistic that you know you are about to wake up.' (*RS* 14) The trouble is, as Michael Newman observes, that to wake up to the reality of these dream-boxes is to watch the Surrealist encounter with the *objets trouvé* meet 'the desire-arousal of mass consumerism'. Cornell creates 'paradises of Symbolist reverie . . . enclosed, with inadvertent irony, in the "packaging" of a box'.[11] Poetry's potential to avoid this literalism is obtained at the cost of low market valuation by comparison with the visual arts. In a sense, neither O'Hara nor Ashbery has gone beyond Baudelaire's uncanny anticipation of these dilemmas. *Les Fleurs du Mal* has proved a ubiquitous influence, but a hard act to follow.

Are the New York poets then trapped in a Cornell box, their rejection of the means-to-end rationality of bourgeois existence a mere refuge in escapism, that colludes at last with mass consumerist palliatives? The criticisms I have levelled at Ashbery are nothing compared to the demolition job on Abstract Expressionism and the idea of an avant-garde supplied recently by Peter Bürger, Serge Guilbaut and others. The remainder of this chapter will be concerned with such critiques, and with the place of New York poetry in what has been called by Jean-François Lyotard, Fredric Jameson and others a Postmodern culture. Does the concept of an avant-garde, mocked already by Baudelaire in his journal references to *la littérature militante*, have any critical reality in these poems of the mountainous island?

POSTMODERNISM AND THE END OF REPRESENTATION

Elsewhere in this study I have looked into the relations between deconstruction and the New York poets. In this context, deconstruction may fairly be said to stand for the aims and tendencies of post-structuralist theory in general. Where structuralism had laid the groundwork for Derrida *et al* in its dismantling of the concept of a subject as epistemological centre, that will-to-deconstruct dried up at the point of identification of so-called systems of representation in the novel/film/fashion. The death of the author, announced by Barthes, co-existed with the birth of the system, a code to be cracked, at least in principle, by the perceiving subject. Derrida and de Man in particular are able to show how the would-be scientific projects of structuralism remain in thrall to metaphysics, through the projection of a totalized system of the signified. By showing, through the workings of difference, how the ceaseless play of the signifier eludes attempts to arrest and stabilize meaning, Derrida brings rigorous criticism to bear on both the idea of representation, and the idea of a coherent, perceiving subject who might be sufficiently present to do the representing. Deconstruction has therefore been receptive to what one might loosely term the avant-garde consensus, seeing in its own procedures and those of progressive art a shared, basically critical attitude, ever ready to expose the contradictions in positions of ideological closure, privileging the pluralities and vagaries of the signifier at the expense of the signified, and (attacks on the concept of the subject notwithstanding), treating alienated subjectivity with a certain mournful relish. Hence, despite the general reluctance of deconstructionist critics to grapple with contemporary writing, the general and automatic enthusiasm for Joyce, Artaud, Bataille, Roussel and Surrealism.

Among recent attempts to produce a theory of the avant-garde implicitly critical of the post-structuralist position, Peter Bürger's is probably the most important. Barely a hundred pages in length, his *Theory of the Avant-Garde* (1974) still provides a dense and thoroughly considered account of such topics as the aesthetics of Kant and Schiller; the later supplanting of realism by aestheticism; Surrealism and Walter Benjamin; and the debates between Adorno and Georg Lukács. Indeed, it is during his engagement with, on the one hand, Adorno's gloomy posture of attentive paralysis on behalf of the social intervention of art, and on the other, Lukács' neo-Leninist faith in vanguard activity, that Bürger forges his central and most contentious postulation of an avant-garde as committed to the re-entry of art into social life. It is a fundamental tenet of Bürger's argument that 'the *autonomy of art* is a category of bourgeois society', reflecting the lifestyles of those free, at least intermittently, from the pressures of the need to survive: within the phenomenological inter-play of art, 'a sensuousness could evolve that was not part of any means-end relationships'. With the realm of the aesthetic set apart in this way from the vulpine rationality of daily bourgeois existence, art has the opportunity to turn in either of two directions. On the one hand, 'it can criticize such an existence'; or, it can succumb to a softer political option:

> Art allows at least an imagined satisfaction of individual needs that are repressed in daily praxis. Through the enjoyment of art, the atrophied bourgeois individual can experience the self as per-sonality. But because art is detached from daily life, this experi-ence remains without tangible effect, i.e., it cannot be integrated into that life. The lack of tangible effects is not the same as functionlessness . . . but characterizes a specific function of art in bourgeois society: the neutralization of critique.

Here, Bürger is building on the critical theory of culture supplied by Marcuse, and the view enunciated by Jürgen Habermas that the secular sanctuary of art permits both a cerebral indulgence of desires that might be quasi-illegal in the world outside, and the miming of spontaneity or solidary communication otherwise frozen out of the social world by bourgeois conformism. Bürger is more unwilling than either to sell art short in order to get on with the main agenda of haranguing the middle class, at least initially.

This close attention to the nexus at which the autonomy of art can either develop a critical edge, or merely concede its own inutility, is of sharp relevance not only to a consideration of the politics of the New York school, but the whole nature of O'Hara's and Ashbery's poetry. Bürger writes of Warhol that 'the painting of 100 Campbell soup cans contains resistance to the commodity society only for the person who wants to see it there'. Might the same be said of the poetry? There are texts by Ashbery from the days of *The Tennis Court Oath* to 'Litany' and beyond, that push or let meaning drift into a zone that Bürger's argument would locate as a more than usually eloquent version of the dampening aporia that has overtaken much recent writing. Bürger's sober analyses of unsober material are frequently persuasive in ways that help locate Modernist poetry, while diminishing the received sense of its achievements. Perhaps more productively, an argument such as Bürger's forces the reader to assess the precise nature of his or her relationship with the selfhood conjured through the poetry; and to see how that textual encounter modifies the reader's sense of selfhood, informed by reading. Put crudely, precisely what should you get out of reading this stuff?

I will try to propose a defence of the poetry, or at least of certain poems, in terms that will do more than merely draw fire away from their limitations. As a first step, it is important to note certain common traits in the theories of the avant-garde supplied by Peter Bürger, Fredric Jameson and others, which stem from a political agenda stretching far beyond the analysis of art works, but which affect their reading of such works deleteriously.

Bürger's model is nothing if not ambitious in its historical scope. He suggests three key phases in the development of art from the Middle Ages to recent times, beginning with sacral art, which he alleges to be collective in both its production and reception. Then comes courtly art, whose semi-detachment from the sacral marks the first stage in the 'emancipation' of art, its emergence as a solitary activity. The third phase is 'the objectification of the self-understanding of the bourgeois class', the stage of the Romantic poem and the realist novel. In the final stage of aestheticism, the apartness which had begun to characterize art in bourgeois society now becomes its content. Although Bürger raises the possibility of a re-entry of vanguard, critical art into the social arena, the examples he analyses (Breton's *Nadja*, Dada, Picasso/Braque, Warhol), fail to fulfil his project, with the partial and predictable exception of Brecht.

To attempt to signal local contradictions and omissions in this account would be a distraction. The deficiency to which I wish to point is not the blindness to factors of political subversion in Renaissance writing, the surprising failure to note the historical link between 'Decadence' and left-wing social critique, or other specific queries. More disturbingly, it is the ambitious scale of the theory that constantly undoes it at the level of detail. The urge to produce a *complete* picture, to propose a historical totality of which art can only ever be the faithful secretary, haunts Bürger's projection of a socially interactive vanguard art, and muddies his analyses of particular works. Despite his reservations over Lukács and the limitations of the realist novel, Bürger is unwilling to free himself from the premises of a *soi-disant* scientific Marxism, and the belief that history is gov-

erned by objective laws of development effectively independent of
human subjectivity. The consistent refusal by artists working in the
twentieth century to shackle themselves to those premisses, combined with the obligation of Marxist theorists to account for work
unfriendly to their own agenda, is responsible for a tension in analyses by Bürger and others damaging to the undeniable ambition and
formal lucidity of their critique. Bürger clearly finds the manifestly
solitary and individualistic aspects of artistic creation intolerable,
and so conjures a mythical Age of Collectivism, (the long-gone 'Sacral'
or the unbuilt Socialist) so as to present much of the art of the last
two centuries as a protracted deformation or mistake.

But it is in their engagement (or failure to engage) with abstraction
in art, that the related critiques of Bürger, Jameson, Guilbaut and
before them, Renato Poggioli, come most palpably unstuck. Bürger's
remarks on the post-Surrealist use of chance procedures in painting
are worth quoting in this context:

> Paint is dripped or splashed on the canvas. Reality is no longer
> copied and interpreted. The intentional creation of a totality is
> largely renounced and makes way for a spontaneity that to a
> considerable extent allows chance to produce the painting. The
> subject that has freed itself of all the constraints and rules of
> creation finally finds itself thrown back into an empty subjectivity.
> Because it can no longer work itself out in something that the
> material, and a specific task, set for it, the result remains accidental
> in the bad sense of the word, i.e., arbitrary. The total protest
> against any and every element of constraint does not take the
> subject to the freedom of creation but into arbitrariness. At best
> this arbitrariness can afterward be interpreted as individual ex-
> pression.[12]

The implied conflation of all post-war abstract tendencies from
Tachism to Pollock and de Kooning is appallingly crude, if inadvertently amusing in its gestures of distaste. The conflation is made
possible not by any historical reality, but by the critic's own refusal
or inability to 'read' a single work.

Let us, briefly, take the case of Jackson Pollock. One does not have
to join the chorus of uncritical admirers in order to see that, although
the bulk of Pollock's work uses abstraction, that unitary term covers
numerous divergent phases of stylistic and thematic experiment.
There are important changes as well as continuities between the

paintings of the early forties such as *The She-Wolf* and *The Moon-Woman Cuts the Circle*, residually figurative works dense with quasi-Jungian Symbolism; works from the high point of Abstract Expressionism such as the 'Number' paintings or *Full Fathom Five* (1947); and the final phase of mysteriously beautiful creations such as *The Deep, Portrait and a Dream* and above all *Easter and the Totem* (all from 1953), where quasi-representational figurations begin to emerge tentatively from the far side of abstraction, a procedure which I will later argue is not without analogues in the poems of Frank O'Hara. Rather than being 'thrown back into an empty subjectivity', Pollock throws himself forward into an astonishing fullness of expression, passionate or excessive according to taste. Bürger's crude dismissal is only possible to a viewer to whom any stress on the subjective is an *a priori* political error. Here we encounter a confusion that is virtually traditional in Marxist critiques of Romantic or modern art: subjectivism is both denounced as a real but reactionary phenomenon, while being dismissed simultaneously as a hallucination.

Pollock's paintings of the early to mid-forties aim to delve into what is (at least in intention) less a private subjectivity than a collective unconscious. This aim, shared at the time by painters such as Mark Rothko and Adolph Gottlieb, was prompted by, but also questions the separation of individual psychologies implicit in earlier works by Max Ernst and Salvador Dali. In only a few years, Pollock's art achieved maturation in very different works such as *Full Fathom Five*. Here the human figure, in one obvious sense abandoned by the development of abstract drip-painting, returns by implication in the rhythms and material scale of paint and canvas respectively. This reintroduction of the human and the personal, given startling emphasis in *Full Fathom Five* by the 'chance' embedding of buttons, coins, matches and cigarette butts in the pigment, points the way to a more effective criticism than Bürger's, by stressing the action, and the materiality, of painting. To these we will return.

Such a materialism should not be confused with Bürger's preference for the set 'specific task', in other words for an art committed as a *raison d'être* to the solution of technical problems. That view, which might gain nourishment from the various Conceptual Art movements, but which has in fact next to no bearing on abstraction, does once again allow the conformation of an allegedly progressive art to a scientific metanarrative, the Marxist view of history. In fact, the works generally hauled in to support the technicist view of twentieth-century art, from Duchamp to Caro and beyond, are only rarely involved at a primary level with problem-solving, and are rather more likely to be objects the artist wished to carry an *atmosphere* of solemn logic.

The same failure to interpret particular works is the least satisfactory aspect of an otherwise persuasive work, Serge Guilbaut's *How New York Stole the Idea of Modern Art: Abstract Expressionism, Freedom, and the Cold War* (1983). Guilbaut's thesis argues the usefulness of a supposed avant-garde, the Abstract Expressionist movement, to a political and commercial establishment avid for the manufacture of cultural, as well as atomic weapons, in the race to win the Cold War. The broad argument regarding the attempted co-option of art by ideology is convincing. Less plausible is Guilbaut's forced insertion of the atomic bomb as subject into an abstract painting by Jackson Pollock:

> In *Shimmering Substance*, the commas of color in the center of the canvas are placed on a dazzling surface created by a grid of thick white strokes and form a luminous yellow circle, a center of energy that can be understood as a sun . . .
> What Pollock depicts is a source of energy that is not merely powerful but also destructive. What is shown, in short, is not the sun but its equivalent, the atomic bomb, transformed into myth.[13]

This is a grossly reductive interpretation, but one typical of the genre. *Sounds in the Grass: Shimmering Substance* (to give it its proper title) is no more disintegratively explosive than a painting such as *The Flame*, made over ten years before the invention of the nuclear bomb. Its dense splashes and trails of colour are no more, and indeed no less, 'like' a nuclear blast or harsh sunlight than they are 'like' cerebral tissue, bacteria seen through a microscope, or the interior of a bird's nest. The polyvalency of this work, confused by Marxist critics with aestheticism or narcissism, was better described by Frank O'Hara as 'a majestic, passionate celebration of matter', suggesting that a successful art of radical ambiguity may not merely issue from, but constantly draw attention to its own materiality. (*AC* 34) Alongside questions of use-value and exchange-value, comes the 'cold materiality of things', cited earlier in relation to Baudelaire's anticipation of our world of mass consumerism. But in the act of painting, Pollock worked against the priorities of that world, however easily its recuperative ideology was able to soak him up. His painting reminds us of the warm materiality of things, and what I am urging here is a quite literal-minded respect for the physicality of that work. Unfashionably, I would suggest that the influential writing on culture emerging around the concept of Postmodernism has tended to neglect the relative independence of the particular painting or text, a sensation of which accompanies even the most contextualizing understanding. *Shimmering Substance* may recall *Eyes in the Heat* or late Turner, or be drawn even as it is seen for the first time into shifting networks of memory, reference and debate beyond the gallery where it hangs. Yet it is also distinctly itself, and not some other painting. Perhaps the recent downplaying of a singular identity for the artwork is itself an aspect of Postmodernism; in diametric opposition to, say, Rilke's writings on Rodin, Wyndham Lewis's comments on the 'vitalist' sculpture of Epstein, and many other manifestations of the period of High Modernism.

In viewing the break between Modernism and Postmodernism as constituted partly by the displacement of the serious and singular work by intertextual play, I echo one of the key arguments in an influential essay, Fredric Jameson's 'Postmodernism, or the Cultural Logic of Late Capitalism', reprinted in overlapping versions but published first by *New Left Review* in 1984. Jameson builds his argument on the narrative logic of the three fundamental movements in capitalism postulated by Ernest Mandel in the book that gives Jameson part of his title. Each of these movements marks 'a dialectical expansion' over the previous stage. The first is market capitalism; the second is the monopoly/imperialist stage. The third, 'wrongly called postindustrial', the stage of late or multinational or consumer capitalism, 'constitutes . . . a prodigious expansion of capital into hitherto uncommodified areas'. This dialectical magnification, far from diminishing culture by marginalizing it in favour of some more unreflectively commercial activity, has by Jameson's account led to a total perfusion of the social by culture. This is no triumph of art, let alone the combative re-entry of the avant-garde into the social arena projected by Bürger, but essentially a process of trivialization, a dissolution of the real into 'so many pseudo-events':

> . . . we must go on to affirm that the dissolution of an autonomous
> sphere of culture is rather to be imagined in terms of an explosion:
> a prodigious expansion of culture throughout the social realm, to

the point at which everything in our social life – from economic value and state power to practices and to the very structure of the psyche itself – can be said to have become 'cultural' in some original and as yet untheorized sense.[14]

Although only a few years old, Jameson's essay has in fact catalyzed an extensive 'theorization' of the Postmodern, much of which turns on this seeming paradox of a ubiquitous saturation-by-culture, productive only of the bitter-sweet and ultimately toxic flavour of an endless stylization. As a consequence of this leakage of the aesthetic into all spheres of activity, Jameson diagnoses a 'waning of affect in postmodern culture' by comparison with art of the earlier twentieth century. One example that he analyses is Edvard Munch's *The Scream*, set against the mere 'decorative exhilaration' of a rather soft target, Andy Warhol's *Diamond Dust Shoes*. The social and epistemological fragmentation taken to be a characteristic of the Postmodern by most commentators is variously located as 'a dialectic between over-organization and deliberate disorder' (J. G. Merquior, paraphrasing Christopher Butler); 'a levelling functionalism' whose paradigm is architecture (Peter Dews); the current expression of the victory of the city over nature (Michael Newman), and so on. The plurality of directions followed by the attempts to define Postmodernism may in part be ascribed to uncertainty over whether or not there is a radical break between the period of Modernism and the current scene. It may be that, to use Merquior's carefully phrased suggestion, 'postmodernism is still largely a sequel to, rather than a denial of, modernism- without any visible improvement of it. The postmodern is at most an ultramodernism – an extremist remake of avant-garde tics'.[15] By these lights, the facetiously ahistorical eclecticism of painting in the eighties had been given a more authoritative rehearsal by Picasso, who was already employing an eclectic blend of Cubist, rococo and classical elements by 1917–18. The use of literary pastiche by A. S. Byatt in *Possession* or by Peter Ackroyd in a number of recent novels might be attractive but it is nothing new, given the virtuoso precedent of Joyce's *Ulysses*. The abrasive fragmentation of poetry by the Language group is anticipated by a range of Modernist poetry from Ezra Pound and *The Waste Land* to Tzara's Dada; and so on.

All such examples may contain some truth to the extent that they identify correctly some artistic precedent or parentage. However, I suspect that there would remain significant differences in the way most people respond to much of the recent work, in whatever artistic medium. Here Jameson's essay is helpful, in the distinction it draws between an art of anxiety, of vertigo, of often monumental emotionalism (Munch, Eliot, Bartók) and the waning of tone, of affect, of obsession, in favour of a playful diversification (Perec, Koons, Cage). The examples are largely mine, and plucked from the air; it is an indication of the usefulness of Jameson's argument that it can immediately find general application beyond the examples he chooses to investigate. It becomes easy to detect the beginnings of Postmodern stylization in Modernism, and more rarely, the residual ability to generate work of Modernist power from a Postmodern frame.

To take a fashionable example: for all its levels of allusive play, autosubversion and what have you, David Lynch's film *Blue Velvet* (1985) is an intensely charged and disturbing work that builds on, without pastiching, Surrealist violence. By contrast the director's follow-up *Wild At Heart* (1989) for all its scenes of decapitation, skull-fracturing, car accidents and near-rape, is a playful, characteristically Postmodernist affair, allowed by the arbitrariness of incident in the road-movie genre to bounce from one cheerful piece of grotesquerie to the next. Significantly, its anchor for allusive reference is *The Wizard of Oz* (right down to the red shoes), where *Blue Velvet* recalled a tradition of serious fetishism from Poe to *Vertigo*, and where redness is more powerfully sanguinary.

Jameson too pays close attention to shoes, and not just Warhol's diamond dusted footwear. An extended account of Van Gogh's painting *Peasant Shoes* shows the ways in which Jameson's argument is disabled finally by its fealty to a political overview to an even greater extent than Bürger's:

> I first want to suggest that if this copiously reproduced image is not to sink to the level of sheer decoration, it requires us to reconstruct some initial situation out of which the finished work emerges. Unless that situation – which has vanished into the past – is somehow mentally restored, the painting will remain an inert object, a reified end-product, and be unable to be grasped as a symbolic act in its own right, as praxis and as production.

Jameson goes on to suggest two ways of reconstructing a context for the work, one of which is a reminder of the world of 'stark rural poverty' and 'backbreaking peasant toil' out of which Van Gogh's work is said to emerge, blazing with hallucinatory colour in a Uto-

pian gesture of sensory compensation for those dismal and inhu-
mane conditions. The other route for reconstruction invokes
Heidegger's very different reading of the shoes as vibrating with
'the silent call of the earth, its quiet gift of ripening corn'. Fortunately, neither interpretation, *an sich*, need detain us in the present
context. What I wish to pause over is Jameson's instinctive, immediate, but highly questionable recourse to a method he describes as
'hermeneutical', one 'in which the work in its inert, objectal form, is
taken as a clue or a symptom for some vaster reality *which replaces it*
as its ultimate truth' (my emphasis). In other words, Jameson engages with the painting in order not to engage with it, but to
dematerialize the thing as rapidly as possible in favour of 'some
vaster reality', which having, as he sanely notes, 'vanished into the
past', must be purely mental. This reading in order not to read, this
looking at a painting purely opportunistically as a cue to a certain
prefixed view of history, sets a strict limit on the credibility of the
essay. In the final paragraph the barely hidden agenda emerges in all
its anthemic, and predictably totalizing rhetoric: 'The political form
of postmodernism, if there ever is any, will have as its vocation the
invention and projection of a global cognitive mapping, on a social
as well as a spatial scale.'[16] Behind Jameson's undoubted (and locally
helpful) alertness to a range of cultural practices wider than those
usually canvassed in an academic discourse, there lies a narrow
adherence to an outmoded politics of art indebted to Lukács and
shadowed by just that brand of Marxian dogma. Jameson joins a
venerable tradition of Marxist critics who have proved to be perfectly incapable of advancing any theory or orientation of artistic
practice beyond the old, lame confinement to representation.

By these dimming lights any attention to a poem or painting will
glance off its surface almost immediately, in order to find a more
comfortable absorption in those external guarantors of meaning that
are always somewhere else, never in the work, but up, out or back
there in some narrative of History. It is this unjustified, almost mystical belief in the rationality of the historical process that reifies the
work, that makes it 'inert', that reduces Van Gogh or the output of
any artist to the miserable level of sheer decoration. Of course,
anyone racing to fill the glaring omissions and contradictions in the
creaking Marxisant adherence to realism/representation with calls
for neo-Derridean 'freeplay', radical 'undecidability', and the ludic
shallowness of much Postmodern manipulation (Jeff Koons and his

ilk) runs every risk of losing all opportunity for art to operate at a
moral level. Althusser's warning that the ideological cutting edge of
the dominant régime will always be there to exploit crises, breaks,
mutations in order to neutralize the effects of those mutations, needs
to be heeded even by those who remain unmoved by Althusser's (or
Jameson's) particular politics.[17] What is needed at this point in the
debate about Postmodernism is a vocabulary which can propose for
art a critical edge and a moral dimension, without at once swerving
into some political master-narrative to which art can only play
handmaiden.

THE FATE OF PERCEPTION: 'SELF-PORTRAIT IN A CONVEX MIRROR'

This section will be concerned with certain poems by Ashbery and
O'Hara, each of which shows an explicit, if ultimately divergent
concern with the material particularity of constructed things.
Unsurprisingly, in both 'Self-Portrait in a Convex Mirror' and 'Joe's
Jacket', this materiality brings with it a capacity for prompt
dematerialization into metaphor, as the things depicted generate a
variety of phenomenological questions and formations. Even in their
moments of most fluid speculation, these are, nevertheless, poems
which in their own quiddity and marked awareness of boundary
and frame draw an illuminating attention to the substance of art, the
labour of its composition and the questionable repose of its finish. It
may be that by attending to the theoretical and self-reflexive aspects
of these texts, ways of reading might be broached which, having
partly emerged from poems, are more likely to stay with poetry,
rather than skidding off the verbal surface into the swirling myths of
history.

Of course, to claim the pathway to one conclusive, accurate engagement with any poem would itself be a chimerical notion, a myth
of reading. A poem is like any other object of attention, in that its
ipseity can never be captured for once and for all. As Maurice
Merleau-Ponty notes in his classic study of the phenomenology of
perception, 'each aspect of the thing which falls to our perception is
still only an invitation to perceive beyond it, still only a momentary
halt in the perceptual process'. Not even the most comprehensively
predatory act of attention could seize its object conclusively, for the
thing 'would cease to exist as a thing at the very moment when we

thought to possess it'.[18] It is what one might term the fate of perception to be led on, and then further on, never to arrive.

To talk of the slippage of the signifier from the signified, to return to a Baudelairean version of the Fall, to cite Merleau-Ponty's phenomenology or Derrida's postulation of *différance*: from their different coigns of historical and methodological vantage, all bear witness to this fate of perception, a negative torsion in the commerce between self and not-self, marking all subject-object and intersubjective relations. The unchallengeable presence of things, requiring a perceiver to bring it to life, maintains a tantalizing and perpetual distance as perception closes in. There is a warning here for readers of poems. Even poems which take that warning as their subject cannot be read transparently. To paraphrase Karl Kraus, the closer one looks at a word, the greater the distance from which it looks back.

> As Parmigianino did it, the right hand
> Bigger than the head, thrust at the viewer
> And swerving easily away, as though to protect
> What it advertises.

So begins John Ashbery's 'Self-Portrait in a Convex Mirror'. The ambiguities of pose and perspective in the original by Parmigianino, which will be referred to much later in the poem as 'shield', 'greeting', and the 'shield of a greeting', display in a particularly concentrated and poignant form what Merleau-Ponty sees as the reluctance of the viewed to yield itself up to the viewer in any act of seeing. Whatever we look at both protects and advertises its being. The singular ingenuity of Parmigianino's mirror-portrait, said to be the first such, frames and locates a pathos in the fate of perception that might otherwise miss its memorial. This act of framing is redoubled in Ashbery's composition of a poem about the painting. And, clearly, the poem is to be an act of self-portrayal by Ashbery, at least as much as it portrays the Renaissance painter's act of self-reflection.

Such an emphasis on artifice and selfhood threatens, in the words of Eliot's Gerontion, to merely 'multiply variety/In a wilderness of mirrors', and like the Hall of Mirrors in the Fun-Fair, leave the spectator a little queasy.[19] The poem would seem at this stage to be courting the contentment with questionable kinds of play and pastiche characteristic of Postmodernism, as distinct from, say, the serious anxieties and moral vertigo that might be seen in Eliot's

poetry. Curiously, Ashbery appears to anticipate both the murky
aspects of Postmodernist style, and the reservations one might have
about it:

> "Play" is something else;
> It exists, in a society specifically
> Organized as a demonstration of itself.
> There is no other way, and those assholes
> Who would confuse everything with their mirror games
> Which seem to multiply stakes and possibilities, or
> At least confuse issues by means of an investing
> Aura that would corrode the architecture
> Of the whole in a haze of suppressed mockery,
> Are beside the point.

There is neither 'haze' in Ashbery's style, nor 'mockery' in his content. 'Self-Portrait' is not without its joky asides, and the donnish
recourse to quotation from Vasari and Sydney Freedberg is a little
tongue-in-cheek. But none of these touches is allowed to impinge on
the serious pathos of the captive soul, transferred by the artist via the
mirror to his painting, and fated, despite being 'treated humanely',
to suspension, 'unable to advance much farther/Than your look as it
intercepts the picture'. Yet the true pathos of the soul is

> that the soul is not a soul,
> Has no secret, is small, and it fits
> Its hollow perfectly: its room, our moment of attention.

This is both the failure and the triumph of painting; that skills of
perspective and depth, of the carefully judged repoussoir, and the
vanishing haze of the horizon line, with its implication of distant
metaphysical resolution – all are, in the end, *trompe l'oeil* effects. It all
comes down to the skilful application of pigment, the creation of an
illusion of deep space, of soul and grandeur, by colour and impasto.
This is likewise the pathos of verse, whose line-breaks, rhythms
and cadence create a 'hollow' for imaginative sympathy from flat
hieroglyphs on a blank page. Everything, to cite one of this poem's
most mournful verdicts, is surface. 'The surface is what's there/And
nothing can exist except what's there.' Yet experience is not depre-
cated as superficial in a pejorative sense. Of the external appearance

of the real, Ashbery writes 'it is not/Superficial but a visible core'. To return to terms used earlier in this study, the urge to provide an art of deep space, of the metaphysical, is therefore subverted by a rueful acknowledgement of the literal nature of the skills and moves that conjure that 'meta', not out of cosmic verities, but from the physical palette of paint or language. All that would seem to be left, at first, is the more modest project of depicting a layered-space world of leaded panes, wooden beams, fur and bits of coral; or the world of contemporary, consumerist New York, that 'logarithm/Of other cities'.

> I feel the carousel starting slowly
> And going faster and faster: desk, papers, books,
> Photographs of friends, the window and the trees
> Merging in one neutral band that surrounds
> Me on all sides, everywhere I look.

This is not so much a layered-space world, as a flat uniformity. Yet there is a crucial element of motion in it. Ultimately this is one of a number of subject-object positions written into the poem, all emphatic, but different and provisional. The moment of initial engagement with the painting, which is also the reader's moment of beginning Ashbery's poem, speaks of 'intercepting' the artwork. In our final glimpse of the painting, it falls back faster than the speed of light 'to flatten ultimately/Among the features of the room'. In between the two, we travel through an extraordinary spectrum of positions vis-à-vis the painting, seen via the poem, vis-à-vis the poem and portrait as analogues, in relation to the poem as containing the flattened picture as would a room, and so on. Here, we may see the 'strict/Otherness of the painter in his/Other room', locked in composition. Elsewhere, 'The balloon pops, the attention/Turns dully away', and it is Ashbery who turns aside from the painting, to think through his own activities of the previous day. At another point, the painting is active, dominant, as it were fleshed-out, and there is in its gaze 'a combination/Of tenderness, amusement and regret, so powerful/In its restraint that one cannot look for long'. Elsewhere, we are once more placed on Parmigianino's side, but only in order to see his consciousness absented in an almost Surrealistic image of absorbed fascination: both the reader and Ashbery reflecting on his day become sunlight and a half-echo of a first line by Emily Dickinson:

> A peculiar slant
> Of memory that intrudes on the dreaming model
> In the silence of the studio as he considers
> Lifting the pencil to the self-portrait.

> (*SPCM* 68–83)

And so on. The poem is a series of such recorded moments of attention, each a temporary arrest in the perceptual process which, to return to Merleau-Ponty's terms, is also a solicitation to proceed. For any moment of encounter half-swerves away from what it meets, like the giant hand to the fore in Parmigianino's mirror-portrait. As Merleau-Ponty goes on to note: 'what makes the "reality" of the thing is therefore precisely what snatches it from our grasp'.[20] It is the almost musical pathos, the self-renewing dance of this meeting only to miss, that the poem charts. The distortions of a convex mirror do make it, as Charles Altieri notes, an apt figure for the philosophical status of figures.[21] Ellman Crasnow places more stress on the relations between the visual and the cognitive.[22] Bloom, on the other hand, stresses the self in the self-portrait.[23] I would suggest that the poem is about the fated nature of encounter, universally applicable to the displacements inhering in any act of perception, be it of self by self, of a loved one, of a painting, of a city. The common element in Ashbery's recorded moments to which attention should be drawn is their mobility.

'Self-Portrait in a Convex Mirror' is a lengthy poem, by the standards of its day, and its formal exoskeleton is grand. It looks like a rival to *Four Quartets*, and arguably is. For the most part, it eschews Eliot's flights into the high rhetoric of Symbolist prophecy in favour of a more cautious tonal range. The productive tension that gives the poem strength, locally, comes on the swing from one line into the next. As with much of Eliot's poetry, a ghostly pentameter remains just within earshot, but Ashbery tends to keep rhythmical impetus on that swing, where Eliot's near-pentameters are more emphatically end-stopped. At the risk of telling only half the story, one might argue that Eliot was a poet of extraordinarily resonant single lines, which he would build, sometimes imperfectly, into a lyrical collage; in certain cases, as we now know, taking years to do so. For Ashbery the line is less discrete, is what makes the next line possible, and for both good and ill, he can always keep on going. There is probably less fatigue in Ashbery than in any poet since Swinburne, a writer he resembles in a number of ways. (Indeed, he appears to be an admirer of the Swinburne generation, frequently using the Rossettian image of drops falling from the eaves as an image of sexual sweetness, and inserting a sentence from Pater's *Plato and Platonism* into the poem 'Houseboat Days'.) But Swinburne, for all the fabulous proliferation of metre and imagery in his paeans to lesbian sadomasochism, sex with a leper *und so weiter*, is usually heading for an important moment of climax-cum-closure, be it a Shelleyan spasm, or the more Victorian, death-desiring sea-murmur. It would be readily agreed that all these things are in short supply in Ashbery (even in 'Litany'). Less obvious but more significant in the present context is the virtual absence of any kind of climactic moment in Ashbery's poetry. No Swinburnian gasp, no chiselled Eliotean fragment, no Rilkean Apollo to blaze out its warning that *Du mußt dein Leben ändern*.[24] In Ashbery, *dein Leben* in the city is 'alive with filiations, shuttlings', in a state of constant, rejuvenating alteration as one threads a way through the metropolitan tapestry.

The refusal of moments of climax or closure, of which this poet's unvarying tone is the guarantor, relates closely to what one might think of as Ashberyan Postmodernism. He would ideally like this to be a world of play, of shifting surfaces and colours; hence, in part, the delight in the giants and castles and fantastic beasts of children's literature. Any impression that Ashbery is capable of a powerful, Modernist poetry of vertigo and belief à la Rilke or Eliot has to contend with all the pressures his invariant tone and deflationary comedy bring to bear against that very possibility. One might guess that Ashbery is led almost reluctantly into Modernist explorations and anxieties, and hence into the construction of his most valuable poems. Something similar may have operated in the case of Frank O'Hara, where fast transitions are the *modus operandi*, on a par with Ashbery's toneless tone. It was when the poetry became almost unwillingly snagged on deeper issues of interiority, morality, and death, that the lunch poems became great poems.

What is it then, that makes 'Self-Portrait in a Convex Mirror' so much more powerful and valuable a work than 'Litany', 'Fantasia on "The Nut-Brown Maid"', or 'The Skaters', poems that by their length and positioning in their respective collections are clearly asking to be given equally serious attention? First, although the attention to a Renaissance portrait gives the poem a 'European' air (and who can doubt the cultural reassurance that would have given the judges of the Pulitzer Prize and other awards won by the book *Self-Portrait* in

1976), it is a profoundly American work, at the level of speculation. Indeed, as Ashbery reminds us during the course of the poem, 'speculation' derives from the Latin word for 'mirror'. While the constant subject of the painting gives this poem a steadiness of focus lacking in the other long poems cited, Ashbery is as close a son of Whitman as ever in the mobility he records as intrinsic to, and ceaselessly at work in, the moment of attention. The poem is no more centred in any of the moments picked out earlier in this reading, than in any other. If it is centred anywhere it is in a pathos of never being centred, the lack inherent in the moment of encounter, which makes the next encounter possible only at the cost of barring access to a stable purchase on anything in our world, imaged at one point as a ping-pong ball, made secure only by 'its jet of water'. The poem, the line within the poem, the painting itself and also the encounter with it, are therefore all microcosms for experience. It is in the refusal of experience to let them nest securely like Chinese boxes that Postmodernist aestheticism is tried, breaks, and is replaced by the more severe and vertiginous perspectives of Modernism.

And yet, if one were to trawl through the lexicon of traditional literary designations for this poem, it could surely be filed under Late Romantic as much as High Modernist. The failure of experience to light on a stable conformation of viewer and viewed, self and other, is evoked neither as an aporia nor the *via negativa* of some modern art, in which alienation proposes itself as its own dark consolation. Rather, the fissure in experience becomes one across which Ashbery lances the poem as existential risk; as an act of belief. In this, pathos is revivified as ethos, bringing to mind the generation of Abstract Expressionist painters Ashbery would initially have seemed to have abandoned in his involvement with Renaissance portraiture. Questioned by the Voice of America's anonymous interrogator as to the risks and beliefs involved in his own projects, Ashbery replied:

> Most reckless things are beautiful in some way and recklessness is what makes experimental art beautiful, just as religions are beautiful because of the strong possibility that they're founded on nothing . . . I feel this also even in the work of great modern painters such as Jackson Pollock or Mark Rothko. Everyone accepts them now as being major artists, and yet, does their work amount to anything? There's a possibility that it doesn't, although I believe in it and want it to exist. But I think that part of the

strength of their art, in fact, is this doubt as to whether art may be there at all.[25]

Once again we are reminded, and usefully so, of the independent, difficult, and 'reckless' *action* of making certain kinds of art. So much recent literary and socially critical theory has stressed the moment of consumption rather than production of art, looking at the work chiefly as a passive channel for ideological pressures and collective practices of signification. Will, intention, the risky creative actions of an intermittently solitary consciousness, are all treated with suspicion and derided as either nineteenth-century or fictional, by an allegedly 'materialist' criticism which is itself, in truth, the loyal slave of a nineteenth-century metanarrative. Where the political almanac of conservative Marxism retains its posthumous and flickering influence, the only theory of art is one whereby it is allocated a subsidiary and eternally retarded position vis-à-vis 'reality'; as if art itself were not a manifestation of the real. The more engaging poems of the New York school follow the example of Abstract Expressionist painting in their stress on a corporeality which, free from the shackles of the old statutes and the old guilt that to think, to write, to create imaginatively are somehow less 'real' activities than mining or mechanical maintenance, can acknowledge that reality is the composition of activities. As James Schuyler wrote, of and in his poetry: all things are real, no one a symbol. To expand a *pensée* of Pascal, one catches the vibration not merely of metaphysics, but of politics, art and the physical world, in the heart's slightest movement.

And yet it is a broken world. We conjure a circle of reciprocating validation around the dual categories, self and other, signifier and signified, nation and nation, to find the circle broken, and yet in that very rupture discover the seed of continuing life. This, which I am setting down as the broad tenor of Ashbery's poem, is not at all unlike what the deconstructionist critic Hillis Miller sees in Shelley's *The Triumph of Life*, where the 'bright destruction' of lovemaking leads, not to a permanent loss of self in Oneness, but some trace, some remnant, foam on the shore that will start up the cycle again. Much the same has been said of *Epipsychidion*.[26] Perhaps, then, without proposing some impossibly ahistorical sameness of procedure, one might argue a persistence of Romanticism as well as Modernism in Ashbery's work. Another piece of art involving the mirror as doorway to dream, was Jean Cocteau's film of *Orphée*. As a young man, Ashbery was immensely struck not only by the wonderful visual effects and oneiric shading of the whole, but by the implications of Orphée's summary of his poetic ambition, given under interrogation by Death: '*Ecrire, et non être écrivain.*' To surrender to the doing, to the writing; not to be that static, dead thing, a writer. In that passionate surrender of self to what will be a more fertile articulation of selfhood, can be seen not only a particular, transhistorical rapport in Cocteau's and Ashbery's affection for illusion, but evidence of a more deeply pervasive continuity of theme and attitude underlying the arts of the last two hundred years. The wished-for integration of the separate self into fusion with another, or with some concept of the all-embracing whole (Nature); the subsequent Fall into the alienation of the ego; the return, through the attempt to heal the fissure by art, that starts the whole cycle again: here may be seen the persistence of Romanticism, from Wordsworth's generation to that of the New York poets.

'Self-Portrait in a Convex Mirror' restates in Modernist terms a traditional and Romantic aesthetic, based on charting the alternating moments of rapport and loss in acts of perception, and subject-object relations. The phenomenology of Merleau-Ponty is directly helpful in supplying a vocabulary with which to clarify this:

> The world is inseparable from the subject, but from a subject who is nothing but a project of the world, and the subject is inseparable from the world, but from a world which it projects itself.[27]

> His body and the distances participate in one same corporeity or visibility in general, which reigns between them and it, and even beyond the horizon, beneath his skin, unto the depths of being.[28]

> We choose our world and the world chooses us.[29]

Merleau-Ponty's phenomenology is closer to the interests of art (and psychology) than to many other schools of philosophy because, like poetry, it constantly seeks the validation of theoretical enquiry in actual human experience. 'Philosophy', Merleau-Ponty argued, 'is indeed, and always, a break with objectivism and a return from *constructa* to lived experience . . .'[30] And there is in his writing an interesting stress on the degree to which we create the reality we inhabit: 'normal functioning must be understood as a process of integration in which the text of the external world is not so much copied, as composed.'[31] This line of thought is not only comfortable with art (and there are illuminating essays by Merleau-Ponty on Da Vinci and Cézanne), but has integrated terms of artistic expression into its depiction of normal life. At such moments in his work we are close to some of Wordsworth's articulations of the nature of perception, as when he writes of sensations 'Felt in the blood, and felt along the heart', as if the latter had its own coastline, mirroring the geography of the outer world.[32] It is a curious fact that Merleau-Ponty – a sometime Marxist, colleague of Sartre, and a sidelong influence on most post-war literary theory in France – should have constructed a body of writing that often recalls the questions and moves characteristic of English Romantic poetry. The general aim of Merleau-Ponty's writing is towards a vocabulary that would reveal the underlying patterns of life, rather than recalling what life can feel like in its more troubled moments. There is a serenity implied by the equilibrium of his assurances (subject/world, body/distances) which may be able to account for our more jarring and painful experiences conceptually, but carries no tone that would correspond with their emotional charge. In this genial philosophy, whose presiding tone is one of quiet rhapsody, there is frequently a pull towards a mirroring division of subject-object relations, in figures of symmetry or chiasmus, which can speak to some but not all of those things that are 'Felt in the blood, and felt along the heart'.

Such, at any rate, is the general tendency of Merleau-Ponty's philosophy, whose phenomenology of perception sits well with Ashbery's poem. Both offer the pleasures, and perhaps the limitations, of a self-circulating system. But Merleau-Ponty's political writing, particularly his examination of the Moscow show trials, *Humanism and Terror* (1947), is more tough and impassioned in tone. The habitual ironies and temperamental reticence of Ashbery's poetry have not, so far, allowed an unequivocal expression of passion, political or otherwise.

THE PERCEPTION OF FATE: 'A WAVE' AND 'JOE'S JACKET'

Although Jean Baudrillard is not a critic of poetry, certain portions of his 1983 essay 'Ecstasy and Inertia' might have been written in direct reaction to John Ashbery's long poem of that period, 'A Wave'. For both writers, an interest in the undecidability of intended meaning coincides with an overwhelming proliferation of data, though what Baudrillard alleges to be collective contemporary practice, Ashbery seems determined to push to an extreme of individual style:

> Every event today is virtually inconsequential, open to all possible interpretations, none of which could determine its meaning: the equiprobability of all causes and of all consequences – multiple and aleatory imputation.
>
> If the waves of meaning, if the waves of memory and historical time are receding, if the waves of causality around the effect are fading (and the event today comes at us like a wave; it doesn't travel only 'over the waves' – it is a wave indecipherable in terms of language and meaning, decipherable only and instantly in terms of color, tactility, ambiance, in terms of sensory effects), it is because light is slowing down, because somewhere a gravitational effect is forcing the light from the event . . .[33]

Beneath his extravagant recourse to the terminology of astrophysics, Baudrillard restates here, in essence, his sense that the Postmodern period has marked the end of representation. But if this results in an 'aleatory imputation' of any and all possible meanings to any and all events, with the concept of the event itself reduced to a ghostly simulacrum of reality, the new equivalence of data grants a paradoxical 'tactility' to any and every drop in the flood of incoming information. To Baudrillard, reality has departed, leaving only a phantom light like that of dead stars; but what has replaced it is irresistible. Cultural coroner of the trivialization he seems at first to endorse, Baudrillard has not let go of the apocalyptic tone made possible by the Marxism in which he can no longer believe; after the death of history's metanarrative, the deluge. Ashbery's 'A Wave' might, as a matter of proper description rather than pejorative comment, be termed a poem of multiple and aleatory imputation, indecipherable in terms of overall narrative meaning, if undeniably rich in 'color' and 'sensory effects'. Yet in the poem there is also a lingering tone, and crucially so, from the world before the deluge, a lyrical tone that in certain respects runs counter to the accompanying proliferation of detail. The excerpt that follows is long, of necessity:

                                  That can't concern us,
However, because now there isn't space enough,

Not enough dimension to guarantee any kind of encounter
The stage-set it requires at the very least in order to burrow
Profitably through history and come out having something to say,
Even just one word with a slightly different intonation
To cause it to stand out from the backing of neatly invented
Chronicles of things men have said and done, like an English horn,
And then to sigh, to faint back
Into all our imaginings, dark
And viewless as they are,
Windows painted over with black paint but
We can sufficiently imagine, so much is admitted, what
Might be going on out there and even play some part
In the ordering of it all into lengths of final night,
Of dim play, of love that at last oozes through the seams
In the cement, suppurates, subsumes
All the other business of living and dying, the orderly
Ceremonials and handling of estates,
Checking what does not appear to be normal and drawing together
All the rest into the report that will finally be made
On a day when it does not appear that there is anything to receive it
Properly and we wonder whether we too are gone,
Buried in our love,
The love that defined us only for a little while,
And when it strolls back a few paces, to get another view,
Fears that it may have encountered eternity in the meantime.

(W 80–1)

A number of important modern writers are allowed some faint echo
here, and deliberately so. Part III of *East Coker* may be heard in the
background orchestration, with its mingling of pulpit rhetoric and
sly satire; and the hope for 'just one word with a slightly different
intonation' that might somehow alter everything, recalls, like many
moments of near-crescendo in Ashbery that fall back into musical
diffidence, J. Alfred Prufrock's unasked but 'overwhelming' question. The conversational manner of the later Auden is also here, to
help (if that is the right term) in the construction of the marathon
sentence. So, less characteristically, in the drawing together of the
final 'report', that will somehow fight off mortality and silence, is the
example of Samuel Beckett, and his many character-writers,
unnameable and otherwise, who can't go on, but must go on, and do

go on. In sum, the echoes are all Christian, or in Beckett's case thoroughly influenced by Christian discourse. And John Ashbery, for all the becalmed artifice and irony of his poetry, anchors his thought in Christian perceptions, as here. Those critics such as Harold Bloom, or David Shapiro, who finds 'parodies of spiritual progress' in Ashbery's *Three Poems*, have missed the wood for the trees.[34] There is no parody, finally, when worldly push comes to cosmic shove, (though there may be scant progress), and the concerns of that intensely Beckettian poem 'The System', 'the age-old problem of what we are to do here and how did we get here', and 'the ever-present issue of our eternal salvation', are also visibly, if not always conventionally, Christian. (*TP* 61) The same tendency of thought is there in the closing words, the near-punning of the end to that extraordinarily long sentence from 'A Wave': to fear, yet to need and need to fear, an encounter with 'eternity in the meantime'.

I am not sure how well it is carried off. The conditions for an American, Christian poem in the 1980s were immaculately unpropitious, to be sure. Given the abolition of strict form in American poetry since Whitman, Ashbery, in one sense free to write in any way he chooses, is precluded from building the un-free discipline of a belief-system into his poetry via the microcosmic structures of metre and rhyme, without at least appearing mawkish or crazed, and so has to resort to an abnormally stretched syntax as the nearest simulacrum of a transcendental rhetoric. What was just possible to Eliot fifty years ago is hardly so now, particularly to a poet of the New York school, wherein an allergy to any kind of bardic tone is ubiquitous. (The serious use of prophetic tones in the poetry of Robert Duncan, on the opposite coast, or the work of the English poet David Gascoyne, would be another story.)

Nevertheless, the postponement of an ending to Ashbery's life-sentence, with its microcosmic implication of an evaded but essential crux in human conduct, does allow him to generate an affecting and lyrical cadence. The piling-up of clauses, by its nature surplus to normal linguistic requirements, turns the marginal strangeness of poetic discourse into an asset, implying a closer proximity of poetry to the things that really matter, beyond the norm. We shall see shortly how Frank O'Hara expresses a quite different sense of the powers of poetry, and a more exploratory attitude to belief, while making use of a comparable device of postponement. In the case of both these poets there is a seriousness at work, one generally absent in the broad mass of poetry of the New York school. Kenward

Elmslie, a prolific writer and editor from this quarter, is typical in using a repertoire of poetic techniques which have made his work instantly recognizable at the expense of all serious expression:

> Submarine dodders movie status Sri A-Frames:
> meaty Gump ion. Bushwah newts at Fiat tempi
>
> ('Four Doors')

> Grasshopper!
> Grasshopper!
> Grasshopper!
>
> ('Nytol')

> Over to picaresque puttering,
> cut off from channel of dubbed-in choice.
> Cut-off point is what I do,
> down to amuse through trapdoor . . .[35]

The examples are recent, though any lines quoted from *Circus Nerves* (1971) or any of the other dozen or so collections by Elmslie would have served as well. There would have been the same deliberate frittering, essentially an extension of the Surrealists' juxtaposition of conventionally unrelated materials, down to new levels of minutiae within the phrase or word. The Surrealists, after all, tended to collage linguistic units which remained intact in themselves, and only startle in their new setting. They therefore left plenty of room for descendants such as Elmslie to play with an endless diffusion of that procedure, carried through the barrier of grammatical cohesion, and right down to the syllable. A 'cut-off point' is therefore what the reader never gets, or, if you like, gets at any moment of the 'picaresque puttering'; the author's tumble through the 'trapdoor' will happen in every phrase, yet never bruise. Would it matter if the first line of 'Four Doors' were rewritten as 'Dreadnought fodders cartoon statute LA B-movie', or perhaps 'Yacht toddles play style Aurobindo X-Rating'? At least in these reduced circumstances poetry becomes a game that all can play, which may be Elmslie's point, repeated *ad nauseam*, but amiably.

The Surrealist interest in dream was combative, at least in part, and certainly never intended as an escape from the social reality it in fact longed to transform. Without resurrecting an old-style theory of representation, it is still hard to read an oeuvre such as Elmslie's as anything other than an evasion of obstreperous life, with all its conflict and difficulty, in favour of Edenic play. What Baudrillard calls our banal condition of acceleration is given ample linguistic expression, here. By a curious twist, the evasion of reality now seems to take place through a verbal scattering, a ceaselessly ludic subtraction of coherence, where earlier forms of middle-class art had tried to make the buffers against conflict and death as solid as oak.

For example, here is Walter Benjamin once more, on the epoch of Baudelaire:

> Since the days of Louis-Philippe the bourgeoisie has endeavoured to compensate itself for the inconsequential nature of private life in the big city. It seeks such compensation within its four walls. Even if a bourgeois is unable to give his earthly being permanence, it seems to be a matter of honour with him to preserve the traces of his articles and requisites of daily use in perpetuity.[36]

It is these *aperçus* that Fredric Jameson may have had in mind by remarking that Benjamin's analysis is both singularly relevant and singularly antiquated. Relevant, perhaps, in that Baudelaire's epoch was also that of the realist novel, which reaches its magnificently suffocating apogee in Proust's itemizing devotions. It is in Proust that a life of thermometers and pocket-watches, cutlery and egg-cups, together with their cases of metal or velvet, and the impression both of touch on those casings, and of those commodities on the middle-class life they furnish, is definitively hymned. There is a touch of this in Ashbery, who also itemizes endlessly, and whose 'Self-Portrait in a Convex Mirror' flattens Parmigianino's mirror-portrait into 'the features of the room', quite as if this rather rare item were something the poet had secured for himself, in a Manhattan sale-room. But the wind of decay dematerializes all objects in Ashbery's world, leaving an age-old question-mark, one aspect of which is the recklessness of belief, the other death. That question-mark does not generally hang over Postmodern writing, which is however equally liable to dematerialize the object. Benjamin's analysis is itself as charmingly antiquated as a grandfather clock in its juxtaposition of heavy ornamentalism and the march of time. If one were to define Benjamin's notion of bourgeois 'compensation' as a list of those things a burglar would be most likely to swipe, cutlery and thermometers have most definitely been replaced by the VCR and the CD player, plastic conduits for fleeting sound and image. It may be that if one were determined to seek a literary analogue for the quantum leap in technological alienation/seduction, to use Jameson's language, or for Jean Baudrillard's diagnosis of cultural ecstasy/inertia, that analogue might be found in the merrily disposable poetry of Elmslie, where signification is eclectic, broken and momentary. But in such large-scale cultural game theory, poetry of any kind is a negligible counter.

In conclusion I want to look at a poem by Frank O'Hara, 'Joe's Jacket', which appears to incorporate a concept of poetry as anchored in the actual minutiae of daily life, and to an almost unprecedented degree, while also pushing to an extreme a neo-Shelleyan perception of life as a ceaseless dance of evanescent forms. The occasion for the poem is an alcoholic-literary weekend in Southampton, carrying faint echoes of Scott Fitzgerald. It is summoned in phrases that also convey a larger view:

> an enormous party mesmerizing comers in the disgathering light
> and dancing miniature-endless, like a pivot

The settings of the poem are all potentially containing and reassuring, from the parlor car of the opening line, in which O'Hara presents himself travelling in the company of his lover Vincent Warren and painter Jasper Johns, to the simpler world of the poet's childhood, 'Barbizonian kiddy days', lit from one simple and parental source. Yet the poem, full of customary activities, of references to literal places and specific individuals, presents them all in an agitated and uncertain light. Containment, desired in the forms of pleasant social ritual and emotional stability, is resisted where it delays confrontation with the real. The only true 'pivot' is the poem.

The fate of perception, the Fall of signifier from signified, lover from loved, is matched by O'Hara's perception of fate. In this chiasmus, a sense of life as a montage of interrelated signs, a deep space of colour, light and sound, is twinned with a disillusioned sense of a 'penetrable' existence, reducible to layered spaces and bald particulars:

no central figure me, I was some sort of cloud or a gust of wind

This Wordsworthian image of childhood lives on in the adult, but
what once spelled freedom and play is now an 'envy of inertia' in a
'strange' and 'mobile' world, where 'coherence' is only lent, by a
creativity which has its own 'flickering' and serpentine duplicities.
Here we may recall the way anxiety and self-distrust coincided with
the multiplications of personality in 'In Memory of My Feelings'.
The recoil from a kaleidoscopic splitting into a more worldly-wise
and contained sense of self, discrete in one sense and indiscrete in
another, is once again Byronic:

I drink to smother my sensitivity for a while so I won't stare away
I drink to kill the fear of boredom, the mounting panic of it
I drink to reduce my seriousness so a certain spurious charm
can appear and win its flickering little victory over noise
I drink to die a little and increase the contrast of this questionable
                                                              (moment

This is truly the most Byronic moment in O'Hara's poetry, as the
probing rhetoric of remorseless self-analysis strips layers from the
performing self, while adding to the strength of that selfhood through
the unflinching nature of the analysis. Reading both draws us nearer
to, and holds us back from, the voice of the poem by virtue of its
articulacy. The closer one gets to O'Hara, the greater the distance
from which he looks back. 'Joe's Jacket' is a poem of 'this questionable moment', in which experience is forever shadowed, fated to be
reached for and lost in a Romantic spirit of *carpe diem*, while being
the opposite of lost, forever here, in a world to which there is no
alternative, and where the surface is all there is. Reading moves in
relation to the poem's voice as the 'I' moves in relation to the things
it both creates and depicts. In consequence and like all great poems,
'Joe's Jacket' is microcosmic, though its fluency and honesty are the
opposite of portentous.

Following the return journey home, the 'forceful histories' of
O'Hara, his relationship with his lover, his probably more important
relationship with the 'sleeping city' New York, whose light alone
'lends things/coherence and an absolute', if only for a questionable
moment as the clock strikes four a.m., reach a point of climactic
expression in the final stanza.

Many of O'Hara's poems of standing still and walking in New York, his 'I do this, I do that' poems, concern waking and sleeping, eating and drinking. Barely more than fifty lines in length, this poem agitates the customary order of those activities, so that going away and coming home are hard to disintricate, there is light and conservation deep in the watches of the night. All this serves to increase the contrast of the questionable moment, and by removing the supposedly ordinary incident from its customary frame, force it to yield something more intense and truthful about experience. 'Joe's Jacket' is one of the great poems of facing up to things. 'Joe' is probably the adopted son of painter friend Larry Rivers, rather than Joe LeSueur, with whom O'Hara once shared an apartment. 'Ashes' is John Ashbery's nickname. The jacket is just a seersucker jacket. It is where it has been, and who O'Hara has been when he borrowed it on past occasions, that count:

when I last borrowed it I was leaving there it was on my Spanish
    plaza back
and hid my shoulders from San Marco's pigeons was jostled on
    the Kurfürstendamm
and sat opposite Ashes in an enormous leather chair in the
    Continental
it is all enormity and life it has protected me and kept me here on
many occasions as a symbol does when the heart is full and risks
    no speech
a precaution I loathe as the pheasant loathes the season and is
    preserved
it will not be need, it will be just what it is and just what happens

(*CP* 329–30)

If 'In Memory of My Feelings' was partly, to revive Grace Hartigan's phrase, about how to be open, then 'Joe's Jacket' is about knowing when to button up the raw and open self inside a jacket of self-preservation. This is a precaution loathsome to O'Hara, who would rather move freely in 'the disgathering light', celebrate the flowing aspects of identity and social relations that retain something of childhood mobility, like that of a cloud or gust of wind. Another poem in defence of the mercurial, beginning 'Krushchev is coming on the right day!' had ended 'and the light seems to be eternal/and joy seems to be inexorable/I am foolish enough always to find it in wind'. (*CP* 340) However reluctantly, O'Hara concedes the foolishness of ignoring the fissures in experience that split self from other, subject from object. The poem's darkest implication is that at times you have to rely on those fissures as a means of survival. The jacket is a reminder of the variousness of identity: my Spanish plaza back and my Kurfürstendamm back are not the same: but it protects against the dangers in what it recalls. It is 'all enormity and life', but at times the single life has to slide along the ground with a cunning self-preservation that will include the venom of self-loathing, if it is to avoid being swallowed by the mesmerizing enormity of the larger Life. And so, in the typically witty and stoical words that come towards the end of the Ode to Michael Goldberg, 'everything is all right and difficult'. (*CP* 297)

Once again, Merleau-Ponty's phenomenology can shed some light on the poetry, both by the way in which it seems to confirm some of O'Hara's conclusions about the nature of experience, and by the ways in which it differs in method and tone:

> In the silence of a country house, once the door has been shut against the odors of the shrubbery and the sounds of the birds, an old jacket lying on a chair will be a riddle if I take it just as it offers itself to me. There it is, blind and limited; it does not know what it is; it is content to occupy that bit of space – but it does so in a way I never could. It does not run off in all directions like consciousness; it remains solidly what it is; it is in itself.[37]

By these lights, the presence of an object becomes an assertion, almost a challenge. The apparent contentment of the jacket weakens slightly the identity of the perceiver, who is reminded by the insistent dumb persistence of the thing that he or you or I are less sure, more fluid, a running consciousness, open 'in all directions'. An element of unease is perpetual in the state of human awareness. The challenge of the mute object, which resides precisely in its silence, is also a reminder that there is a real world continuing beyond the horizon of one individual's perception. An object's identity deprives me of mine, reminds me of the larger world, an enormity promising my death. And yet what can raise the jacket or any dumb object to this status of challenge, this reality, except my or someone's perception of it? Without that human validation, the world is not nothing, but it is as nothing; unimaginable, asleep. The fate of perception is its uneasy containment of a mingled antagonism and need.

The world and I are not on a see-saw, where self and other can slide nearer to each other or further away, like children at play in a disequilibrium that is never truly disturbing. Or perhaps life is like that, but only intermittently: the knowledge that fundamental disturbance does exist, that the challenge of existence can kill, may affect the degree of agreement we can reach with Merleau-Ponty's phenomenology. Philosophy can only describe the real; art enacts it. In its distance from normal discourse, the language of poetry does of course defamiliarize its material. It is precisely in the act of distancing from the norm that the truth-claims of poetry lie. For example, in 'Joe's Jacket' the lack of punctuation and breathless disruptions of syntax make a positive and identifiable contribution to a poem that will conclude with a recorded moment where the heart is full, and risks no speech:

> no central figure me, I was some sort of cloud or a gust of wind
> at the station a crowd of drunken fishermen on a picnic Kenneth
> is hard to find . . .

Is the gust of wind in O'Hara's past, or at the station where he can't at first find Kenneth Koch, or both? The confusion is fertile, and helps to embody the poem's exploratory world-view.

The crucial moments of self-anchorage in that poem, and indeed all the moments of self-presentation in the poetry of Frank O'Hara, operate in historical descent from a Romantic prioritization of the ego, but cannot be confused with the 'egotistical sublime'. The more modern conjuration of the sublime in the paintings of Abstract Expressionism, particularly the work of Jackson Pollock, was of recent and crucial importance to O'Hara. The re-emergence of representation from the far side of abstraction in those canvasses of the early fifties, such as *Easter and the Totem*, is in a sense matched by the ways O'Hara presents his poetic 'I' as emerging from a background of varied and mobile material. That background – the city of New York, say – both gives rise to his individual voice, and is made significant by that printed voice. To that extent the reciprocity of phenomenology speaks accurately enough to the workings of his poetry. But New York is not an easy place, is not a country house where one can close the door against the intrusive odours of the shrubbery. You can still hear the sirens wail when the door has closed. That constancy of interruption, intrusion, challenge, is vital to O'Hara's poetry. It renews the possibility of poetry in each poem. Nothing is more or less material than anything else in the poem, including its 'I'. It is all verbal substance, here producing pain, there a colour or a jacket or a mixture of the three. His poetry was far-sighted in its anticipation of the playfulness and rapid-fire brilliance of Postmodernism; but what to O'Hara was a way of keeping himself entertained, a flashlight for use under the stifling bedclothes of the fifties, turned out to be something like the dominant style of the 1980s. His earlier work does foreshadow at times the weaker poetic culture of today. But he could, and generally did, pull away from that into a more anxious and difficult and durable poetry, whose critical edge lies in its individualistic materiality.

To speak of the death of representation is another way of marking the death of humanism. The alleged division between art and life was partner to another lie, the radical severance of Man, the centre of his world, from all of the non-human, which was there to be crushed, farmed or moulded. O'Hara was not a prelapsarian Romantic poet, seeking mystical reintegration into all that was not him. He was a champion of the City, more so in fact than any poet writing now. He is made up of bits of it; and it is only through such poetry that people in the future will think that life in New York City in the fifties and sixties must have been good. But his work does more than this; the poetry of Frank O'Hara has an incomparable warmth and humanity. These are not Victorian qualities, crying out to the reader that they are orphaned, and that it is snowing outside. Coalescing from the far side of neo-Surrealist abstraction, gathered out of forces that had seemed just blown about leaves in the air, they are suddenly there as a figure who seems to step, alive and breathing, through the revolving glass door on West 53rd St. and into the theatre of silent reading.

Postscript:
Going Around Cities

> So going around cities
> To get to other places you found
> It all on paper but the land
> Was made of paper . . .
>
> (John Ashbery, 'Rivers and Mountains')

Ted Berrigan (1934–83) was wont to say that he invented the New
York School of poetry. And there is psychological, though not historical truth to this. His poems do not simply issue from such an
idea, but also take it on as their subject matter; saying it, to make it
happen. Born in Providence, Rhode Island, Berrigan moved to New
York in the early sixties and met Frank O'Hara, whom he venerated.
Chiefly from his reading of the older poet, Berrigan developed a
poetry that could move easily from neo-Surrealist snapshot effects to
autobiographical narrative, transcribed talk, and the collaging of
'found' texts – including recognizable chunks from the work of
Ashbery and O'Hara. An early poem presents Berrigan on a 'Whirl
thru mad Manhattan dressed in books/looking for today', and an
analogue for his co-opting of found materials occurs in the periodic
references to 'liberating' the physical book from the bookstore.
Berrigan's liberation of bits of O'Hara is strictly an act of de-libera-
tion, the first example historically of the older poet being laundered
and turned into a reusable influence. The begetter of Berrigan's
demi-Surrealist non sequiturs and flip one-liners is immediately
apparent: 'It's not exciting to have a bar of soap/in your right breast
pocket/it's not boring either/it's just what's happening in America,
in 1965'. This sits on page 132 of Berrigan's Selected Poems, *So Going
Around Cities*. On the opposite page sits a piece called 'Frank O'Hara's
Question from "Writers and Issues" by John Ashbery', which turns
out to be a cut-up à la William Burroughs of Ashbery's obituary for
O'Hara, done for *Book Week*, with bits of the latter's poems. The only
'original' line is a slight misquotation, presumably deliberate, of a
line from 'Biotherm'. Dangerously loose in one way, it is all rather
claustrophobic in another.

177

Berrigan did have a likeably dry wit. A late poem called 'Angst' goes, in its entirety, 'I had angst'. This streamlined Haiku was something he began trying in the sixties: one poem runs thus; 'Morning/ (ripped out of my mind again!)'. Berrigan certainly captures aspects of the Zeitgeist. Overall, what he did was to dig into O'Hara's general approach to poetry, so that it fanned out into a repertoire recalling its component historical parts; Dada, transcribed conversation, and so on. One of the more interesting facets of Berrigan's work is the way in which he writes details from the daily life in which he was dealing with those reading materials into the poetry itself, so that what constitutes Art and what Life are not so much blurred, as set going in a perpetual race. There is undeniable skill in the way reading is caught slightly off-balance, as seemingly referential statements are allowed to ripple weirdly, without (at least in the best poems) evaporating into the aleatory. Berrigan's most sustained work, 'A Boke', a poetic narrative of life on the reading circuit, does this superbly:

> What is his life like? Where will he die?
> Who is this nun giving him a calm
> sense of proportion? and who leaves him; and
> this time he is really in a
> deserted landscape with dead corn in the
> building and no one knows him –
> "Come home." And who is that thin
> serious boy with the crewcut?'

Ted Berrigan saw that, since poetry in the sixties was, with the exception of one or two harrassed celebrities such as Ginsberg and Lowell, a côterie affair, one had to either ignore that evidence, or push it for all it was worth. His long-term gamble lay in taking the second route. Writers, friends and readers were the same figures appearing at different moments on the poem's turning wheel. Berrigan is the obvious figure with whom to begin this final chapter, which will deal with what became of the New York School of poetry, and its contemporary influence. His involvement with the (still functioning) St Mark's Poetry Project in New York was crucial to its development, as were the sporadic activities of his own 'C' press, which published Padgett's *In Advance of the Broken Arm* (1965), Steve Carey's *The Lily of St. Mark's* (1978), and between the two, Berrigan's own most influential collection, the 1964 version of *The Sonnets*.

Leaving aside the O'Hara connexion, Berrigan was an important mover and shaker in New York poetic culture, at the mid-point between the generation of Paul Blackburn and Joel Oppenheimer, and the present. The unashamed promotion of the côterie of poets as such probably reached its high-point with Berrigan. More frequently in New York and New York-influenced poetry, stress has been laid on the marginalization of the art. The panoply of Postmodernism does not know what to do with a creative labour so worthless in the market that its new product cannot be corrupted and canonized by the media. The two assessments that follow make one similar and one crucially different point: 'Eclecticism is the degree zero of contemporary general culture: one listens to reggae, watches a western, eats McDonald's food for lunch and local cuisine for dinner, wears Paris perfume in Tokyo and "retro" clothes in Hong Kong; knowledge is a matter for TV games. It is easy to find a public for eclectic works.'[2] Thus, Jean-François Lyotard. Here is the British poet Tom Raworth: 'And the bottle stands on the table (the wood of which came from Finland) next to the empty cigar box ('Elaborados a mano' in Cuba) near the Olympia typewriter (from West Germany). Until finally writing becomes the only thing that is not a petroleum by-product, or a neat capsule available without prescription.'[3] It is not easy to find a public for poetic works which, *elaborados a mano*, keep a critical edge in their relations with the degree zero of contemporary general culture. Not that Raworth's tone is ever one of regret, or lament. Like a number of well-established and independent English poets whose work is closer to the New Yorkers than to Faber and Faber, Raworth has built an understanding of the cultural and political destination of poetry into the production of the text, and to memorable effect.

Largely ignored, the poet is, after all, exempt from public and editorial pressure. In the world of the 'small presses', where most significant postwar American and British poetry has at least originated, this control extends to dissemination, as the poet or his or her friends often run the press also. Imprints such as Burning Deck, Roof, The Figures or Potes & Poets Press are the intrepid contemporary heirs of Corinth Books, Tibor De Nagy Editions, The Poet's Press, C, Angel Hair Books and other small-scale outfits that published the new American poetry of the 1960s. Some of these newer presses border on solvency, some have been reliant since the mid-seventies on subsidy from the National Endowment for the Arts; either way, limitations on financial outlay have in many cases not compromised the visual presentation of the text, at all. (This has been duly noted in the book trade: many small-press owners report that, while the lay readership is numerically small, the more alert second-hand book dealers will order a copy of a new publication sight unseen, for 'laying down'.) Adventurous book design is frequently possible in this sphere that metropolitan houses would reject as inefficient; for example Tom Raworth's epic poem *Writing*, published by The Figures in 1982, has a page width of 13½ inches, making it impossible to stack vertically on a conventional bookstore shelf. By contrast his collection *Common Sense*, published a few years earlier by a truly fugitive press, Zephyrus Image, is beautifully produced, but in the form of a miniature, spiral-bound notepad, again resistant to stacking. Yet these two obstreperously unconventional items might well figure in any serious account of the transatlantic avant-garde, post-1945. In short, where movie-makers or television scriptwriters bemoan the recycling of distribution values into production, so that (in theory at least) only the sure-fire commercial success gets beyond the planning stage, the financial write-off of small press poetry may make of it the last refuge of artistic control; an oasis of art in a desert of culture.

The problem here is that the isolation forced on serious writing by market forces can sound wilful, mandarin, high-art and Eliotean, leaving poetry in a posture of Olympean paralysis. To counter this, the American poets associated with the 'Language' label have persevered in the attempt to repoliticize poetry, poetics, and the question of their institutional and market dissemination. However variable their achievements in poetry as such, the Language group are undoubtedly at the cutting edge of current debate about these matters. There is no space in this context to do anything resembling justice to the range of provocative materials produced since Charles Bernstein and Bruce Andrews opened the first issue of *L=A=N=G=U=A=G=E* in February 1978 with a text by Larry Eigner.[4] In addition, many of the crucial names on the Language roster, for example Steve Benson and Stephen Rodefer, live on the West Coast; more importantly, their writing builds on earlier poetics which were rooted in California. It is the Language group, for example, who are responsible for keeping Jack Spicer's work in the arena of debate, and who have helped clear an access to Robert Duncan's poetry that avoids the equally distracting mythologies of San Francisco occultism and Black Mountain College. Nevertheless, Charles Bernstein, Clark Coolidge, Ron Silliman and others have never ceased to lay stress on the importance of O'Hara's and John Ashbery's work, through both Language criticism and poetry.[5]

The political consensus of Language writing lies on the radical Left, though it is generated by a critical absorption of Marxist and Structuralist theory, much more than by any revival of interest in the American traditions of socialism and anarchism. (One would have to look to the neo-Sandbergian poem-chants of Ed Sanders, rather than the Language group, to find mention of Emma Goldman or Morris Hillquit.)[6] There is in consequence a vehement opposition to socialist realism, and the sub-stratum of nostalgia persisting in, say, Fredric Jameson's thinking. Language theory offers a critique of any referential or transparent model of communication which would dematerialize linguistic reality at the expense of the referent. In this it shares the tendency of much Modernist and recent poetry. What is new is the explicit politicization of the communicative act, in the articulated clash of terms drawn from commodity capitalism, as well as Marxian theory. In the terms used by the Language group, the new stress is on the poetic demystifying, unveiling and sharing of meaning, in contrast to a view of language that has to do with ideological closure, fixed meaning as the expression of power relations, and communication as a mere 'exchange of prepackaged commodities'.[7] The group could certainly not be faulted on its efforts in getting poetry, and these debates about its contexts, out into the working world; the quantity of interviews, transcriptions of panels and workshops, statements and other back-up materials, is breathtaking. The clear intention is to rejuvenate the idea of a successful social intervention by a poetic vanguard movement.

The reality is more problematic. Bernstein's and Andrews' exhortations to agitate in the workplace, the emphasis on collective practice, the manifestos and statements, combine to stage a pre-emptive strike on any individual reader thinking that he or she dare make his or her own way into the poetry, without the cellophane-wrapped Information Pack. Even the Pack reneges on its own most progressive tendencies, as when Ron Silliman, asking for a recognition of poetry as the 'philosophy of practice in language', lays down the following prescription: '(1) recognition of the historic nature and structure of referentiality, (2) placing the issue of language, the repressed element, at the center of the program, and (3) placing the program into the context of conscious class struggle.'[8] Going on to quote Marx's *Eighteenth Brumaire*, Silliman asserts that revolution cannot draw its poetry from the past, but only from the future. Some would say that if it draws its program from the past ('class struggle'), there isn't going to be a revolution anyway. And the emphasis placed on an allegedly dialectical relationship between political theory and poetic practice does serve to distract attention from a certain thinness in the poetry. This is not at all a ubiquitous flaw, but would be true in the case of Bernstein, for example, whose prose is constantly engaging and illuminating in its shrewdness and Puckishness. ('We don't know what "art" is or does but we are forever finding out.')[9] His poetry, by contrast, is tricked out in a one-size-fits-all subversiveness, in which the poet hopes to outpace whatever old-fashioned preconception a jog-along reader can be led into confessing and shedding.

How should we read the following page, from Craig Watson's *After Calculus*?

but not what you say that you want and

not what you *say* that[10]

This is not from Watson's most impressive book to date (*Discipline*), but it is a representative page of the long sequence from which it is drawn. I would suggest that, without backup from the Information Pack, one would be hard put to know whether the poet subscribed to any political program whatsoever, and whether the minimalism of his writing made of him a surfer on the flood-tide of Postmodernism, a disciple of Robert Creeley, or an enigmatic interloper. Watson's startlingly tentative management of the poem at the level of its emergence, his shifting of the ground from a familiar self-reflexiveness to a new interiority, where the *urge* to write has become writing's subject, would seem to confirm Peter Bürger's worst fears regarding the entrenchment of aestheticism in modern poetry, rather than Bernstein's high hopes for a freshly politicized art.

Under the Language banner, the most effective poetry has so far been of two kinds. One, typified by the work of Stephen Rodefer, Clark Coolidge and above all Ron Silliman, had been under way before Language was invented (as it were) and does in many respects issue from, and press further, the innovations of the New York school. Coolidge's rather icy experimentalism has been seen as descending from the work of Ashbery, in his *Tennis Court Oath* phase.[11] Silliman, by contrast, provides a much more genial poetry of observation, particularly in the massive sequence *The Alphabet*, now running to a number of volumes. This is a short section from a work of over two hundred pages, *Tjanting* (1981):

> What then? This is a nic fit. The shirt settles lightly over the sunburn. We will remember with difficulty how it was spelld. Film cranes oversaw each intersection. When you come back later none of it's the same. That there are pelicans in Minnesota surpasses the imagination. It is a game children call four-square. A pleasant sort of numbness as prelude to feeling. An inexplicable pillar not at the center of the rotunda. While you read this you continue thinking, composing your own poem as you go. The blue light flickerd. It was a species that for centuries had sat in one chair with its hind feet raised into another, gazing into books. Somewhere heretofore unexplored. Thus it happend that we had enterd into an undeclared game with secret rules, whose payoff wld be unknown, tho specific. Birds hung in the trees like drops of water. Simile became a mask.[12]

One abiding uncertainty with many of the writers published alongside Silliman hovers around the question of whether disruption of conventional syntax, parataxis, and the rest of the grab-bag of explosive devices, are to be taken more as futuristic pointers or instances of present-tense vandalism. (With the weaker poets the kneejerk recourse to 'subversive' mannerism gives the devices a decidedly past-tense air.) If the Barthesian concept of writing is pushed to an extreme, do the rents that it discloses in ideology reveal Utopia; or are they just holes? These problems are engaged by Silliman's practice, as distinct from his theory, in part by the deployment of more traditional poetic skills than the Information Pack would comfortably wish to claim. Though his program, including some explicit remarks in *Tjanting*, rejects representational aesthetics as repressive, the poetry tends regularly to exploit the traditional moves and pleasures of a descriptive and observational art, then by some twist in the tail – perhaps just in spelling – relocate the reader at a critical distance. While in one sense the sentence is the poetic unit here, end-stopped and discrete, in another sense provisional units of meaning and design are to be formed by a self-conscious and analytical reading across the text at different points. In the above passage, one can single out and link the statements that seem to concern the act of reading, itself; or one could pick out the 'game' references: or one could decide that those two sets definitely were, or were not, related. The textual surface is multiple and self-divergent, but not random in its effects, à la Kenward Elmslie. The decisions taken in reading about what to link, and what to see released, are exposed as such. Whether this results in an effective political poetry is another question. Silliman appears to locate, but does not ultimately base his poetry in the interactive, social networks of language and gesture. The apartness of an idiosyncratic and personal coign of vantage is at least as integral to the pleasures of *Tjanting*, or the equally extended and enlivening *What* (1988). Notwithstanding the gaps between theory and practice, (which may work to the poetry's advantage), Silliman's is still the only body of work to live up to anything like the range of ambitions to which the Language debates have aspired.

It is clear that the airy structures of Frank O'Hara's city poems have helped facilitate these recent developments. In his poetry the 'I' can appear as the abrupt concretization of different discourses that were in the air, and in relation to which the I stands variously as self and other, producer and product. In a poem such as 'Essay on Style' (*CP* 393) this aspect of writing, which is also a question of reading, offers the reader different words to move around, delete or consider. This both is and is not a game, and the poem, as so often with O'Hara, lives up to both the serious and joky implications of its title. The argument is not that Silliman was definitely influenced by that poem, but that from the present perspective, it appears to be O'Hara's work among the New Yorkers that suggests the most productive ways forward to American poetry today.

Born in 1956, Diane Ward is one of the youngest writers associated with Language, and her work also appears to build in productive and unforseen ways on some of O'Hara's mobility and interest in decentring experience. In particular, her way of handling pronouns and the whole grammar of familial relations is delicate in its tonal approach, but powerful in the immediate repercussions for reading. This is perhaps most true of a recent sequence, *Relation* (1989); in this case the memory of the poetry, and of poems as wholes, seems more important to their workings than a brief quotation would be able to suggest. Ward's 1984 collection *Never Without One* is often brilliant, locally, and so lends itself to excerpt:

> Last night I was the mouth pressed to the shoulder
> blade at the same time I was the hardest edge

of the bone itself. I was two figures, no three,
shrinking away toward the distant line labeled
horizon, known to trade its place with you.
    The three figures were drawn together twice:
First, as stick figures or in full perspective
    on white paper by the hand that's free to dream,
    clearing the way for the second drawing,
the moment that imagination always knew could
    include you, me, and the spectrum of pronouns
    conducting a conversation as background to
    the ragged line of isolated bodies moving as
    one, voluntarily bunched together then released.[13]

As much as Silliman's, though in a more lyrical and indeed Romantic fashion, the poem conveys a heightened awareness of the constitutive reality of language. But if the way the 'conducting' voice moves onward, pausing and flowing in turn, is phenomenologically exacting and analytical, watching itself beg to differ, seeing others in its replication, there is also an air of marvellous improvisation, almost of automatic writing, as the 'hand that's free to dream' dictates the release of its terms as the terms of its release. Diane Ward's poetry is one of trading places, where the exchange of prepackaged meaning as a commodity is replaced by seeing through other eyes. 'And whenever one whoever touches makes up dialogue in me', as one poem has it.[14]

   Michael Davidson, a critic sympathetic to the Language poets, sees in their work an interest in the social rules and context of utterance, along lines indicated by Structuralism and Speech Act theory, as opposed to 'an expressivist aesthetics derived from Romanticism' which characterized earlier avant-garde formations such as the New York or Black Mountain groupings. Davidson suggests that the concept of gesture, with its implication of bodily action, is vital to developments as various but close in time as Abstract Expressionist painting and Charles Olson's Projective Verse. The primacy of gesture, authenticity and artistic individualism has now, he argues, been put into question by Language, 'which offers the most thorough critique of expressivism in postwar writing, even while building upon the earlier generation's accomplishments'.[15] A less charitable assessment might read in the stronger Language poets a gestural and 'expressivist' art of considerable stylistic individualism,

(Ward's poetry is nothing like Silliman's), but one which remains contained to a large extent by the more powerful and groundbreaking achievements of Frank O'Hara and his generation. There is a partial critique of, but not yet a release from the persistence of Romanticism, in the attempted reorientation of poetry towards speech acts, rather than the privileged action of poetic speech. One problem, as Davidson concedes, is the stultification that ensues when the terms for reading have already been built into the formal design of a poem. Having grasped the rules of the language-game, and identified the particular devices of disruption in play, the reader is left with little to do. The whole operation is as guided, though by different rules, as a puzzle-poem by Craig Raine – or, ultimately, a Movement exercise in controlled irony.

The influence of New York poetry is of course not confined to America. There was more of a transatlantic shuttle in poetry around the mid-point of the 1960s than obtains today, despite the valiant efforts of such magazines as *Reality Studios*, *Spectacular Diseases* and more recently *Archeus* and *fragmente* to keep the British on a state of alert. Twenty or so years ago, presses such as Fulcrum had the resources to fulfil a tripartite schedule: to present the work of neglected Modernist poets in an authoritative form, as was done with Basil Bunting and George Oppen; to publish the work of Americans such as Edward Dorn and Robert Duncan, then at the height of their powers; and to present the work of younger British poets such as Tom Raworth and Lee Harwood in a context that suggested affinities with the other two groupings. So Lee Harwood's *The White Room*, published by Fulcrum in 1968, carried commendations from Dorn and Ashbery; Harwood's second pamphlet *The Man with Blue Eyes* had been published in New York two years previously by Anne Waldman and Lewis Warsh's press Angel Hair, and included poetry written in collaboration with John Ashbery. At this stage in his career Harwood was writing lyrical collages that had clearly been set free by an encounter with O'Hara's and Ashbery's work, from the strictures and structures imposed on English poetry by the Movement. While the tone of Harwood's poetry is often unironically and openly lyrical, that simplicity is offset by devices of self-conscious artifice, Surrealistic scene-switching and *trompe l'oeil* effects. The latter takes more firm control in some of his most accomplished poetry, the sequence *The Sinking Colony* published by Fulcrum in 1970:

> As strange as the white cargo boat
> heading east along the coast
> two speed-boats named "Dark Red" and "Dark Blue"
>   shooting off
> in glorified arcs of spray   like you
> naked again   beyond the Green Mountains' snow
> licked clean   puzzled
> running out of petrol smells[16]

Significantly, Harwood's enthusiasm for the writing of the New Yorkers partly accompanied and partly disclosed the influence on their writing of continental Modernist developments, chiefly Tristan Tzara's poetry, and Surrealism. Harwood's and Tom Raworth's first books did therefore have the effect of rejoining British poetry to European traditions, however brief the reunion.

John James began to publish at about this time, and in his work there is an even more explicit and continuing debt to Frank O'Hara, as there is to Tzara: James's *Letters to Sarah* (1973) incorporates a certain amount of translation. Indeed, John James's poetry is translative at all levels, and in the fuller and older sense of translation; involved in changing, shake-up, transference, of gender, language, politics. His sense of Englishness is plural, and dissents from the allegation of a dominant class or voice, as is clear from the clash of cultures in such titles as *The Ghost of Jimi Hendrix at Stokesay Castle* (1988), and most of all *War* (1978). From O'Hara he draws an emphasis on the single, upbeat line as a poetic unit, but in this case the impetus of the line has always been towards social provocation. Often James employs a tone of baleful dandyism, at which he has always excelled, sharply alternated with a more thuggishly tendentious tone. Settled pronominal and other relations are set flying like bottles in a bar-room punchup: 'listen kid, when you're in love with a married woman/you shouldn't wear mascara'.[17] James produced some of his strongest work to date in the wake of Punk Rock which, like his poetry and contrary to popular belief, combined the intimate yell of Mayakovsky with a constant, po-faced humour and subtle attention to social detail. The poetry of John James builds on Walter Benjamin's belief that 'The poets find the refuse of society on their street and derive their heroic subject from this very refuse. This means that a common type is, as it were, superimposed upon their illustrious type.'[18]:

> your grand desire rises in my throat & my heart
> pulses on into its thirty-sixth year like an indifferent
> steam-engine while milky tea embalms the organ
> a woman feels very cold around the buttocks
> once in a while & yet your laugh brings light to me
> cause you're the first good man I've found
> pressing the glossy black embellishments to the hand
> under the gentle curtain imagery of the gasfire & the
> dusty smell of old red velvet cinema seats
>   but still this hanging over
>   of the female in the man
>   means maybe
>   rather than[19]

There is a deal of what Michael Davidson might identify as 'expressivist' swagger in James's poetry – which is none the worse for that. His work does also offer strong evidence that O'Hara's influence can be 'common' in humanity, as well as 'illustrious' in style; all of which he surely would have relished.

In conversation with Anne Waldman, Edwin Denby said the following about Frank O'Hara and the New York school of poets:

> So the New York School was a cluster of poets and it was through Frank O'Hara that the uptown poets and the downtown poets got together and eventually the West Coast too, plus the painters and Frank was at the center and joined them all together. After his death there was no center for that group. He had started giving big parties at his loft on Broadway after he started making enough money working very hard at the Museum of Modern Art. No one was grateful for it. He was writing less and working hard. He really wanted to establish the painters he liked.[20]

O'Hara is now himself 'established' as a continuing influence on uptown, downtown, West Coast and even British poets. His bequest is much more than a repertoire of devices, rather a zest – and something paradoxical, a grand intimacy, impossible to conceive outside an aesthetics of gesture, stylistic individualism and expressive authenticity. That no subsequent American poetry has been as powerful is partly to do with O'Hara's equation of poetry, truth, and passionate speech seeking a response, as in the closing lines of 'Ode: Salute to the French Negro Poets' (CP 305):

> the only truth is face to face, the poem whose words become
>   your mouth
> and dying in black and white we fight for what we love, not are

Notes

INTRODUCTION: THE NEW YORK SCHOOL OF POETS

1. Harold Rosenberg, *The Anxious Object* (Chicago and London: Chicago U. P., 1982 rept.), p. 61.
2. For more detailed analysis of the relationship between the Federal Art Project, the Surrealist influence and the development of Abstract Expressionist art, see Dore Ashton, *The New York School: A Cultural Reckoning* (Harmondsworth and New York: Penguin, 1979) and Serge Guilbaut, *How New York Stole the Idea of Modern Art: Abstract Expressionism, Freedom, and the Cold War* (Chicago and London: Chicago U. P., 1983).
3. Dore Ashton, *The New York School*, (1983 rept.), p. 233.
4. Charles Baudelaire, 'Les Sept Vieillards', *The Complete Verse* (London: Anvil Press, 1986), p. 177.
5. David Trotter, *The Making of the Reader: Language and Subjectivity In Modern American, English and Irish Poetry* (London and Basingstoke: Macmillan, 1984), p. 156.
6. Harold Bloom, ed., *Modern Critical Views: John Ashbery* (New York: Chelsea House, 1985), p. 6.
7. A number of books by Harold Bloom contain chapters or sections on John Ashbery. Bloom's Introduction to the *Modern Critical Views* anthology is probably the essay most explicitly antagonistic to the idea of a New York School of poets. The tenor of the essays collected in *Agon* (1982) is also one of opposition to the concept of collective, avant-garde poetry in America.
8. Jean-François Lyotard, *The Postmodern Condition: A Report on Knowledge* (Manchester: Manchester U. P., 1989), p. xxiv.
9. Anne Waldman, 'Paraphrase of Edwin Denby Speaking on the "New York School"', in B. Berkson and J. LeSueur (eds), *Homage to Frank O'Hara* (Bolinas: Big Sky 11/12, 1978), p. 32.
10. The poems by Kenneth Koch cited in this Introduction may be found in his *Selected Poems 1950–1982* (New York: Random House, 1985).
11. The comments by John Bernard Myers given in this Introduction may be found on pages 7, 8 and 23 of his *The Poets of the New York School* (Philadelphia: Pennsylvania U. P., 1969). Further details of Myers' publishing and gallery activities may be found in his 'Frank O'Hara: A Memoir', in *Homage to Frank O'Hara*.

1: JAMES SCHUYLER AND THE RHETORIC OF TEMPORALITY

1. Harold Rosenberg, *The Anxious Object*, p. 114. I have extended for my own purposes terms used by Rosenberg solely to clarify a point concerning the work of Willem de Kooning.
2. For a fully developed argument linking Abstract Expressionism to the Romantic landscape tradition, see Robert Rosenblum, *Modern Painting and the Northern Romantic Tradition: Friedrich to Rothko* (London: Thames and Hudson, 1975).
3. See Serge Guilbaut, *How New York Stole the Idea of Modern Art*, esp. Chapter Four.

4.   William Carlos Williams, *The Collected Poems 1909–1939* (Manchester: Carcanet Press, 1987), p. 174.
5.   Paul de Man, 'Lyric and Modernity', in *Blindness and Insight: Essays in the Rhetoric of Contemporary Criticism* (London: Methuen, rev. ed., 1983), p. 184. For comments by O'Hara on Auden, see the interview with Edward Lucie-Smith in *SSWNY*.
7.   Bill Berkson, 'Frank O'Hara and his Poems', *Homage to Frank O'Hara*, p. 162.
8.   W. H. Auden, *Collected Poems* (London: Faber, 1976), p. 132.
9.   Charles Baudelaire, *The Complete Verse*, tr. Francis Scarfe (London: Anvil Press, 1986), pp. 262 and 159.
10.   Charles Baudelaire, 'Of the Essence of Laughter, and generally of the Comic in the Plastic Arts', *Baudelaire: Selected Writings on Art and Artists*, tr. P. E. Charvet (Cambridge: Cambridge U. P., 1981), p. 143.
11.   Paul de Man, 'The Rhetoric of Temporality', *Blindness and Insight*. Quotations from the essay used in this chapter are from pp. 206 and 196.
12.   Barbara Johnson, 'Rigorous Unreliability', *Yale French Studies* 69, (1985), p. 74.
13.   Christopher Norris, 'Some Versions of Rhetoric', in R. C. Davis and R. Schleifer (eds), *Rhetoric and Form: Deconstruction at Yale* (Norman: Oklahoma U. P., 1985), p. 201.

2: FRANK O'HARA: ACCIDENT AND DESIGN

1.   Larry Rivers, 'Speech Read at Frank O'Hara's Funeral', *Homage to Frank O'Hara*, p. 138.
2.   Waldo Rasmussen, 'Frank O'Hara in the Museum', ibid., p. 86.
3.   O'Hara's worksheets and personal memoranda relating to the major exhibitions at MOMA with which he was involved, were sorted after the poet's death (presumably by Renée Neu). The papers have been retained by the Museum as part of Frank O'Hara's 'employee's file'.
4.   Joe LeSueur, 'Four Apartments', in *Homage to Frank O'Hara*, p. 47.
5.   O'Hara died of massive internal injuries after being knocked down by a beach buggy in the dark, on Fire Island. See J. J. Mitchell, 'The Death of Frank O'Hara', in *Homage to Frank O'Hara*.
6.   Edward Lucie-Smith, 'An Interview with Frank O'Hara', *SSWNY*, p. 13. For a more positive view of O'Hara by Olson, see the *Paris Review* interview with Charles Olson by Gerard Malanga (April, 1969).
7.   Frederick Page, ed., *Byron: Poetical Works* (Oxford: Oxford U. P., rev. ed. 1970). All further quotations from Byron's poetry are from this edition.
8.   Jacques Derrida, *Speech and Phenomena: and other Essays on Husserl's Theory of Signs*, tr. D. B. Allison (Evanston: Northwestern U. P., 1973), p. 108.
9.   Paul de Man, 'Shelley Disfigured', in Harold Bloom et al, *Deconstruction and Criticism* (London and Henley: Routledge and Kegan Paul, 1979), p. 69.
10.   Barbara Johnson, *The Critical Difference: Essays in the Contemporary Rhetoric of Reading* (Baltimore and London: Johns Hopkins U. P., 1980), p. xi.
11.   J. Hillis Miller, 'The Critic as Host', in *Deconstruction and Criticism*, pp. 217–55.
12.   Barbara Johnson, *The Critical Difference*, p. 6.
13.   Roland Barthes, *Roland Barthes*, tr. R. Howard (London and Basingstoke: Macmillan, 1979), p. 69.
14.   Donald M. Allen, ed., *The New American Poetry* (New York: Grove Press, 1960).
15.   Donald Allen and George F. Butterick (eds), *The Postmoderns* (New York: Grove Press, 1982).
16.   R. D. Gooder, 'After the Deluge, Me: Some Reflections on the Poems of Frank O'Hara', *The Cambridge Quarterly*, XIV (2), 1985, p. 99.

17. A. Walton Litz and Christopher MacGowan (eds), *The Collected Poems of William Carlos Williams: Volume I, 1909–1939* (Manchester: Carcanet Press, 1987), p. 21.
18. Ibid., p. 42.
19. Ibid., p. 65.
20. Kenneth Koch, 'A Note on Frank O'Hara in the Early Fifties', in *Homage to Frank O'Hara*, p. 27.
21. *The Collected Poems of William Carlos Williams: Volume I*, p. 178.
22. Ibid., p. 372.
23. Jacques Derrida, *Speech and Phenomena*, p. 107.
24. Ibid., p. 147.
25. *The Collected Poems of William Carlos Williams: Volume I*, p. 249.
26. See for example Bram Dijkstra, *The Hieroglyphics of a New Speech: Cubism, Stieglitz and the Early Poetry of William Carlos Williams* (New Jersey: Princeton U. P., 1969), esp. Chapter I.
27. Francis Scarfe (ed.), *Baudelaire: The Complete Verse* (London: Anvil Press Poetry, 1986) p. 61.
28. *New York Review of Books*, 31 March 1966, p. 20.
29. 'It all comes back to that, to my and your "fun" – if we but allow the term its full extension . . .' Henry James, Prefaces to the New York Edition, *European Writers and the Prefaces* (Cambridge U. P., New York: The Library of America, 1984) p. 1338.
30. Paul de Man, *Blindness and Insight*, p. 206.
31. *The Collected Poems of Wallace Stevens* (London and Boston: Faber and Faber, 1984) p. 1.
32. Alex Smith, p. 246.
33. Barbara Johnson, 'Rigorous Unreliability', *Yale French Studies* 69, p. 74.
34. Paul de Man, *Allegories of Reading: Figural Language in Rousseau, Nietzche, Rilke, and Proust* (New Haven and London: Yale U. P., 1979) p. 17.
35. Barbara Johnson, *A World of Difference* (Baltimore and London: Johns Hopkins U. P., 1987) p. 17.
36. Paul de Man, *Allegories of Reading*, p. 19.
37. The statement by Ed Dorn is taken from the dustjacket of the British edition of Tom Raworth, *A Serial Biography* (London: Fulcrum Press, 1969). Dorn's observations on the shared mind and other localities are contained in an interview for *VORT* magazine, reprinted in Edward Dorn, *Interviews* (Bolinas: Four Seasons Foundation, 1980).
38. Thomas H. Johnson (ed.), *The Complete Poems of Emily Dickinson* (London: Faber and Faber, 1975) p. 333.
39. David Gascoyne, 'And the Seventh Dream is the Dream of Isis', *Collected Poems 1988* (Oxford and New York: Oxford U. P., 1988) p. 25.
40. As given by Charles Rosen and Henri Zerner, *Romanticism and Realism: The Mythology of Nineteenth Century Art* (London and Boston: Faber and Faber, 1984) p. 25.
41. *Poems of André Breton: A Bilingual Anthology*, tr. Jean-Pierre Cauvin and Mary Ann Caws (Austin: Texas U. P., 1982) pp. 62–3.
42. Kenneth Koch, 'A Note on Frank O'Hara in the Early Fifties', *Homage to Frank O'Hara*, p. 27.
43. Ezra Pound, Canto LXXXI, *The Cantos of Ezra Pound* (London: Faber and Faber, 1968) p. 553.
44. George F. Butterick (ed.), *The Collected Poems of Charles Olson, excluding the Maximus Poems* (Berkeley: California U. P., 1988) pp. 172–3.
45. T. S. Eliot, *Collected Poems 1909–1962* (London: Faber and Faber, 1963) p. 217.
46. Reginald L. Cook (ed.), *Ralph Waldo Emerson: Selected Prose and Poetry* (New York: Holt, Rinehart and Winston, 1969) p. 42.

47. Grace Hartigan to Marjorie Perloff, 14 March 1976. As given by Perloff, *Frank O'Hara: Poet among Painters* (Austin: Texas U. P., 1977) p. 215.

3: ASHBERY AND INFLUENCE

1. *Guardian*, 20 September 1984.
2. Craig Raine, 'The Sylko Bandit', *Rich* (London: The Poetry Book Society, 1983) p. 88.
3. *Sunday Times*, 23 September 1984.
4. Algernon Charles Swinburne, *Under the Microscope* (London: D. White, 1872) p. 49.
5. Harold Bloom, 'The Charity of the Hard Moments'. In Bloom (ed.), *Modern Critical Views: John Ashbery* (New York: Chelsea House Publishers, 1985) p. 58.
6. *Quarto*, 17, May 1981, p. 15.
7. Philip Larkin, *Collected Poems* (London/Boston: The Marvell Press/Faber and Faber, 1988) p. 165.
8. Allen Ginsberg, *Collected Poems 1947–1980* (Harmondsworth/New York: Viking, 1984) p. 128.
9. 'Spring and All, xviii'. *The Collected Poems of William Carlos Williams: Volume I*, p. 217.
10. Philip Larkin, *Collected Poems*, p. 165.
11. *Quarto* interview, p. 14.
12. The quotations are from Stephen Fredman, *Poet's Prose: The Crisis in American Verse* (Cambridge: Cambridge U. P., 1983) p. 6; and Andrew Ross, *The Failure of Modernism: Symptoms of American Poetry* (New York: Columbia U. P., 1986) p. 160.
13. Göran Printz-Pahlson, 'Surface and Accident: John Ashbery', *PN Review*, 46, 1985, p. 36.
14. Andrew Crozier and Tim Longville (eds) *A Various Art* (Manchester: Carcanet, 1987).
15. As given by Edward Mendelson, *Early Auden* (London/Boston: Faber and Faber, 1981) p. 96.
16. Edward Mendelson, ed., *The English Auden: Poems, Essays and Dramatic Writings 1927–1939* (London: Faber and Faber, 1977) p. 46.
17. Ibid., p. 62.
18. As given by Marjorie Perloff, *The Poetics of Indeterminacy: Rimbaud to Cage* (New Jersey: Princeton U. P., 1981) p. 249.
19. Ibid., p. 250.
20. The quotations are drawn from various lyrics written around 1930 and reprinted in the *The English Auden*.
21. Edward Mendelson, *Early Auden*, p. 10.
22. Lawrence Norfolk, 'Forever coming closer', *Times Literary Supplement*, 17–23 June 1988, p. 681.
23. Ron Padgett, *Toujours l'amour* (New York: Sun, 1976) p. 78.
24. *The Collected Poems of Wallace Stevens*, p. 237.
25. 'John Ashbery in conversation with John Ash', *PN Review*, 46, p. 31.
26. Veronica Forrest-Thomson, *Poetic Artifice: A theory of twentieth-century poetry* (Manchester: Manchester U. P., 1978) p. 156.
27. Ibid., p. 155.
28. Veronica Forrest-Thomson, *Language-Games* (Leeds: School of English Press, University of Leeds/New Poets Award 2, 1971) p. 6.
29. Veronica Forrest-Thomson, *On the Periphery* (Cambridge: Street Editions, 1976) p. iii.

30. Harold Bloom, 'The Charity of the Hard Moments'. *Modern Critical Views: John Ashbery*, pp. 51–5.
31. *Quarto*, 17, p. 14.
32. David Shapiro, *John Ashbery: An Introduction to the Poetry* (New York: Columbia U. P., 1979) p. 54.
33. *Quarto*, 17, p. 14.
34. *PN Review*, 46, p. 32.
35. *Quarto*, 17, p. 14.
36. *The Collected Poems of Robert Creeley 1945–1975* (Berkeley and Los Angeles: California U. P., 1982) p. 105.
37. Harold Bloom, *Deconstruction and Criticism*, p. ix.
38. Imre Salusinszky, *Criticism in Society: Interviews with Jacques Derrida, Northrop Frye, Harold Bloom, Geoffrey Hartman, Frank Kermode, Edward Said, Barbara Johnson, Frank Lentricchia, and J. Hillis Miller* (New York and London: Methuen, 1987) p. 61.
39. Paul de Man, *The Rhetoric of Romanticism* (New York: Columbia U. P., 1984) p. vii.
40. Imre Salusinszky, *Criticism in Society*, pp. 66–7.
41. Harold Bloom, *The Anxiety of Influence: A Theory of Poetry* (London/Oxford/New York: Oxford U. P., 1973) p. 11 ff.
42. Paul de Man, *The Resistance to Theory* (Manchester: Manchester U. P., 1986) p. 6.
43. Imre Salusinszky, *Criticism in Society*, p. 65.
44. Paul de Man, *Blindness and Insight*, p. 273.
45. Seamus Heaney, *The Makings of a Music: Reflections on the Poetry of Wordsworth and Yeats* (Liverpool: Liverpool U. P. [Kenneth Allott Lectures I], 1978).
46. Cyril Connolly, *Enemies of Promise* (1938) (Harmondsworth: Penguin, 1978) p. 59.
47. R. K. R. Thornton (ed.), *Poetry of the 'Nineties* (Harmondsworth: Penguin, 1970) pp. 25–6.
48. Charlie Shively, 'Stephen Jonas', *Fag Rag/Gay Sunshine*, special issue, 1974, p. 19.
49. *Locus Solus*, II, 1961, p. 196; p. 8.
50. Joseph Conrad and F. M. Hueffer, *The Nature of a Crime* (London: Duckworth, 1924) p. 8.
51. Ford Madox Ford, *Joseph Conrad: A Personal Remembrance* (London: Duckworth, 1924) p. 141.
52. Conrad to Garnett, 31 March 1899. As given by Zdzislaw Najder, *Joseph Conrad: A Chronicle* (Cambridge: Cambridge U. P., 1983) p. 259.
53. 'In Memory of W. B. Yeats'. Edward Mendelson (ed.), *W. H. Auden: Collected Poems* (London: Faber and Faber, 1976) p. 197.
54. Harold Bloom, *Agon: Towards a Theory of Revisionism* (Oxford: Oxford U. P., 1982) p. 270 ff.
55. Lawrence Norfolk, 'Forever coming closer', *Times Literary Supplement*, 17–23 June 1988. p. 681: Helen Vendler, 'Understanding Ashbery', in Bloom (ed.), *Modern Critical Views: John Ashbery*, p. 188.
56. David Shapiro, *John Ashbery*, p. 7.
57. Harold Bloom, *Agon*, p. 272.

4: LYRIC POETS IN THE ERA OF LATE CAPITALISM

1. Ron Padgett, *The Big Something* (Great Barrington: The Figures, 1990) p. 23.
2. John Ashbery, 'Frank O'Hara's Question', *Book Week*, 25 September 1966, p. 6.

Notes

195

3.   Andy Warhol, *From A to B and Back Again: The Philosophy of Andy Warhol* (London: Picador, 1976) p. 66.
4.   Elaine de Kooning, *Homage to Frank O'Hara*, p. 97.
5.   See Edward Lucie-Smith, 'An Interview with Frank O'Hara', *SSWNY*.
6.   Walter Benjamin, *Charles Baudelaire: A Lyric Poet in the Era of High Capitalism*, tr. H. Zohn (London: Verso, 1983) esp. 'The Paris of the Second Empire in Baudelaire'.
7.   Jean Baudrillard, *Simulations*, tr. P. Foss, P. Patton and P. Beitchman (New York: Semiotext[e], 1983) pp 2, 25, 146, 136.
8.   *Ralph Waldo Emerson: Selected Prose and Poetry*, p. 75.
9.   Jean Baudrillard, *Fatal Strategies*, tr. P. Beitchman and W. G. J. Niesluchowski (New York/London: Semiotext[e]/Pluto, 1990) pp. 116–17.
10. As given by Baudrillard, *Fatal Strategies*, p. 116.
11. Michael Newman, 'Postmodernism'; in Lisa Appignanesi (ed.), *Postmodernism: ICA Documents* (London: Free Association Books, 1989) p. 130.
12. Peter Bürger, *Theory of the Avant-Garde*, tr. M. Shaw (Manchester/Minneapolis: Manchester U. P./Minnesota U. P., 1984) p. 10 ff.
13. Serge Guilbaut, *How New York Stole the Idea of Modern Art: Abstract Expressionism, Freedom, and the Cold War* tr. A. Goldhammer (Chicago and London: Chicago U. P., 1983) p. 97.
14. Fredric Jameson, 'Postmodernism, or the Cultural Logic of Late Capitalism', *New Left Review* 146, 1984 p. 78; p. 87.
15. Lisa Appignanesi (ed.), *Postmodernism: ICA Documents*, passim.
16. Fredric Jameson, 'Postmodernism or the Cultural Logic of Late Capitalism', passim.
17. My argument at this stage is indebted for its reference points to Warren Montag's essay 'What is at Stake in the Debate on Postmodernism?', in E. Ann Kaplan (ed.), *Postmodernism and its Discontents: Theories, Practices* (London/New York: Verso, 1988).
18. Maurice Merleau-Ponty, *Phenomenology of Perception*, tr. C. Smith (London: Routledge and Kegan Paul, 1962) p. 233.
19. T. S. Eliot, *Poems 1909–1925* (London: Faber and Gwyer, 1925) p. 42.
20. Merleau-Ponty, *Phenomenology of Perception*, p. 233.
21. Charles Altieri, *Self and Sensibility in Contemporary American Poetry* (Cambridge: Cambridge U. P., 1984) p. 157.
22. Ellman Crasnow, 'Figure and Ground in Modern American Poetry', in Marc Chénetier (ed.), *Critical Angles: European Views of Contemporary American Literature* (Illinois: Southern Illinois U. P., 1986).
23. Harold Bloom, 'The Breaking of Form', in *Deconstruction and Criticism*, pp. 1–39.
24. Rainer Maria Rilke, *Gesammelte Gedichte* (Frankfurt-am-Main: Insel-Verlag, 1962) p. 313.
25. 'An Interview with John Ashbery'. *American Writing Today*, I (Washington: Forum Series, 1982) p. 270.
26. See *Deconstruction and Criticism*, Chapter 5, esp. pages 236–7.
27. Merleau-Ponty, *Phenomenology of Perception*, p. 430.
28. M. Merleau-Ponty, *The Visible and the Invisible*, tr. A. Lingis (Evanston: Northwestern U. P., 1968) p. 149.
29. Merleau-Ponty, *Phenomenology of Perception*, p. 454.
30. M. Merleau-Ponty, *Signs*, tr. R. C. McCleary (Evanston: Northwestern U. P., 1964) p. 112.
31. Merleau-Ponty, *Phenomenology of Perception*, p. 9.
32. William Wordsworth, 'Lines written a few miles above Tintern Abbey . . .' E. de Selincourt (ed.), *The Poetical Works of William Wordsworth*, II (Oxford: Clarendon Press, 1944) p. 260.

33. Jean Baudrillard, *Fatal Strategies*, pp. 17–18.
34. David Shapiro, *John Ashbery*, p. 7.
35. Kenward Elmslie, *Communications Equipment* (Providence: Burning Deck, 1979) (unpaginated)
36. Walter Benjamin, *Charles Baudelaire*, p. 46.
37. Maurice Merleau-Ponty, *Sense and Non-Sense* tr. H. L. and P. A. Dreyfus (Evanston: Northwestern U. P., 1964) p. 29.

POSTSCRIPT: GOING AROUND CITIES

1.   Ted Berrigan, *So Going Around Cities: New & Selected Poems 1958–1979* (Berkeley: Blue Wind Press, 1980) passim. 'Angst' is from the posthumous collection *A Certain Slant of Sunlight* (Oakland: O Books, 1988).
2.   Jean-François Lyotard, *The Postmodern Condition: A Report on Knowledge* tr. G. Bennington and B. Massumi (Manchester: Manchester U. P., 1986) p. 76.
3.   Tom Raworth, *Logbook* (Berkeley: Poltroon Press, 1976) p. 301.
4.   A selection of texts from the first three volumes of L=A=N=G=U=A=G=E has been published as Bruce Andrews and Charles Bernstein (eds), *The L=A=N=G=U=A=G=E Book* (Carbondale and Edwardsville: Southern Illinois U. P., 1984).
5.   See *The L=A=N=G=U=A=G=E Book*, passim, and Ron Silliman, *The New Sentence* (New York: Roof, 1987).
6.   See Ed Sanders, 'Yiddish Speaking Socialists of the Lower East Side', in André Codrescu (ed.), *Up Late: American Poetry Since 1970* (New York: Four Walls Eight Windows, 1989) pp. 22–32.
7.   Bruce Andrews, 'Writing Social Work & Political Practice', *The L=A=N=G=U=A=G=E Book*, p. 133.
8.   Ron Silliman, 'Disappearance of the Word, Appearance of the World', ibid., p. 131.
9.   Charles Bernstein, 'Optimism and Critical Excess (Process)', *Critical Inquiry*, 16(4) Summer 1990, p. 845.
10. Craig Watson, *After Calculus* (Providence: Burning Deck, 1988) p. 26.
11. For comments by Ashbery on this development, see the interview by John Ash in *PN Review*, 46.
12. Ron Silliman, *Tjanting* (Great Barrington: The Figures, 1981) p. 47.
13. Diane Ward, 'Nine-tenths of our Body', *Never Without One* (New York: Roof Books, 1984) pp. 45–6.
14. Diane Ward, 'Never Without One', ibid., p. 41.
15. Michael Davidson, '"Skewed by Design": From Act to Speech-Act in Language Writing'. *fragmente*, 2, 1990, p. 45.
16. Lee Harwood, 'Cargo' *The Sinking Colony* (London: Fulcrum Press, 1970) p. 13.
17. John James, *War* (London: A Grazed Avocado, 1978) (unpaginated).
18. Walter Benjamin, *Charles Baudelaire*, p. 79.
19. John James, 'Sister Midnight', *Berlin Return* (Matlock/London/Liverpool: Grosseteste/Ferry/Délires, 1983) pp. 73–4.
20. Anne Waldman, 'Paraphrase of Edwin Denby Speaking on The "New York School"', *Homage to Frank O'Hara*, p. 32.

Select Bibliography

Abrams, M. H. *Natural Supernaturalism: Tradition and Revolution in Romantic Literature* (New York and London: W. W. Norton, 1971).

Allen, Donald (ed.). *The New American Poetry* (New York: Grove Press, 1960).

Allen, Donald and Butterick, George F. (eds). *The Postmoderns: The New American Poetry Revised* (New York: Grove Press, 1982).

Altieri, Charles. *Self and Sensibility in Contemporary American Poetry* (Cambridge: Cambridge U. P., 1984).

Andrews, Bruce and Bernstein, Charles (eds). *The L=A=N=G=U=A=G=E Book* (Carbondale and Edwardsville: Southern Illinois U. P., 1984).

Appignanesi, Lisa (ed.). *Postmodernism: ICA Documents* (London: Free Association Books, 1989).

Ashbery, John. *Turandot and Other Poems* (New York: Editions of the Tibor de Nagy Gallery, 1953).

Ashbery, John. *Some Trees* (New Haven: Yale U. P., 1956; reprinted, New York: Corinth Books, 1970; and New York: Ecco Press, 1978).

Ashbery, John. *The Tennis Court Oath* (Connecticut: Wesleyan U. P., 1962).

Ashbery, John. *Rivers and Mountains* (New York: Holt, Rinehart and Winston, 1966; reprinted, New York: Ecco Press, 1977).

Ashbery, John. *The Double Dream of Spring* (New York: Dutton, 1970; reprinted, New York: Ecco Press, 1976).

Ashbery, John. *Three Poems* (New York: The Viking Press, 1972).

Ashbery, John. *The Vermont Notebook* (Los Angeles: Black Sparrow Press, 1975).

Ashbery, John. *Self-Portrait in a Convex Mirror* (New York: The Viking Press, 1975).

Ashbery, John. *Houseboat Days* (New York: The Viking Press/Penguin, 1977).

Ashbery, John. *Three Plays* (Vermont: Z Press, 1978).

Ashbery, John. *As We Know* (New York: The Viking Press, 1979).

Ashbery, John. *Shadow Train* (New York: The Viking Press/Penguin, 1981).

Ashbery, John. *A Wave* (New York: The Viking Press, 1984).

Ashbery, John. *Selected Poems* (London: Paladin Books, 1987).

Ashbery, John. *April Galleons* (New York: Viking Penguin, 1987).

Ashbery, John. *Reported Sightings: Art Chronicles 1957–1987*, ed. David Bergman (New York: Knopf, 1989).

Ashbery, John and Schuyler, James. *A Nest of Ninnies* (New York: Dutton, 1969; reprinted, Vermont; Z Press, 1975; Manchester: Carcanet, 1987).

Ashbery, John. 'Frank O'Hara's question', *Book Week* (25 September 1966).

Ashbery, John. 'In Conversation with John Ash', *PN Review*, 46 (1985).

Ashbery, John (ed.). *Penguin Modern Poets 24: Kenward Elmslie, Kenneth Koch, James Schuyler* (Harmondsworth: Penguin Books, 1974).

Ashton, Dore. *The New York School: A Cultural Reckoning* (Harmondsworth and New York: Penguin, 1983 rept.).

Auden, W. H. *The English Auden: Poems, Essays, and Dramatic Writings 1927–1939* (ed.). Edward Mendelson (London: Faber, 1977).

Auden, W. H. *Collected Poems* (London: Faber, 1976).

Auden, W. H. and Isherwood, Christopher. *Plays and Other Dramatic Writings by W. H. Auden 1928–1938* ed. Edward Mendelson (London: Faber, 1989).

Barthes, Roland. *A Lover's Discourse: Fragments*, tr. R. Howard (London: Jonathan Cape, 1969).

Barthes, Roland. *Roland Barthes*, tr. Richard Howard (New York: Hill and Wang, 1977).

Barthes, Roland. *The Grain of the Voice: Interviews 1962–80*, tr. L. Coverdale (New York: Hill and Wang, 1985).

Baudelaire, Charles. *The Complete Verse*, tr. Francis Scarfe (London: Anvil Press, 1986).

Baudelaire, Charles. *Selected Writing on Art and Artists*, tr. P. E. Charvet (Cambridge: Cambridge U. P., 1981 rept.).

Baudrillard, Jean, *Simulations*, tr. P. Foss, P. Patton and P. Beitchman (New York: Semiotext[e], 1983).

Baudrillard, Jean. *Fatal Strategies*, tr. P. Beitchman and W. G. J. Niesluchowski (New York/London: Semiotext[e]/Pluto, 1990).

Benjamin, Walter, *Charles Baudelaire: A Lyric Poet in the Era of High Capitalism*, tr. H. Zohn (London: Verso, 1983).

Berkson, Bill and LeSueur, Joe (eds). *Homage to Frank O'Hara* (Bolinas: Big Sky 11/12, 1978).

Bernstein, Charles. 'Optimism and Critical Excess (Process)' *Critical Inquiry*, XVI(4) (1990).

Berrigan, Ted. *The Sonnets* (New York: C Press, 1964).

Berrigan, Ted. *So Going Around Cities: New and Selected Poems 1958–1979* (Berkeley: Blue Wind Press, 1980).

Berrigan, Ted. *A Certain Slant of Sunlight* (Oakland: O Books, 1988).

Bloom, Harold. *The Anxiety of Influence: A Theory of Poetry* (New York: Oxford U. P., 1973).

Bloom, Harold. *A Map of Misreading* (New York: Oxford U. P., 1975).

Bloom, Harold. *Figures of Capable Imagination* (New York: Seabury Press, 1976).

Bloom, Harold. *Agon: Towards a Theory of Revisionism* (New York: Oxford U. P., 1982).

Bloom, Harold (ed.). *Modern Critical Views: John Ashbery* (New York: Chelsea House, 1985).

Bloom, Harold (ed.). *Deconstruction and Criticism* (London and Henley: Routledge and Kegan Paul, 1979).

Breton, André. *Poems of André Breton: A Bilingual Anthology*, ed. J. -P. Cauvin and M. A. Caws (Austin: Texas U. P., 1982).

Breton, André and Eluard, Paul. *The Immaculate Conception*, tr. Jon Graham (London: Atlas Press, 1990).

Bürger, Peter. *Theory of the Avant-Garde*, tr. M. Shaw (Minneapolis/Manchester: Manchester U. P., 1984).

Burroughs, William. *The Naked Lunch* (Paris: The Olympia Press, 1959).

Byron, Lord. Ed. F. Page, corrected by J. Jump, *Byron: Poetical Works* (London, Oxford, New York: Oxford U. P., 1970).

Carey, Steve. *The Lily of St. Mark's* (New York: C Press, 1978).

Codrescu, Andrei (ed.). *American Poetry Since 1970: Up Late* (New York: Four Walls Eight Windows, 1990).

Connolly, Cyril, *Enemies of Promise* (London: Routledge and Kegan Paul, 1938; reprinted, Harmondsworth: Penguin Books, 1979).

Conrad, Joseph and Hueffer, Ford M. *The Inheritors* (London: William Heinemann, 1901).

Conrad, Joseph and Hueffer, Ford M. *Romance: A Novel* (London: Smith, Elder, 1903).

Conrad, Joseph and Hueffer, Ford M. *The Nature of a Crime* (London: Duckworth, 1924).

Creeley, Robert. *The Collected Poems 1945–1975* (Berkeley and Los Angeles: California U. P., 1982).

Crozier, Andrew and Longville, Tim. *A Various Art* (Manchester: Carcanet Press, 1987).

Davidson, Michael. 'Skewed by Design: from Act to Speech in Language Writing', *fragmente*, 2 (1990).

Davis, Robert Con and Schleifer, Ronald (eds). *Rhetoric and Form: Deconstruction at Yale* (Norman: Oklahoma U. P., 1985).

Dawson, Fielding. *An Emotional Memoir of Franz Kline* (New York: Random House, 1967).

de Man, Paul. *Blindness and Insight* (London: Methuen, 1983).

de Man, Paul. *Allegories of Reading: Figural Language in Rousseau, Nietzche, Rilke, and Proust* (New Haven and London: Yale U. P., 1979).

de Man, Paul. *The Rhetoric of Romanticism* (New York: Columbia U. P., 1983).

de Man, Paul. *The Resistance to Theory* (Manchester U. P., 1986),

de Man, Paul. 'Shelley Disfigured', in H. Bloom et al, *Deconstruction and Criticism* (London and Henley: Routledge and Kegan Paul, 1979).

Derrida, Jacques, *Speech and Phenomena*, tr. D. B. Allison, (Evanston: Northwestern U. P., 1973).

Dickinson, Emily. *The Complete Poems of Emily Dickinson* ed. T. H. Johnson (London: Faber and Faber, 1975)

Dijkstra, Bram. *The Hieroglyphics of a New Speech: Cubism, Stieglitz and The Early Poetry of William Carlos Williams* (New Jersey: Princeton U. P., 1969).

Dorn, Edward. *Gunslinger* (Durham and London: Duke U. P., 1989).

Eliot, T. S. *Collected Poems 1909–1962* (London: Faber, 1963).

Eliot, T. S. 'Tradition and the Individual Talent', in *Selected Essays* (London: Faber, 1951).

Elmslie, Kenward. *Pavilions* (New York: Tibor de Nagy Editions, 1961).

Elmslie, Kenward. *Power Plant Poems* (New York: C Press, 1967).

Elmslie, Kenward. *Circus Nerves* (Los Angeles: Black Sparrow Press, 1971).

Elmslie, Kenward. *The Orchid Stories* (New York: Doubleday/Paris Review Editions, 1973).

Elmslie, Kenward. *Communications Equipment* (Providence: Burning Deck, 1979).

Emerson, Ralph Waldo. *Selected Prose and Poetry*, ed. R. L. Cook (New York: Holt, Rinehart, and Winston, 1969).

Ford, Ford Madox. *Joseph Conrad: A Personal Remembrance* (London: Duckworth, 1924).

Forrest-Thomson, Veronica. *Poetic Artifice: A Theory of Twentieth-Century Poetry* (Manchester: Manchester U. P., 1978).

Forrest-Thomson, Veronica. *Language-Games* (University of Leeds: School of English Press, 1971).

Fredman, Stephen. *Poet's Prose: The Crisis in American Verse* (Cambridge U. P., 1983).

Gascoyne, David. *Collected Poems 1988* (Oxford and New York: Oxford U. P., 1988).

Ginsberg, Allen. *Collected Poems 1947–1980* (New York: Harper and Row, 1985).

Gooder, R. D. 'After the Deluge, Me: Some Reflections on the Poems of Frank O'Hara', *The Cambridge Quarterly*, XIV (2) (1985).

Guilbaut, Serge. *How New York Stole the Idea of Modern Art: Abstract Expressionism, Freedom, and the Cold War*, tr. A. Goldhammer, (Chicago and London: Chicago U. P., 1983).

Hartman, Geoffrey. 'The Voice of the Shuttle', in *Beyond Formalism* (New Haven and London: Yale U. P., 1970).

Harwood, Lee. *The Man with Blue Eyes* (New York: Angel Hair Books, 1966).

Harwood, Lee. *The White Room* (London: Fulcrum Press, 1968).

Harwood, Lee. *The Sinking Colony* (London: Fulcrum Press, 1970).

Heaney, Seamus. *The Makings of a Music: Reflections on the Poetry of Wordsworth and Yeats* (Liverpool: Liverpool U. P., 1978).

Jakobson, Roman and Lévi-Strauss, Claude. '"Les Chats" de Charles Baudelaire', *Questions de Poétique* (Paris: Editions du Seuil, 1973).

James, Henry. *European Writers and the Prefaces* (New York: Library of America, 1984).

James, John. *Letters from Sarah* (Cambridge, U. K.: Street Editions, 1973).

James, John. *War* (London: Grazed Avocado, 1978).

James, John. *Berlin Return* (Matlock: Grosseteste, Ferry, Délires, 1983).

James, John. *The Ghost of Jimi Hendrix at Stokesay Castle* (Cambridge, U. K.: Avocado Sandwiches, 1988).

Jameson, Fredric. 'Postmodernism, or the Cultural Logic of Late Capitalism', *New Left Review*, 146 (1984).

Johnson, Barbara. *The Critical Difference: Essays in the Contemporary Rhetoric of Reading* (Baltimore: Johns Hopkins U. P., 1985).

Johnson, Barbara. *A World of Difference* (Baltimore and London: Johns Hopkins U. P., 1987).

Johnson, Barbara. 'Rigorous Unreliability', *Yale French Studies*, 69 (1985).

Kaplan, E. Ann (ed.). *Postmodernism and Its Discontents: Theories, Practices* (London and New York: Verso, 1988).

Kermani, David K. *John Ashbery: A Comprehensive Bibliography* (New York and London: Garland, 1976).

Kerouac, Jack. *On The Road* (New York: Viking Press, 1957).

Koch, Kenneth. *Thank You and Other Poems* (New York: Grove Press, 1962).

Koch, Kenneth. *The Pleasures of Peace* (New York: Grove Press, 1969).

Koch, Kenneth. *The Art of Love* (New York: Random House, 1975).

Koch, Kenneth. *The Red Robins* (New York: Random House, 1975).

Koch, Kenneth. *Days and Nights* (New York: Random House, 1982).

Koch, Kenneth. *Selected Poems 1950–1982* (New York: Random House, 1985).

Koch, Kenneth. *On the Edge* (New York: Penguin, 1986).

Koch, Kenneth (ed.). *Locus Solus*, II (collaborations issue) (Lans-en-Vercors, 1961).

Kostelanetz, Richard (ed.). *American Writing Today*, I (Washington: Forum Series, 1982).

Lang, V. R. *Poems and Plays* (New York: Random House, 1975).

Larkin, Philip. *Collected Poems* (London: The Marvell Press/Faber, 1988).

Lehman, David (ed.). *Beyond Amazement: New Essays on John Ashbery* (Ithaca and London: Cornell U. P., 1980).

Lyotard, Jean-François. *The Postmodern Condition: A Report on Knowledge*, tr. G. Bennington and B. Massumi, (Manchester: Manchester U. P., 1989).

Mendelson, Edward. *Early Auden* (London and Boston: Faber, 1981).

Merleau-Ponty, Maurice. *Phenomenology of Perception*, tr. Colin Smith (London: Routledge and Kegan Paul, 1962).

Merleau-Ponty, Maurice. *Sense and Non-Sense*, tr. H. L. and P. A. Dreyfus (Evanston: Northwestern U. P., 1964).

Merleau-Ponty, Maurice. *Signs*, tr. R. McCleary (Evanston: Northwestern U. P., 1964).

Merleau-Ponty, Maurice. *The Visible and the Invisible*, tr. Alphonso Lingis (Evanston: Northwestern U. P., 1968).

Merleau-Ponty, Maurice. *Humanism and Terror: An Essay on the Communist Problem*, tr. J. O'Neill (Boston: Beacon Press, 1969).

Miller, J. Hillis. *Fiction and Repetition: Seven English Novels* (Cambridge, Mass.: Harvard U. P., 1982).

Miller, J. Hillis. 'The Critic as Host', in H. Bloom et al., *Deconstruction and Criticism* (London and Henley: Routledge and Kegan Paul, 1979).

Myers, John Bernard (ed.). *The Poets of the New York School* (Philadelphia: Pennsylvania U. P., 1969).

Najder, Zdzislaw. *Joseph Conrad: A Chronicle* (Cambridge: Cambridge U. P., 1983).

Norfolk, Lawrence. 'Forever coming closer', *Times Literary Supplement*, 17–23 June 1988.

O'Hara, Frank. *A City Winter and Other Poems* (New York: Tibor de Nagy Gallery, 1952).

O'Hara, Frank. *Meditations in an Emergency* (New York: Grove Press, 1957).

O'Hara, Frank. *Jackson Pollock* (New York: George Braziller, 1959).

O'Hara, Frank. *Odes* (New York: Tiber Press, 1960).

O'Hara, Frank. *Second Avenue* (New York: Totem/Corinth Press, 1960).

O'Hara, Frank. *Lunch Poems* (San Francisco: City Lights Press, 1964).

O'Hara, Frank. *Love Poems (Tentative Title)* (New York: Tibor de Nagy Editions, 1965).

O'Hara, Frank. *In Memory of My Feelings* (New York: Museun of Modern Art, 1967).

O'Hara, Frank. *The Collected Poems of Frank O'Hara*, ed. Donald Allen (New York: Knopf, 1971).

O'Hara, Frank. *The Selected Poems of Frank O'Hara*, ed. Donald Allen (New York: Random House, 1974).

O'Hara, Frank and Bill Berkson. *Hymns of St. Bridget* (New York: Adventures in Poetry, 1974).

O'Hara, Frank. *Standing Still and Walking in New York*, ed. Donald Allen (Bolinas: Grey Fox Press, 1975).

O'Hara, Frank. *Art Chronicles 1954–1966* (New York: George Braziller, 1975).

O'Hara, Frank. *Poems Retrieved*, ed. Donald Allen (Bolinas: Grey Fox Press, 1977).

O'Hara, Frank. *Early Writing*, ed. Donald Allen (Bolinas: Grey Fox Press, 1977).

O'Hara, Frank. *Selected Plays* (New York: Full Court Press, 1978).

Olson, Charles. *The Collected Poems of Charles Olson excluding the Maximus Poems* (Berkeley, Los Angeles, London: California U. P., 1987).

Padgett, Ron. *In Advance of the Broken Arm* (New York: C Press, 1965).

Padgett, Ron with Berrigan, Ted and Brainard, Joe. *Bean Spasms* (New York: Kulchur Press, 1967).

Padgett, Ron. *Great Balls of Fire* (Chicago, New York, San Francisco: Holt, Rinehart and Winston, n.d. [1969?]).

Padgett, Ron and Shapiro, David (eds). *An Anthology of New York Poets* (New York: Random House, 1970).

Padgett, Ron and Jim Dine. *The Adventures of Mr. & Mrs. Jim and Ron* (New York: Grossman/Viking, 1970).

Padgett, Ron and Tom Veitch. *Antlers in the Treetops* (Toronto: The Coach House Press, 1973).

Padgett, Ron. *Toujours l'amour* (New York: Sun, 1976).

Padgett, Ron. *Triangles in the Afternoon* (New York: Sun, 1979).

Padgett, Ron. *Tulsa Kid* (Vermont: Z Press, 1979).

Padgett, Ron. *The Big Something* (Massachusetts: The Figures, 1990).

Pater, Walter. *Plato and Platonism: A Series of Lectures* (London: Macmillan, 1910).

Perloff, Marjorie. *Frank O'Hara: Poet Among Painters* (Austin and London: Texas U. P., 1977).

Perloff, Marjorie. *The Poetics of Indeterminacy: Rimbaud to Cage* (New Jersey: Princeton U. P., 1981).

Pound, Ezra. *The Cantos* (London: Faber, 1964).

Printz-Pâhlson, Göran. 'Surface and Accident: John Ashbery', *PN Review*, 46 (1985).

Raine, Craig. *Rich* (London: Poetry Book Society, 1983).

Raworth, Tom. *Logbook* (Berkeley: Poltroon Press, 1976).

Raworth, Tom. *Common Sense* (California (?): Zaphyrus Image, 1976).

Raworth, Tom. *Writing* (Berkeley: The Figures, 1982).

Rilke, Rainer Maria. *Gesammelte Gedichte* (Frankfurt am Main: Insel-Verlag, 1962).

Rosen, Charles and Zerner, Henri. *Romanticism and Realism: The Mythology of Nineteenth Century Art* (London: Faber, 1984).

Rosenberg, Harold. *The Anxious Object* (Chicago and London: Chicago U. P., 1982 rept.).

Rosenblum, Robert. *Modern Painting and the Northern Romantic Tradition: Friedrich to Rothko* (London: Thames and Hudson, 1975).

Ross, Andrew. *The Failure of Modernism: Symptoms of American Poetry* (New York: Columbia U. P., 1986).

Roussel, Raymond. *Locus Solus*, tr. R. C. Cuningham (London/New York: John Calder/Riverrun Press, 1983).

Salusinszky, Imre (ed.). *Criticism in Society* (New York and London: Methuen, 1987).

Sandler, Irving. *Abstract Expressionism: The Triumph of American Painting* (London: Pall Mall Press, 1970).

Schubert, David. *Works and Days* (Princeton: *Quarterly Review of Literature* Contemporary Poetry Series, 1983).

Schuyler, James. *Freely Espousing* (New York: Doubleday/Paris Review Editions, 1969).

Schuyler, James. *The Crystal Lithium* (New York: Random House, 1972).

Schuyler, James. *Hymn to Life* (New York: Random House, 1974).

Schuyler, James. *The Home Book: Prose and Poems, 1951–1970* (Vermont: Z Books, 1977).

Schuyler, James. *What's For Dinner?* (Santa Barbara: Black Sparrow Press, 1978).

Schuyler, James. *The Morning of the Poem* (New York: Farrar, Straus and Giroux, 1980).

Schuyler, James. *Early in '71* (Berkeley: The Figures, 1982).

Schuyler, James. *A Few Days* (New York: Random House, 1985).

Schuyler, James. *Selected Poems* (New York: Farrar, Strauss and Giroux, 1988).

Shapiro, David. *John Ashbery: An Introduction to the Poetry* (New York: Columbia U. P., 1979).

Shively, Charles. 'Stephen Jonas', in *Fag Rag/Gay Sunshine* (1974).

Silliman, Ron. *Tjanting* (Berkeley: The Figures, 1981).

Silliman, Ron. *The New Sentence* (New York: Roof Books, 1987).

Silliman, Ron. *What* (Great Barrington: The Figures, 1988).

Silliman, Ron. 'Disappearance of the Word, Appearance of the World', in *The L=A=N=G=U=A=G=E Book*, ed. B. Andrews and C. Bernstein.

Smith, Alex. *A Bibliography of the Work of Frank O'Hara* (Available through the British Library).

Sommer, Piotr. 'John Ashbery in Warsaw' (interview) *Quarto* 17 (1981).

Stevens, Wallace. *Collected Poems* (London: Faber, 1955).

Swinburne, A. C. *Under the Microscope* (London: D. White, 1872).

Symons, Arthur. *Silhouettes* (London: Leonard Smithers, 1896).

Thornton, R. K. R. (ed.). *Poetry of the 'Nineties* (Harmondsworth: Penguin, 1970).

Trotter, David. *The Making of the Reader: Language and Subjectivity in Modern American, English and Irish Poetry* (London and Basingstoke: Macmillan, 1984).

Waldman, Anne. *The World Anthology: Poems from the St. Mark's Poetry Project* (Indianapolis and New York: Bobbs-Merrill, 1969).

Ward, Diane. *Never Without One* (New York: Roof Books, 1984).

Ward, Diane. *Relation* (New York: Roof Books, 1989).

Warhol, Andy. *From A to B & Back Again: The Philosophy of Andy Warhol* (London: Michael Dempsey/Cassell, 1975).

Watson, Craig. *Discipline* (Providence: Burning Deck, 1986).

Watson, Craig. *After Calculus* (Providence: Burning Deck, 1988).

Whitman, Walt. *The Complete Poems*, ed. Francis Murphy (Harmondsworth: Penguin, 1989 rept.).

Wieners, John. *The Hotel Wentley Poems* (San Francisco: The Auerhahn Press, 1958).

Wieners, John. *Behind the State Capitol or Cincinnati Pike* (Boston: The Good Gay Poets, 1975).

Wieners, John. *Selected Poems 1958–1984*, ed. R. Foye (Santa Barbara: Black Sparrow Press, 1986).

Williams, William Carlos. *The Collected Poems 1909–1939*, ed. Litz, A. Walton and MacGowan, Christopher (Manchester: Carcanet Press, 1987).

Wordsworth, William. *Poetical Works*, ed. E. de Selincourt and H. Darbishire (Oxford U. P., 1940–9).

Index